QL
638
A1
G6.7

Functional Morphology
and Classification of
Teleostean Fishes

Functional Morphology and Classification of Teleostean Fishes

William A. Gosline

HONOLULU
THE UNIVERSITY PRESS OF HAWAII
1971

Library of Congress Catalog Card Number 77-151454
Published by The University Press of Hawaii
(formerly University of Hawaii Press, ISBN 0-87022-300-3)
Copyright © 1971 by William A. Gosline

Contents

Preface

In recent years functional morphology has had something of a vogue. Books on various aspects of the subject that deal at least in part with fishes have been written by Aleev (1963), Hertel (1966), and Alexander (1967a, 1968). The aspect developed in the present work is the interrelationship between functional morphology and the classification, that is, evolution, of teleostean bony fishes. That such a book seems warranted can be attributed in large part to two fairly recent shifts in zoological thinking.

It used to be stated that an animal existed because it was better adapted to some ecological niche than its competitors. Attention then became focused on the nature of the niche, and the animal occupying it tended to be lost from sight. For active forms, at least, a far more illuminating concept is that of Manton (1959) that a species survives only if it is adept at something. This viewpoint focuses attention on the animal and opens up vistas of investigation that were closed, or at best sidetracked, under the older "niche" approach.

It also used to be stated that taxonomists should use nonadaptive characters insofar as possible as a basis for classification. This probably remains valid advice in those portions of taxonomic practice that have to do with the separation of units. But the objective of higher classification is to depict phylogenetic relationships. Traits that are not and never have been adaptive play at best a coincidental role in evolutionary history. Rather, it is the adaptive traits that are selected and that, passed on to subsequent generations, determine the course evolution will take. Indeed, Svetovidov (1946, 1948, 1952) believes that the classification of any group of fishes should be based on those characteristics functionally associated with the most important biological peculiarity of that group. Essentially, Svetovidov is saying that Manton's concept should be used as a basis of classification.

In point of fact people have always grouped animals according to their chief biological peculiarities. Perhaps the main value of

Svetovidov's precept is to identify exactly what it is that we have been doing. Once this is realized, many of the empirical data upon which classification has been constructed take on a coherence, and indeed a predictive value, that they did not formerly have.

Unrelated groups have of course developed similar biological peculiarities, and the old problem remains of distinguishing the results of convergence from traits which indicate the origin and relationships of the group. But if the chief biological peculiarity of a group can be correctly postulated, then the adaptations to which this peculiarity has probably given rise can be more readily recognized as such and separated from those characteristics that represent inheritance and are hence better indicators of origin and relationships.

The principal justifications for the present book lie in what has been said above. One limitation to a functional approach to teleostean classification should also be noted. Such an approach depends on and can only add insight into the data of competent descriptive morphology. Since the existing body of morphological knowledge for teleostean fishes is greatest for the skeletal system, and indeed for fossil forms is limited to that system, bony structures take up a large proportion of the space here. Other systems are, of course, equally important to the fish and, when better known, may prove to be equally important to modern fish classification.

The book is divided into two related parts. The first takes up those aspects of functional morphology that seem to bear on an understanding of teleostean evolution. The second part deals with the classification of modern teleosts. Various classifications are already available (Jordan 1923; Regan 1929; Berg 1940; Tretiakov 1944; Schultz, in Schultz and Stern 1948; Matsubara 1963; Greenwood et al. 1966; etc.). That adopted here is eclectic, and the major effort has been placed on clarifying the zoological problems underlying it.

This book was conceived more than ten years ago. Since that time I have had the opportunity of more or less critically examining at least the basal forms of many of the groups of fishes dealt with. This would not have been possible without funds provided by the University of Hawaii sabbatical leave program and fellowships from the Guggenheim Foundation and the Smithsonian Institution, or without space and facilities provided by the fish divisions of the British Museum (Natural History), the Museum of Zoology of the University of Michigan, the U.S.

National Museum, and most recently by the U.S. Bureau of Commercial Fisheries Biological Laboratory at Woods Hole. To all of these institutions and their staffs I am most grateful. I am also indebted to students and to colleagues innumerable for help and discussions regarding various matters taken up. I can only express my appreciation, and, if I have inadvertently absorbed ideas without giving credit, I apologize. Specifically, I wish to extend my thanks to Dr. J. J. Magnuson and Dr. E. D. Stevens for their comments on portions of the manuscript, to Dr. C. L. Hubbs for critically reading the whole of it, and to my wife for typing all of it.

Honolulu, Hawaii
April 1970

FUNCTIONAL MORPHOLOGY

ONE

Introduction

The evolution of any animal group is governed by inheritance, which determines the biological capabilities of the animals, and by the environment, which selects from among the various expressions of these capabilities the ones to be passed along to succeeding generations. It seems appropriate to review briefly certain aspects of the aquatic environment fishes inhabit, and the major features of their basic vertebrate inheritance.

LIMITATIONS AND ADVANTAGES
OF AQUATIC EXISTENCE

The differences between the terrestrial environment, in which man lives, and the aquatic environment, in which the fish lives, are reflected in every aspect of existence of both animals, and neither fish nor man has ever had much success in invading the habitat of the other. Nevertheless, these differences are primarily ones of degree, not of kind. Thus water is more dense than air and less compressible; it transmits light less well and contains less oxygen; and so forth.

Because of the greater density of water, far less effort is required of a fish to keep it from sinking through still water than is needed to keep a bird aloft in still air. Also, the same amount of thrust is far more immediately effective pushing against water than against air (as a landed fish beating its tail and going nowhere will sufficiently testify).

Water is a solvent for materials needed in metabolism. Thus, in respiration, oxygen and carbon dioxide pass across the gill membranes in aqueous solution. However, the maximum amount of oxygen that water can carry in solution is far less than is found in an equivalent quantity of air. This lower availability of oxygen in water places a far more stringent limit on the rate of continuous muscular activity possible for a fish than for an air-breathing animal, for instance, a whale or a porpoise. Furthermore, the

3

amount of dissolved oxygen in many areas of the sea, though rarely prohibitively low, is often well below maximum saturation. In such areas the continuous activity in fishes must be even further restricted. However, decomposing organic material in many fresh waters, particularly in the tropics, may use up most or practically all of the oxygen available. Fishes can live in such areas only if they have developed some system of breathing surface air, which they have frequently done.

In the aquatic environment all light except that provided by bioluminescense comes from the surface. Once in the water, light is extinguished relatively rapidly and it is almost gone below about 1,000 feet in even the clearest of seas. Some fishes live far below this level—but they live in the dark, except again for bioluminescense. The main effect of the absence of light, however, is not on the fishes directly but on their food supply. In the sea, as on land, the primary source of food is the green plants that can carry on their photosynthetic activities only in the presence of light, hence in the surface layers.

Water differs greatly from air or any other gas in that it is almost incompressible. (What little compressibility water does possess is responsible for its ability to transmit sound.) Its relative incompressibility has been used by fishes and other aquatic animals in connection with three functional systems. One is the so-called hydrostatic skeleton (Chapman 1958; Clark 1964), which seems to be represented in vertebrates by the notochord. The second is the lateralis sensory system. Because of the virtual noncompressibility of water, when any particle of water is moved, it in turn moves the particles of water around it. Thus any movement a fish makes causes, at least temporarily, the physical displacement of the water particles in the surrounding area. Fishes have made use of this attribute of water as one basis for perceiving, via the lateralis system, the items in their vicinity. Such a sensory system is not feasible in the far more compressible air and, except for those portions of it that have been incorporated into the inner ear, it has been lost by the terrestrial vertebrates.

Third, most teleosts apply the "pipette" principle in feeding, at least to some extent. By this system, water with the included food items, is sucked into the mouth. The feasibility of such a method of feeding depends in part on the fact that the displacement of water in any one area, in this case at the front of the mouth, is transmitted almost directly to the surrounding water. In the far more compressible (or expansible) air, a similar suction is not as effectively transmitted to surrounding areas, and consequently terrestrial animals must have a different method of feeding. A toad, for example, will often approach a fly and then extend its tongue to capture it. This would not work in water, where protrusion of the tongue would force the water forward away from the mouth, pushing the prey out of range. A teleost fish, by contrast, approaches the prey and then sucks it into the mouth. This basic difference in feeding methods between teleosts and terrestrial vertebrates is reflected in rather extensive differences in the mouth and jaw construction (chap. 3) in the two groups.

VERTEBRATE INHERITANCE

Fishes are active, free-swimming animals. Although the major adaptations for this mode of life, for example, the sense organs and brain, appear to have been developed within the vertebrates, a basal body plan inherited from prevertebrate ancestors would seem to have made a free-swimming existence possible. Among the features of this basal body plan are the dorsal nerve cord, the notochord, a series of "gill" slits perforating the gut wall, and segmented musculature. Of these, the "gill" slits are associated with feeding, but the others, judging from amphioxus, are related to locomotion. Presumably, the notochord represents the primary skeleton (Clark 1964, and other papers; but see Gutman 1966); the muscular segmentation has evolved independently in the chordate stock in association with an undulatory type of locomotion (Goodrich 1930); and the nerve cord integrates and controls muscular activity.

The major features that differentiate the vertebrates from amphioxus are those that have made them more adept at an active, free-swimming existence. To accomplish this change, improvements of two basic types were required: increased locomotor power and control, and improved ability, on the basis of sensory perception, to determine where the increased muscular activity should take it.

Since muscular power increases with the amount of musculature, additional locomotor power is most easily attained by increasing the size of the animal. This in turn involved the vertebrates in basic alteration of several amphioxus features. One is respiration. In an animal as small as amphioxus, where the surface area is relatively great in proportion to its volume, an adequate supply of oxygen for respiration could be obtained by a simple diffusion of oxygen through the skin. For a larger animal (with a larger volume-to-surface ratio), this system is inadequate. Fishes have compensated for this inadequacy in part by the development of specialized respiratory surfaces—the gills—which seem to have originated in connection with the feeding apparatus of amphioxus. In that animal water with the contained food particles is brought into the mouth, and the water is passed out the numerous "gill" slits by ciliary action. The more or less continuous flow of water through the "gill" slits preadapts them, as it were, as a location for specialized respiratory surfaces, and the vertebrates have used them for that purpose. However, cilia seem to be limited in absolute size, and they can move water efficiently only through spaces of small diameter. Fishes, with their larger gill chambers, substituted a muscular pumping system for ciliary action to move water through the gill slits. Such a pumping system has also permitted a great reduction in the number of gill slits as compared with amphioxus.

In the excretory system, also, vertebrates have substituted a force-pump for the essentially ciliary mechanism of amphioxus. The excretory system of amphioxus consists of segmental nephridia with solenocytes. Vertebrates have glomerular kidneys, in which, essentially, the smaller molecules are pressure-forced across the walls of capillaries of the circulatory system and into the excretory tubules (Robertson 1957). Such a system requires pressure in the circulatory system, and Ride (1954) has suggested that the vertebrate heart evolved as a force pump to provide this pressure.

With regard to sense perception, it is notable that the major sensory systems of the vertebrates—vision, olfaction, hearing, the lateralis system—provide distance perception. These systems do not occur, at least beyond a rudimentary stage, in amphioxus, a partly burrowing animal that could hardly do much about distant stimuli if it received them. The fish brain, basically an expanded portion of the nerve cord, seems to serve primarily for the interpretation of stimuli received from the sensory systems.

As might be expected, the areas of the environment of particular importance to an actively moving animal are those in front of it, and the organs of distance perception (except for part of the lateralis system) are concentrated at the anterior end of the animal. Support and protection for these organs are provided by the cranium. However adequate the notochord may be as an axial skeleton, it always remains a tubular structure that seems incapable of the complex configurations needed to support and protect the sense organs of the head. It is perhaps in this connection that another important vertebrate attribute, the cartilaginous and bony skeleton, has been developed.

SUPPORTING AND PROTECTING STRUCTURES

The primary requirement of supporting and protecting structures is firmness, at least relative to the firmness of the features around them. Aside from the so-called connective tissues, there are three main classes of supporting and protecting materials in fishes: notochord, cartilage, and bone. In a general way, and in this order, these three form an increasing series in regard to strength, rigidity, and density. There are other significant differences between them. Such strength as the notochord has seems to depend on the enclosure of free water in strong, elastic membranes, and it is this construction that may limit the shape the notochord can take. Cartilage also contains much water, but it is held in the form of organic gel. Cartilage can and does take various shapes, but cartilaginous projections, when they occur, are blunt. Bone may form fine splints, as in the intermuscular bones or fin spines, probably because bone, unlike ordinary uncalcified cartilage, contains considerable quantities of mineral salts, the crystals of which may align themselves as spicules, etc. (This same mineralization accounts for the fact that bone fossilizes, whereas cartilage ordinarily does not, a matter of importance to the student of fish if not to the fish itself.)

A major difference between cartilage and bone, probably associated with the mineralization of bone, lies in the manner of growth. Cartilage-forming cells produce around themselves the matrix that provides the actual "body" of cartilage. The living cells within this matrix are able to acquire such materials as they need by diffusion through the matrix. Growth takes place by the division of the cartilage-producing cells, with the daughter cells from each division separating and continuing to surround themselves with matrix. Thus growth is internal; cartilage expands from within. Bone-producing cells also develop a matrix around themselves. But when mineral salts are laid down in this matrix, it entombs that particular cell. In fishes, further increase in bone size can take place only around the outside of previously formed bone (which gives rise to the concentric rings seen on the scales, otoliths, operculi, and similar structures of many fishes). Also, the metabolic needs of bone cells cannot be supplied adequately by diffusion through a bone matrix, and must be provided through vascular channels.

This difference in diffusion through cartilaginous vs. bony matrices may have something to do with the locations of the two substances in the body. Cartilage never appears on external surfaces; bone, vascularized from below, frequently does. Indeed, it may be that all bone originates in the outer layer of the dermis (Jarvik 1959).

Comparative chordate anatomy suggests that the notochord provided the original vertebrate skeleton. But as far back as the vertebrates can be traced, dermal bone, with its superficial layers of dentine and enamel, formed a source of dermal armor for fishes (Ørvig 1958, 1967). In the group that includes the earliest vertebrates (the heterostracan ostracoderms), however, an internal head skeleton has never been found; it was presumably cartilaginous (Stensiö 1958). Thus the earliest known vertebrates probably had a notochord, cartilage, and bone. Even today, nearly all fishes retain these same three categories of skeletal material, at least at some stage in their ontogenetic development. In the course of ontogeny, however, there is usually considerable displacement of one skeletal material by another. In bony-fish ontogeny, the notochord is ordinarily replaced by the cartilaginous vertebral column which becomes bony; in the head, the original cartilage is more or less supplanted by a bony head skeleton. However, the end result varies greatly among the different fish groups (Holmgren and Stensiö 1936; Stensiö 1963).

There seem to be a number of factors that determine the extent to which skeletal material of one type displaces that of another (Schaeffer 1961). One factor is the apparently inverse relationship between development of bony external armor and of the axial skeleton, and the general trend in the course of fish evolution to strengthen the axial skeleton and diminish the armor. As already noted, the oldest known fish remains consist entirely of external hard parts. These presumably served as protective armor, although Gutman (1967) has suggested that this exoskeleton may have played an additional supporting role. Somewhat later in the fossil record, forms with a bony cranium as well as dermal armor occur (cephalaspid ostracoderms). So far as the known record goes, the last major skeletal feature to appear is the vertebral column. Furthermore, *Palaeospondylus*, one of the earliest fishes for which a vertebral column is recorded, seems to have had no dermal exoskeleton (Moy-Thomas 1940). The same inverse relationship between dermal armor and vertebrae appears in the prototeleosts. In this lineage, the bony vertebral column develops first among forms that are losing the dentine and enamel layers in the scales (Woodward 1895; Patterson 1968).

Whatever its causes, the gradual replacement of an external bony skeleton by an internal one during the course of fish evolution seems to be functionally appropriate. An internal axial skeleton is a supporting structure and needs only to be relatively firmer than the musculature it supports. In the small amphioxus or weakly swimming, deep-sea fishes (Denton and Marshall 1958), no great axial strength is needed. On the other hand, the external skeleton of fishes apparently acted as protective armor, and the effectiveness of such armor would be determined by its absolute strength and rigidity. In this connection it is perhaps significant that the armor of early fishes consisted of three layers of increasing hardness—bone, dentine, and enamel—with the hardest (enamel) layer on the outside, and the bone on the inside. During the course of evolution, fishes have come to rely more on escape and less on armor as a means of thwarting enemies. In this process, not only has the reliance on external armor been downgraded, but greater strength in the axial skeleton to support the increasingly powerful body musculature has become necessary.

The vertebral column is discussed in the next chapter, but the history of the dermal armor will be traced a little further here. Such armor covered the head as well as the body of early fishes. In the higher fishes, the armor of the head has developed into the dermal bones of the skull, jaws, etc. That of the body has given rise to the scales, fin rays, teeth, and dermal bones of the pectoral girdle. These various dermal elements have of course become greatly differentiated from one another in consistency, size, and method of growth. Only two aspects of this differentiation will be mentioned. First, in teleosts only the teeth retain their original external layers of dentine and enamel (Peyer 1968). This is probably related to the fact that, whereas bony armor is progressively reduced in the course of fish evolution, teeth retain their original importance. The second aspect is the size attained by any particular dermal element, which is related to the amount of flexibility required in its area. Thus, those elements of the head that provide rigid structural supports for the cranium (e.g., the parasphenoid) form relatively large, stiff units. Conversely, in the branchiostegal membranes, which must be moved over a curved surface during respiration (see chap. 3), the supporting struts, that is, the branchiostegal rays, remain flexible, separately movable elements. Undulation of the body has always required flexibility of the dermal covering. The geometric pattern of squamation (Breder 1947) seems to be at least partly associated with this requirement, as is the relatively small size of the individual scales.

To return to the contrast between bone and cartilage, a quite different aspect of the relationship between them has to do with the relative weights of the two substances. The density of seawater (as compared with that of fresh water) is about 1.03; that of cartilage, 1.1; and that of bone 2.0 (Alexander 1967a). For fishes that ordinarily live in direct contact with the bottom, as most ostracoderms apparently did, the relatively high density of bone presents no particular problem. Bone weight would, however, create more serious difficulties for free-swimming fishes, especially for those, like the sharks, that have no swim bladder. But even among those fishes in which the density of bone is neutralized by a gas-filled swim bladder, filling the swim bladder requires metabolic effort, and the amount of effort required increases with depth. It works out that many of the deeper-living bathypelagic fishes have lost their swim bladders and show relatively slight skeletal ossification (Denton and Marshall 1958).

Teleosts have also alleviated the problem of buoyancy in another way—by making lighter the bone that does occur. Thus, not only have teleostean scales lost the external enamel (ganoin) and dentine (cosmine) layers, but the "bony" layer that remains is flexible and unmineralized. Some of the higher teleosts, such as *Lophius* and *Mola* (see, for example, Studnicka 1916), have the whole skeleton made up of light, fibrous bone with little mineralization.

The neotenous fishes, which retain larval or juvenile characteristics in the sexually mature individuals, are a second group of fishes that, apparently for a different reason, continue to have a relatively large proportion of cartilage in the adult. Neoteny occurs here and there among modern fishes, for example, the clupeiform genus *Cromeria* (d'Aubenton 1961), the beloniform *Belonion* (Collette 1966), and the perciform *Schindleria* (Gosline 1959).

There is still another phenomenon concerned with the balance between cartilage and bone in adult fishes. Repeatedly in fish evolution the earlier members of a lineage are bonier than the later members. This seems to have happened in lampreys (but see E. I.

White 1946), sharks, lungfishes, sturgeons and, judging by comparative anatomy, also in a number of modern teleostean lines, among them those leading to the Dalliidae and Icosteidae.

Finally, it should be noted that under certain conditions, for example, during the upstream migration of salmon (Tchernavin 1938), previously formed bones may actually be resorbed.

The interrelationships between the notochord, cartilage, and bone are highly complex, and the extent of displacement of one skeletal material by another in the different fishes varies greatly. The complexity would be increased if calcified cartilage were taken into account, but it has been omitted because it seems to play at best a minor role in teleosts. In this discussion an attempt has been made merely to indicate some of the phenomena involved.

TWO

Locomotion

DRAG

Fishes are and always have been actively swimming organisms. Whether a fish is a tuna being chased by a swordfish or a guppy about to go over a dam, there will be times in its life when it proves advisable to move with all possible speed. The maximum speed attainable depends upon two opposing forces. One is the power of the propulsive effort and the efficiency with which it is transformed into forward locomotion. The other is the drag of the water, which slows the progress of any object moving through it.

From the point of view of hydrodynamics (Hertel 1966; Alexander 1968) there are two types of drag: friction drag and pressure drag. Water immediately surrounding any moving body moves with the object and forms a boundary layer, while water farther away is not affected. The viscosity of the water between the boundary layer and the still water farther away causes friction drag. The amount of friction drag rises with increasing surface area of the moving body. But Alexander (1968, p. 219) notes: "Roughness has little effect on drag unless the irregularities of the surface are big enough to protrude from the boundary layer. Since the boundary layer gets thinner as (speed of movement through the water) increases, irregularities that are unimportant at low speeds may have a serious effect at higher ones."

The other source of drag is that which sets up eddies in the water alongside or behind a moving body. The energy used in creating such eddies is lost, and this loss, or pressure drag (Alexander 1968), increases with the amount of eddying. So long as small bodies are moved through the water at low speeds, there is no eddying along their sides; the flow is laminar, and roiling occurs only as a wake. If two rigid bodies are towed through the water at a moderate speed, the one that is more nearly streamlined will cause the least wake, that is, the least pressure drag. If, however, a larger body is towed at a faster rate, the water along its sides also

12

will at some point begin to form eddies, and the type of flow will change from laminar to turbulent. At this point, pressure drag will begin to occur along the sides as well as in the wake.

Several complicating factors seriously hamper any effort to calculate the actual effect of drag on a moving fish. One is the matter of interaction between the various sources of drag (Alexander 1968). Probably more serious is the fact that up to now all measurements of drag have been made in experiments with rigid bodies (in such devices as wind tunnels), whereas a fish is constantly changing its own configuration as it moves through the water. Suffice it for the moment to say that even the fastest moving of fishes have quite varied shapes. Tunas have the classic streamlined form that might be expected, on a priori grounds, of all fishes. Barracudas, however, are essentially spear shaped; dolphins (*Coryphaena*) taper gradually from front to rear; and spearfishes are needle nosed.

The wake, as a type of drag, appears to have influenced the shape of fish in another way. Aleev (1963) pointed out that an eddying wake will have a disturbing effect on any structure moving through it. In fishes the structure primarily affected by such turbulence is the tail. In slowly moving fishes, which create relatively little wake, its effect on the tail will be slight. The tails of slowly moving fishes are of various shapes. In fast moving fishes, the greater wake presumably creates a more serious problem, and Aleev (1963) suggests that the broadly forked tails of such fishes permit at least the outer parts of the caudal lobes to project into the undisturbed water above and below the wake area. He also hypothesizes that the narrow caudal peduncles of many such fishes minimize the depth of the wake band.

FORWARD PROPULSION

Locomotion is usually thought of in terms of the forces giving rise to forward progress. However, control over that progress—that is, the ability to determine where the animal will actually proceed to—is equally important. These two aspects of locomotion are inseparable so far as the existence of any fish is concerned, but for purposes of exposition it is necessary to separate them.

Almost all forward movement of fishes originates in the contraction of body musculature. That sidewise undulation of the body—throwing the body into successive S-shaped curves (fig. 1)—is the basal type of fish locomotion is attested by at least two

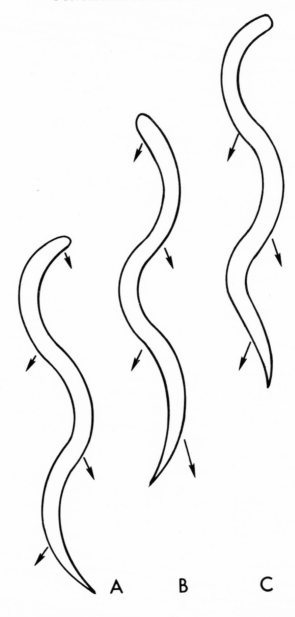

Figure 1. Oversimplified diagram of undulating locomotion. As an eel-like fish moves a series of alternate flexures back along the body in the sequence *A–C*, it pushes against the water in the areas of the flexures indicated by the arrows.

lines of evidence. First, undulation is used in varying degrees by all of the primitive living fishes, from the lampreys, sharks, and lungfishes to the lower teleostean types, for instance, the trout (Gray 1933). Second, vertebrate segmentation is developed principally in the musculature and nervous system, which would suggest a relationship to undulating locomotion (Clark 1964).

In discussing movement of fish, locomotion of the eel, which greatly exaggerates the sidewise swinging of the body (fig. 1), is the easiest place to start (Gray 1933; see also Gadd 1952; Taylor 1952). As the eel moves forward, successive waves of muscular contraction pass backward along alternate sides of the body. If the eel is motionless in the water, the moving body flexures will press against the water behind them as indicated by the arrows in the figure. The lateral components of force on the two sides of the body will cancel out, and the resultant movement will be forward.

So long as the eel passes the flexures backward through the water faster than it is moving forward, it will increase or maintain its speed. To slow down or stop, the eel can simply hold the S-curved body rigid, in which event the water will push against the front rather than the rear of each bend. Backward progression can be accomplished by passing the flexures along the body from back to front.

Forward movement of the usual tail-wagging fish appears to be quite different from that of the eel, but in principle it is the same. The differences are due to the distribution of body bulk, most of which in the fish is forward, providing a steadying fulcrum, and to the fact that the effect of contracting the body muscles is concentrated in the tail region. These changes are in part the result of alteration in the configuration of the muscle segments. In the lower fishes and amphioxus the muscle segments are short, and contraction of one of them affects only a small lateral portion of the body. The individual segments of higher fishes, however, have become complexly folded into elongated cones (Nursall 1962*b*). In such a fish as the tuna, the muscle bulk is forward, but contraction pulls forward on tendons that extend through the narrow caudal peduncle to the base of the tail on either side.

The fish tail itself is so constructed as to give maximum forward push. The way in which this is accomplished is illustrated in part by figure 2. Ignoring the flexure of the body, one might envision a boat with a stiff rear rudder that can be moved back and forth, as in figure 2*A*. When this rudder is moved from position *1* to position *3*, there is a slight forward component of force, though

A   B

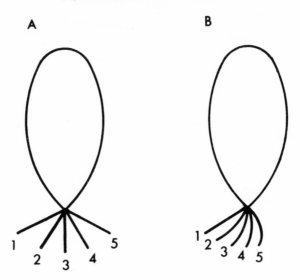

Figure 2. Forward thrust with a rigid *(A)* and a flexible *(B)* tail. As the tail is swung through the series *1–5,* there is always some portion of the tail, if it is flexible, that exerts a backward push against the water.

most of it is sideward; but when the rudder moves from position *3* to *5* the only component of force in addition to that to the side is a backward one. Actual experiments with models (Breder 1926) have shown that they do move forward a little, but most of the motion is from side to side. The caudal fin of fishes is not a stiff blade, but a flexible one (Bainbridge 1963) that moves more nearly as shown in figure *2B.* In all positions from *1* through *5* there is some backward component of thrust; at the same time the sidewise component of force has been reduced, with the result that there is less sidewise flopping of the posterior end of the body. The forward component of force is also increased in the living fish because the body is not rigid, but somewhat flexed.

In the course of fish evolution there has been a gradual shift from the undulating type of locomotion found in amphioxus toward the caudal type of propulsion found in such teleosts as the bass. In a sense, undulation is more efficient than caudal locomotion because a larger proportion of the body surface is used in the process. Alexander (1968, p. 277) points out that, because of hydrodynamic laws, "a given force can be obtained more economically by accelerating a lot of water to a low velocity than by accelerating less water to a higher velocity." Thus, other things being equal, the larger the propelling surface the more efficient it is. Aleev (1963) makes the same point in a somewhat different way.

It would seem to follow that those forms for which speed is not important or is unattainable, for example, larval stages, will move most efficiently by undulation. The basic advantage of caudal locomotion, so far as fishes are concerned, is that a far greater speed can be attained than is possible by undulation. No doubt several factors are involved; perhaps the most obvious is that a forward thrust from the tail moves the body almost directly forward through the water, while in undulation the body must traverse a series of bends to attain any forward distance.

THE AXIAL SKELETON AND BODY MUSCULATURE

As previously noted, the original vertebrate axial skeleton was the notochord. Assuming that the water in the cell vacuoles in the notochord can move in any direction, it follows that pressure exerted at any point on the notochord will be transmitted equally to all points along it. Hence a notochord can be only as strong as the weakest area in the membrane that encloses it. So long as an animal moves by undulation, the pressures on the notochord are principally lateral and more or less equally distributed along it. But with the development of cephalization and the trend toward concentration of the propulsive forces at the rear of the fish, the problem of the axial skeleton becomes less that of providing resilience to lateral bending and more that of giving resistance to longitudinal compression. What is needed in such forms is a strut that will permit lateral flexure but resist telescoping. A notochord would seem to be poorly designed to meet the latter requirement.

The vertebral column, which replaces the notochord as the axial skeleton of all modern fishes except a few deep-sea forms, is built on a different mechanical principal. In essence, the vertebral column consists of a series of rigid blocks separated by joints. (The fingers of one's hand are constructed on the same principle and meet analogous problems of providing lateral flexibility while resisting compression.) In the vertebral column (as in the fingers) the skeletal blocks abut or nearly abut against one another, so that any longitudinal thrust is resisted by what is essentially a single rigid column. The jointing between the units of this column, however, permits lateral bending.

Certain points about the intervertebral jointing deserve comment. In the first place, an intervertebral joint, like any other has the dual function of permitting a certain amount of motion between rigid elements and of holding these elements in place in relationship to one another. There is thus a strong membrane between the ends of adjacent vertebrae, which holds them in alignment.

Apparently the intervertebral joints of fishes serve still another function—that of shock absorbers. If a forward thrust is exerted against the end of a straight column (fig. 3A, upper), the force of that thrust is presumably distributed throughout the transverse area of the column. In the case of a moving fish, however, any forward thrust is exerted against an at least slightly bent vertebral column (fig. 3A, lower) and hence against only the lateral rim of any individual vertebra. Thus, were it not for the nature of the intervertebral joints, only the two lateral rims of the vertebral column would receive the entire force of any forward thrust. In the ontogeny of fishes, the vertebrae replace the notochord, but even in adults, portions of the original notochord are retained in the intervertebral spaces (fig. 3B). These remnants apparently serve as water-filled cushions between rigid elements. Insofar as pressure exerted at one point on such a cushion is transmitted equally in all directions, such cushions serve, when the column is bent (fig. 3B, lower), to receive the force from one rim of a

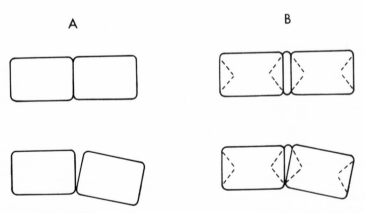

A   B

Figure 3. Diagram to illustrate the shock-absorbing effect of the portion of the notochord (shown between the rectangular blocks in B) retained between adjacent vertebrae. The blocks represent two vertebrae, seen from above. If the body is bent in swimming (lower figures in A and B), any forward thrust is transmitted entirely through one rim in A, but is distributed more or less evenly across the intervertebral surfaces in B.

vertebral pair and distribute it over the full face of the adjacent vertebra.

At least in the teleostean lineage, the change from a cartilaginous vertebral column to one made up of bony elements seems to be associated with the perfection of the teleostean caudal fin (see below). There may well be a functional reason for this. So long as the tail maintained its ancestral heterocercal form (see fig. 9) and forward locomotion was of a more or less undulating type, the force of the forward thrust was at least partially distributed over a number of vertebrae. But with the development of the teleostean caudal skeleton and the reduction in body undulation, most of the forward thrust became concentrated on one or a very few vertebral centra at the base of the tail. This concentration of force may be associated with the substitution of the structurally stronger bone for cartilage in the vertebral column of the forms at the bottom of the teleostean series (Patterson 1968*a*).

The progressively increasing emphasis on caudal locomotion in teleostean evolution is also associated with the general trend toward reduction in the number of vertebrae. Theoretically, the flexibility of the vertebral column needed by an undulating fish could be attained by creating large bends between relatively few vertebrae. In practice, large bends between individual vertebrae would probably tend to dislocate them in relation to one another, to reduce the effectiveness of the notochordal shock-absorbing system, and to shear the nerve cord passing through the neural arches. In any event, increased flexibility in fishes is attained not by enlarging the bends in the individual joints but by increasing the number of joints. Thus the undulating eels may have hundreds of vertebrae, whereas the relatively stiff-bodied, tail-swinging higher teleosts often have 24 or fewer.

The vertebral column did not, of course, develop independently of other body structures; some of these structures can best be dealt with at this point.

Amphioxus is an essentially bilaterally symmetrical animal. A vertical membranous septum divides the body into two halves, except for the notochord and the abdominal region, and each half is made up mostly of segmented musculature, with individual muscle fibers running longitudinally between the transverse membranes separating the segments (fig. 4). Vertebrates have a far more complicated muscle arrangement. In the first place, the individual segments develop considerable distortion (Nursall 1962*b*), and the muscle fibers extending between the septa

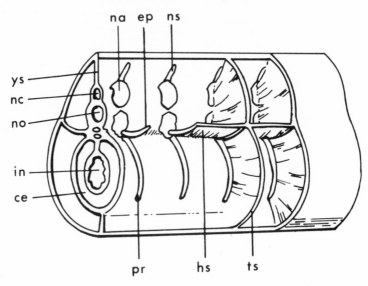

Figure 4. Diagram of vertebral column, ribs, and septa in the abdominal region of a higher teleost (based on Goodrich 1909, fig. 40). *ce*, Body cavity; *ep*, epipleural intermuscular bone; *hs*, horizontal septum; *in*, intestine; *na*, neural arch; *nc*, nerve cord; *no*, notochord; *ns*, neural spine; *pr*, pleural rib; *ts*, transverse septum; and *ys*, vertical septum.

bordering the segments become similarly complex (Alexander 1969). Second, a horizontal septum develops in gnathostomes dividing the musculature of each side into an upper and lower portion (fig. 4). Third, the muscles to the fin rays, which start out as extensions of the body segments, become pinched off and specialized. Fourth, some of the anterior body musculature develops attachments to the posterior surface of the head.

All of the various elements of the axial skeleton seem to form in the membranes that separate the segments of body musculature and are hence basically intersegmental (fig. 4). (What has been said previously about the vertebral column refers primarily to its centrum elements.) But other units become attached to and eventually fuse with the centra. In a generalized teleost such as *Alepocephalus* there seem to be four such units per centrum anteriorly (Gosline 1969), one above and one below on either side. Two spines project from the upper unit that is embedded in each centrum, one extending up and back, and a lower one, laterally and back. On more posterior centra along the column, the upper unit usually fuses with its fellow from the other side to form the

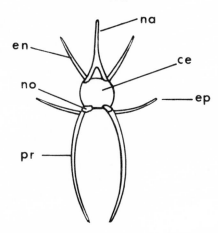

Figure 5. Abdominal vertebra of *Salmo,* frontal view (based on Goodrich 1909, fig. 305). *ce,* Centrum; *en,* epineural; *ep,* epipleural; *na,* neural arch and spine; *no,* nodule of bone probably representing a hemal arch element; and *pr,* pleural rib.

neural arch and spine (fig. 5). The nerve cord extends along under the neural arch. The laterally extending spine becomes the epineural intermuscular bone (fig. 5) of higher teleosts, which may lose more or less completely its basal articulation with the vertebra. The lower of the two bony platelets on the side of the vertebra has two projecting spines movably articulating with it. Anteriorly, the lower of the two projections extends around the body cavity and forms the pleural rib (figs. 4, 5). The upper becomes the epipleural intermuscular bone (figs. 4, 5), which extends out into the horizontal septum. Behind the abdominal cavity the pleural ribs disappear and each vertebra has a hemal arch and spine opposite the neural arch and spine. The dorsal aorta extends back through the hemal arches.

Lateral undulation requires lateral flexibility in all parts of the body skeleton. Thus, those parts of the axial skeleton that extend sideward from it must either have movable basal articulations, as do the ribs, or be completely free from one another, as are the intermuscular bones in some fishes. By contrast, lateral undulation requires no vertical changes in the body shape and no swiveling on the axis. Indeed, it is probably advantageous to the fish to minimize such changes, any of which would only decrease the efficiency of lateral undulation; the overlapping extensions (zygopophyses) at the tops and bottoms of adjacent vertebrae minimize vertical distortion in the column and probably strengthen the alignment between vertebrae.

The fact that the body axis is relatively stiff vertically but flexible horizontally has a number of consequences. For one thing, there is no need for movable articulations in the vertical projections on the vertebrae (i.e., the neural and hemal spines). Indeed such articulations would merely decrease their effectiveness as supporting structures.

Also, and more important, the vertical stiffness of the body as contrasted with its lateral flexibility makes lateral changes in the forward trajectory much easier to accomplish than vertical changes (Aleev 1963). When a moving fish turns laterally, it merely bends its head to one side. This bend is then moved back along the body until the whole fish has swung around the curve and is moving in the same direction as the head. This is not possible with vertical turns. Here, lowering or raising the front or rear of the body during forward progress has the effect of pushing the other end of the body in the opposite direction, but, in any event, the whole body must make any vertical change in trajectory as a single, relatively rigid unit. The effect is the same as changing the forward course of a boat by means of a rudder, which is correspondingly inefficient so far as abrupt turns are concerned. It is probably for this reason that a fish in executing an abrupt vertical turn frequently rotates onto its side and then bends its body laterally (Aleev 1963).

The one point at which the axial skeleton often shows relatively great vertical flexibility is at the junction between the head and the vertebral column. Examples are found in myctophids (Gosline, Marshall, and Mead 1966; see also, Fishelson 1968). This flexibility permits the head to make at least an upward movement in relation to the rest of the body, a motion that may facilitate the capture of upwardly darting prey, as well as upward changes in forward trajectory. Quite possibly, an area of the vertebral column just ahead of the caudal skeleton also has more than usual vertical flexibility (e.g., in tunas).

FINS AND THEIR SUPPORTING STRUCTURES

Fins comprise one of the most ubiquitous of fish structures, and only a few burrowing forms are completely without them. Among teleosts, increasing functional efficiency and specialization of the individual fins seems to have been one of the major evolutionary themes.

All fish fins, with the exception of the adipose, have two skeletal components—a median endoskeletal supporting structure and external fin rays. The median endoskeletal portion is laid down as cartilage and usually remains at least partly cartilaginous throughout life. Embryologically, the fin endoskeleton seems to originate in the median mesenchyme between the muscle buds that project from the myotomes into the embryonic fin (Harrison 1895; Goodrich 1904, 1906; François 1956; and others)

The external fin rays are of several types, but all have the same ontogenetic origin in the outer (corium) layer of the dermis (Goodrich 1904; Jarvik 1959). In the larval fin fold, in the adipose fin, and at the very edges of the other fins of most teleosts, there is a series of minute, scleroprotein struts, the so-called ceratotrichia (actinotrichia). For the adult, at least, a far more important type of support for the fins is provided by the bony ray. This may be a stiff spine or a soft ray. The soft rays of teleosts have been called lepidotrichia (Goodrich 1904; Jarvik 1959) because they resemble fish scales in various ways. But there are basic differences between scales and fin rays, notably in the method of growth.

Each soft ray consists of two portions which grow out as the two halves of a hollow cylinder on opposite sides of the median fin membrane (fig. 6). At intervals during its growth, the bone that constitutes each half cylinder forms a joint, then continues growing outward toward the border of the fin as a new segment.

Basally these dermal rays ride over and articulate with a median endoskeletal nodule (fig. 6). In teleosts, the whole fin can be raised or lowered, more or less like a partially collapsible fan. The soft rays may also be swung from side to side by contraction of muscles attached to the ray base.

The efficiency of the fin (as compared to a stiff paddle) depends upon a combination of flexibility and elasticity. The importance of these factors for caudal swimming has been noted above. But even where the fins are used only to stabilize a previously developed trajectory, the same two attributes are important, just as feathers on arrows make better stabilizers than do rigid vanes.

The flexibility of a fin ray is presumably provided by the jointing between segments, but the way in which elasticity has been attained is more difficult to understand. Because there are no muscles within the dermal ray (fig. 6C shows how elasticity theoretically could be provided by musculature), and no ligaments along it, the elasticity must be a function of the dermal ray

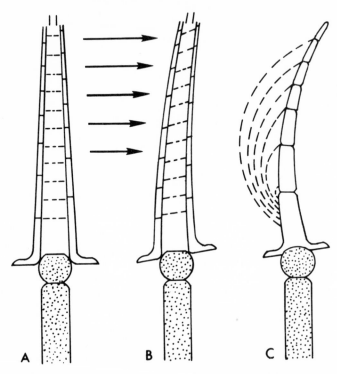

Figure 6. Diagram to illustrate that, as a fin ray is swung from right to left (in *B*), the resistance of the water increases toward its periphery (where its walls are also thinnest). Unless some counteracting, stiffening force also increases toward the periphery, the outer portion of the ray would presumably fold over and become almost or quite ineffective. Possibly, the membrane that unites the two halves of the ray, indicated by the dashed lines between the two halves, provides such a force (see text). An alternative method which might be used for stiffening a segmented, columnar structure is shown in C, where the dashed lines represent hypothetical separate muscles extending from the base to each segment. Such a method seems to be used in the pectoral axis of lungfishes (see Braus 1900) but apparently does not occur elsewhere among fishes.

elements and their membranes. As the dermal rays themselves are bony, hence presumably nondistensible, the elasticity must be provided by their membranes. These are of two types: (1) the membranes between adjacent segments of each half of the ray, and (2) the membranes holding together the two halves of any dermal ray. When any ray is bent to the right by the force of the water pushing against it (fig. 6*B*) the membranes between the segments of the left half of that ray may be slightly expanded. If so, and if these membranes are elastic, then they will tend to pull the ray back to an erect position. But also, if the ray is bent, its two halves will tend to shear in relation to one another (fig. 6B). If the membranes that unite the two halves are elastic, they will tend to counteract this shearing, again bringing the bent ray back to an upright position. How a ray actually attains its elasticity has not been investigated. It is probably significant, however, that all soft rays have separate right and left bony halves.

Though both flexibility and elasticity are requirements of any soft fin ray, the relative importance of the two factors would seem to depend in part on the use made of the particular fin (Harris 1953). Thus most filefishes and triggerfishes swim by passing undulations backward (or forward) along the dorsal and anal. Since the bases of the two fins remain linear, undulations in these fins can be developed only by the peripheral areas of the fin—the more peripheral the greater the potential undulation. However, flexibility of the individual fin rays will only diminish the amount of undulation produced in the fin as a whole. Fishes that move in this way tend to have relatively short, stiff, closely spaced, unbranched rays. It is significant that those triggerfishes that move forward by swinging their fins back and forth rather than by moving undulations along the fins (e.g., *Canthidermis*) have much longer dorsal and anal fin rays. Here, the flexibility factor is more important.

Where flexibility and elasticity are not desirable, the soft ray has been replaced by fin spines. These spines, though they have been developed a number of times in a number of ways, usually lack the segmentation and always lack the double structure and branching of soft rays. When fin spines have a primarily defensive function, they tend to be stiff and pungent. There are occasions, however, when fin spines seem to serve other purposes, and in such instances it may be difficult to differentiate them from soft rays.

All fish fins (except perhaps the adipose) have certain basic similarities, and certain factors, starvation, for example, seem to affect the pattern of growth in the rays of all fins simultaneously. Nevertheless, whether the fin ray is represented by a spine, a soft ray, or ceratotrichia, and the manner of articulation of the dermal rays with their endoskeletal supports will vary considerably, depending on the functional specialization of the particular fin. Only a general account of this differentiation will be given at this point.

The old shark and chondrostean fin type, with numerous

dermal rays basally overlapping relatively few endoskeletal blocks that extended well out into the fin, would seem to provide relatively little fin flexibility. Such flexibility as exists must be restricted largely to the edge of the fin, and there would seem to have been little possibility of raising or depressing the fin on its longitudinal axis.

Considerable functional improvement in flexibility of fins seems to have occurred in "holosteans." In those fishes each ray movably articulates with its own skeletal support, which does not protrude into the fin. In the "holosteans" there developed a one-to-one relationship between rays and endoskeletal supports not only in the dorsal and anal, but in the caudal fin as well, and such a condition was at least approached in the pectorals and pelvics. Though teleosts retain the one-to-one ratio between dermal rays and endoskeletal supports in the dorsal and anal, a number of rays frequently articulate with a single endoskeletal support in the other fins. The reasons for this can best be taken up in the accounts of the individual fins.

THE INDIVIDUAL FINS

Fish fins, though they may also serve other functions, are basically concerned with locomotion. In this regard they play a number of roles. Forward movement of the fish must be generated; there must be a method of guiding its course; and finally there should be some system of braking or indeed of backing up. So long as a fish, for example, an eel, moves only by undulation, the various requirements of locomotion are distributed along the length of the body and there is little differentiation of fins. But with the trend toward emphasis on caudal locomotion and a relatively rigid, heavy body, the various fins become specialized for particular functions. This is related to the fact that in this type of locomotion certain of the fin functions can be most effectively carried out by fins placed over definite regions of the body (Aleev 1963). Thus, in caudal locomotion the fins concerned with forward thrust are, by definition, at the posterior end. Fins that stabilize the course of forward movement, as do the feathers of an arrow, must be behind the center of gravity. Fins that function as rudders, controlling and changing the direction of movement, are most effectively placed at the greatest possible distance from the center of gravity, either anterior or posterior to it. Finally, if a fin is to function as a keel its most effective position is at the level of the center of gravity. On the basis of these differences in fin function Aleev (1963) has divided the fish body into four regions: (1) an anterior zone of rudders (and their functional equivalents, lift surfaces), (2) a zone of keels, (3) one of stabilizers, and (4) one of locomotor organs and posterior rudders. This differentiation of zones provides a useful conceptual framework providing it is understood (1) that a fin or fins may serve additional functions, such as braking, that are not zonally differentiated, (2) that a single fin may and usually does serve more than one function, and (3) that this zonation applies only to those forms that emphasize caudal locomotion.

THE DORSAL AND ANAL FINS

The typical dorsal and anal remain the least specialized of fins. If one considers fins to have arisen as folds extending the body surfaces of an undulating fish, the dorsal and anal, among teleostean fins, retain most nearly the original function. For purposes of simplicity, it would be pleasant to think of the dorsal and anal fins as providing functional opposites to one another on the dorsal and ventral rims of the body. However, this is only partially so. When the dorsal and anal fins aid in forward propulsion or in braking, or function as stabilizers, they tend to act as symmetrical opposites. But the extent of the symmetry is limited by two perhaps related factors. One is the usual vertical asymmetry of the body form (see below). Second, the visceral organs and anus are ventral to the body axis, essentially limiting the forward origin of the anal, but not of the dorsal, fin. Therefore, though the dorsal and anal may be symmetrical posteriorly, the dorsal, if it extends anteriorly, acquires functions (e.g., as a keel or anterior rudder) unattainable to the anal fin. Thus the dorsal and anal may become partially or wholly asymmetrical in relation to one another.

In the sharks, which combine a large component of body undulation with caudal locomotion, the short posterior dorsal and anal are essentially symmetrical opposites. They may be used during swimming partly to aid forward locomotion and partly to offset the sidewise push of the swinging tail. It would seem from the photographs of swimming sharks given by Gray (1933, pl. III) that the dorsal and anal may be far enough ahead of the caudal to be in the opposite phase of undulation from it. Thus, when the caudal is pushing the body forward and to the left, the dorsal and anal would be pushing it forward and to the right, and vice versa (fig. 7A).

In some higher teleosts the posterior ends of the dorsal and anal

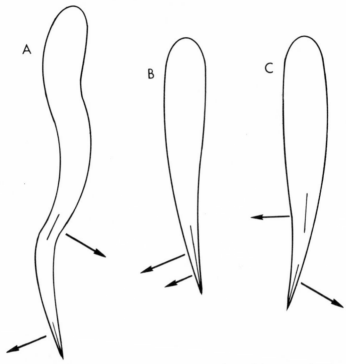

Figure 7. Diagram illustrating the possible function of the posterior dorsal (or anal) fin in *A*, a shark; *B*, *Chaetodon*; and *C*, most teleosts (e. g., a black bass). All three figures represent dorsal views; the median lines represent the posterior dorsal (or anal) fins. The upper arrows show the direction of push of the dorsal (or anal) against the water, the lower arrows that of the caudal fin in a swimming fish. In *A*, the dorsal and anal apparently help to generate the forward thrust, but by pushing in an opposite direction from the caudal, also stabilize the forward trajectory. In *B*, the dorsal and anal help to generate the forward force, but since they move together with the caudal the back end of the fish wobbles from side to side. In *C*, the dorsal and anal act independently of the caudal; they do not help to generate the forward force, and probably diminish it to some extent through friction, but by increasing the vertical surface of the posterior portion of the body, they tend to prevent that portion of the body from being pushed sideways by the lateral force generated by the caudal.

are so close to the caudal that they appear to be nearly in phase with it. Thus a fish like the butterfly fish, *Chaetodon*, moves forward by swinging its soft dorsal and anal back and forth with the caudal; the result is a flapping of the whole posterior end of the body and a wobbling sort of forward progress (fig. 7*B*). So far as the position of the posterior dorsal and anal are concerned, the

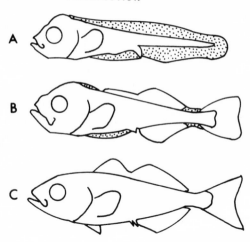

Figure 8. Developmental stages of *Trachurus mediterraneus ponticus* (based on Aleev 1963, fig. 108). *A*, 0.28 cm; *B*, 0.68 cm; and *C*, 1.00 cm. Fin fold stippled.

sharks and *Chaetodon* seem to represent extremes, with most teleosts somewhere in between.

Breder (1926) has shown that the usual teleost can slow its forward trajectory by swinging its dorsal and anal fins to one side and its caudal to the other. Presumably in teleosts, but not in sharks, any opposing movements of these two suites of fins will slow the forward trajectory. If, however, the dorsal and anal are swung only slightly to the opposite side from the caudal, the disadvantage of increased drag would seem to be offset by the advantage gained through stabilization of the forward course. (The same offsetting advantage is gained by adding feathers to an arrow.) If this is so, the posterior portions of the dorsal and anal may serve as stabilizing rudders (fig. 7*C*) to diminish yawing, just as the rudder of a boat may be used for the same purpose.

This stabilizing-rudder concept of the posteriorly placed dorsal and anal fins may be carried one step further. In the early life histories of most teleosts there is a stage in which a continuous fin fold extends vertically around the whole posterior end of the animal (fig. 8*A*). Presumably the fish moves at this stage by undulation, and the fin fold, as in most adult eels, forms a dorsoventral extension of the body that adds to the amount of surface pressed against the water. In such a fish as a bass, the dorsal, anal, and caudal fins grow out and back into the fin fold (fig. 8*B*), and the portions of this structure between these three fins is resorbed (fig. 8*C*). Why, in the adult, are the three fins discontinuous, whereas the fin fold was continuous? A possible answer lies in the changeover from undulating locomotion in the juvenile to caudal locomotion in the adult. In undulation, the lateral force generated by a bend to one side is counteracted by a bend to the other side farther along the body (fig. 1). In caudal locomotion the lateral force generated by swinging the caudal fin to one side is not thus counteracted, or only to a lesser extent. To diminish the yawing of the body during caudal locomotion, the posterior portions of the dorsal and anal seem to be used as stabilizing rudders (fig. 7C). (In this connection, it may be significant that the posterior dorsal and anal rays extend backward from a base on the body ahead of the swinging caudal axis, i.e., the caudal peduncle.) These fins would not be able to act as stabilizers if they were part of a continuous fin fold; indeed, any stabilizing action they may have depends on their being able to counteract, and hence be free from, the swinging of the caudal fin.

The fishes in which the greatest asymmetry between dorsal and anal occurs are certain of the lower teleosts. In these fishes (e.g., *Elops, Chanos, Clupea, Salmo*) there is very frequently a single dorsal fin of moderate length over approximately the center of the back. Presumably this is the old, more posteriorly placed dorsal of the earlier actinopterygians, moved forward to serve as a keel. A keel, however, has limited usefulness for fishes. It serves to diminish the overshooting of curves, but the only fishes for which the tendency to overshoot curves is a serious matter are those that develop considerable forward trajectory in relation to the body surface that is exposed to the curve the fish goes around. The tendency to overshoot, as with a car going round a curve, is due to momentum, which increases with the size and speed of the object. Thus a keel would seem to be of little use to a small and/or slowly moving animal. Nor would a keel be of use to an animal like an eel, even if the animal were large enough and fast enough to develop significant momentum. This is because the eel already has so much body surface to expose to any curve that the problem of overshooting is practically eliminated. In actinopterygian fishes a short dorsal fin placed over the center of gravity is present primarily in relatively large forms having a powerful caudal thrust.

A dorsal keel may be highly advantageous to the adult *Elops, Chanos, Clupea,* or *Salmo* but can hardly serve any purpose in the weakly swimming early stages of these same fishes. Indeed, in *Elops,* and to a lesser extent in *Chanos* and *Clupea,* the dorsal fin first develops ontogenetically well behind the final adult position (Gosline 1969). Assuming that the dorsal fin in its adult forward position functions as a keel, what is the significance of the ontogenetically earlier, more posterior position of the dorsal fin?

Before attempting to answer this question, it may be well to take up another, probably related, matter. In those members of the Salmoniformes and Cypriniformes that have an anteriorly placed dorsal, the fin originates in the adult position. However, in most Salmoniformes and Cypriniformes there is, behind the rayed dorsal, a small, so-called adipose (but see Weisel 1968) fin. Is the adipose the functional equivalent of the more posteriorly placed dorsal of the juvenile *Elops, Clupea,* and *Chanos,* none of which have an adipose fin? If so (or if not) what function does the adipose serve?

No really satisfactory answers to the questions in the last two paragraphs can be given. But since these matters are of importance for the interpretation of lower teleostean evolution, they require some discussion. It seems best to deal with them in relation to ontogeny.

In the newly hatched teleost, the only finlike structure is the so-called fin fold (fig. 8A). The fin fold has no skeletal structure aside from ceratotrichia.

From the ontogenetically earliest, undulating type of locomotion, most teleosts develop a progressively emphasized caudal type of locomotion. This does not take place in a single step (or lurch) and it seems possible that the posteriorly placed dorsal of *Elops, Clupea,* and *Chanos,* and the adipose of Salmoniformes, Myctophiformes, and Cypriniformes are functionally significant during these transitional stages.

It would certainly appear that the adults of *Elops, Clupea, Chanos,* and *Salmo* can and do effectively counteract any imbalance caused by the asymmetry of the vertical fins. They do this, presumably, by appropriately extending the paired fins, by increasing the strength of the vertebral axis, etc. But what of the juvenile forms? Might not the posterior dorsal of the early *Elops* and the adipose fin of *Salmo* serve as counterbalance to the asymmetrically placed anal fin in the early transitional stages of organization?

The structure of the adipose is such as to support the hypothesis that this fin is significant chiefly in the juvenile stages. Like other fins, it differentiates within the fin fold, but unlike them, it rarely develops dermal rays other than the ceratotrichia, and it never has any endoskeletal supports. Thus, though the adipose arises early, it never attains the developmental completion that occurs in other fins (Wassnetzov 1935).

There is of course a danger of placing too much emphasis on the functional significance of the relatively posterior position of the dorsal fin of *Elops* and the adipose of *Salmo*. In this connection it may be recalled that the dorsal fin of cyprinids originates in its final anterior position and that the adipose has been lost. However, it does appear that it has taken the teleosts a considerable length of time to work out satisfactorily the cyprinid solution to the problem.

In the acanthopteran fishes the short, keel-like dorsal of early teleosts has been further transformed in both form and function. In higher teleosts the dorsal fin frequently extends farther forward over the anterior part of the body. With such anterior extension the dorsal fin comes to serve as a rudder as well as a keel. The requirements of structural efficiency in an anterior rudder are somewhat different from those of a keel. It would seem that a keel functions best as a relatively homogeneous unit, and that it needs only enough flexibility to permit it to swing with the body. If the keel is over the center of the body it tends neither to stabilize the forward course, as a more posteriorly located fin would do, nor to deflect it, as an anteriorly located fin would do. Thus, aside from drag, there is no particular reason to fold away a keel at any time. An anteriorly placed rudder, by contrast, has the tendency to deflect a straight, forward course, as the feathers at the *front* of an arrow would do (see Alexander 1968). This, together with drag, makes it highly desirable that a forward rudder be folded away during straight, forward progress. Presumably for these reasons, the dorsal fin of many higher teleosts is divided into two, often separate, parts—an anterior spinous rudder-keel that is folded away during forward progress, and a posterior soft portion that is not folded away and which, in conjunction with the anal, is used to stabilize the forward course, to aid forward locomotion, or for braking.

Certain other requirements of an anterior dorsal fin, if it is used as a rudder, deserve comment. Such a rudder, when erect, provides a dorsal extension of the midline over the anterior portion of the body. When a fish makes a left turn during forward progress, it bends its head to the left and erects its dorsal fin. As noted above, the flexure between the head and the body is moved back along the body as the fish passes around the bend. If the dorsal fin is to aid in this process, the flexure that passes back along the body must be duplicated in the dorsal fin. The ability to swing the anterior portion of the dorsal fin to the right or left of the posterior portion and to move this flexure backward is provided by the movable articulation between successive spines and their endoskeletal supports and by the fin membrane between adjacent spines. If longitudinal flexibility is needed, lateral flexibility in the individual spines would only diminish the usefulness of the fin as a rudder. Lateral rigidity of the fin is provided by the bony, monolithic nature of its spinous supports, which have lateral flanges basally on each side firmly propped against lateral projections from the endoskeleton of the fin (Bridge 1896). These lateral flanges at the base of each dorsal spine are thus functionally very different from the lateral flanges at the base of each soft ray (fig. 6). The former hold the spine erect; the latter serve as muscle attachments that enable the soft ray to be swung from side to side.

The anal fin, in contrast with the dorsal, is more or less restricted to a posterior position, that is, behind the anus. Despite this restriction, the anal fin is seldom lost in fishes. The possible functions of an anal fin would seem to be the same as those of a posteriorly placed dorsal fin (fig. 7).

Usually, as previously noted, the posterior portions of the dorsal and the anal are symmetrical. In many of those lower teleosts in which this is not true, it has been suggested that a more posteriorly placed dorsal fin in the juvenile form *(Elops)* or an adipose fin furnishes a partial offset for the asymmetrically placed anal fin. The only question that remains is what possible effect this asymmetry may have.

If such an anal fin created a powerful thrust directed straight forward, the effect would be to lower the posterior portion of the body (just as the action of a heterocercal tail tends to raise it). But there is no reason to believe that the anal fin creates such a thrust. If, however, the anal fin functions as a stabilizer, rudder, or brake, its asymmetrical location below the body axis may, by the drag created during these processes, tend to raise the posterior end of the body. The extent to which such a tendency, if it exists, is offset by the greater convexity of the dorsal surface of the body and by the dorsal fin remains unknown. But also, if an asymmetrical anal fin were used for braking, as a rudder, or even as a stabilizer, it would tend to twist the rear of the fish. Perhaps this is the most serious effect such a fin might have on a fish, at least until its vertebral column is firmly formed.

THE CAUDAL FIN

The perfection of caudal locomotion has probably been the single greatest achievement of the teleostean fishes. Functionally as well as structurally, the heterocercal tail of sharks and early bony fishes seems to be a sort of halfway point between body undulation and the swinging of the teleostean caudal fin. A reason why the teleosts have inherited an axial skeleton that extends along the dorsal rim of the caudal fin, rather than one with the axis through the center (as in *Latimeria* and modern lungfish) or along the ventral border (as in the extinct pteraspids), may be as follows.

Aleev (1963) has shown that a fish that has more dorsal than ventral body surface will (because of differential friction) tend to turn upward during forward progress. This tendency is usually counteracted by concentrating most of the forward-directed locomotor force above the body axis. Forms which live near the bottom, as vertebrate ancestors presumably did, naturally have a flat ventral surface, and any protrusions are on the dorsal surface, as in the modern sturgeons. The heterocercal caudal fin of sturgeons does not seem to provide any great lift for the posterior end of the body (Aleev 1963), but instead it directs a forward force above the body axis, thus counteracting the excess drag of the dorsal surface during forward movement. In the related but free-swimming *Polyodon*, in which there is less asymmetry between dorsal and ventral surfaces, the caudal fin is far more symmetrical than that of the sturgeons. It has frequently been noted (e.g., Patterson 1968a) that certain neutrally buoyant fishes continue to have somewhat heterocercal fins, and it may well be, as Aleev implies, that such fins have more to do with body shape than with providing a lift force for the posterior end of the fish.

Such lift force as a heterocercal fin supplies would seem to arise from the fact that the caudal rays extend downward as well as backward from the caudal axis (fig. 9B). When the axis is swung through a lateral arc, the tips of these rays, insofar as they are flexible, will swing through the arc somewhat later than the axis (fig. 9A). As a result the tail will be forced somewhat upward as well as forward. Aleev (1963) pointed out that the teleost can and does bring about the same upward force by voluntarily swinging its lower caudal lobe through any lateral arc somewhat later than the upper.

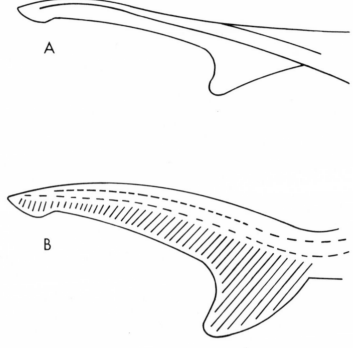

Figure 9. Heterocercal fin of a shark in dorsal view *(A)* and lateral view *(B)* with the rays and axis indicated. As the axis of the fin is swung from right to left (bottom to top of page), the lower edge of the fin trails somewhat behind, but also the anterior portion of the axis precedes its tip in any one cross stroke and the total sidewise distance traveled is less at the base than at the tip.

However, a teleost can also force the tail down, and hence the head upward, by swinging the lower caudal lobe through a lateral arc somewhat in advance of the upper. It would be difficult for a fish with a heterocercal fin to do this; upward turns in sharks and sturgeons apparently must be accomplished entirely by means of the paired fins (though possible the fish can change somewhat the axis of the tail). The essentially symmetrical caudal fin of the higher teleosts may provide other advantages. First, a teleost, by differential swinging of the individual caudal rays, can cause undulations to pass up and down the fin. The force created by such undulations is almost entirely vertical. Teleosts frequently use this method of adjusting the position of the posterior end of the body while maintaining a stationary position in the water. Second, and more important, a teleost, for forward progression, can swing both caudal lobes back and forth synchronously, both lobes generating a directly forward force. A fish with a heterocercal tail cannot easily do this because the endoskeletal supports for the rays of the lower caudal lobe articulate farther forward along the axis than do those of the upper lobe (fig. 9B). Hence any swinging of the axis affects the lower lobe first and makes exact synchronization of the two lobes difficult if not impossible.

In the preceding paragraphs, the heterocercal caudal fin of such a fish as a sturgeon has been contrasted with the externally symmetrical tail of a teleost. There are, however, transitional stages between these two.

In such "holosteans" as *Amia* and *Lepisosteus,* the caudal fin, like the dorsal and anal, has achieved a one-to-one relationship between the rays and their endoskeletal supports, in this case hypurals (fig. 10A). The external outline of the caudal fin is also much more nearly symmetrical than that of the sturgeons. Undoubtedly this change permits a much greater flexibility in the fin for purposes of creating vertical forces, downward or upward, at the posterior end of the animal. Each of the hypurals, however, retains a basal articulation with a separate centrum, which means that the endoskeletal supports to the lower caudal rays articulate farther forward on the vertebral column than do those of the upper caudal rays. In short, as compared with sturgeons, *Amia* and *Lepisosteus* have improved the caudal flexibility, but still seem to retain some of the old inefficiency in the generation of a synchronized forward force.

Both *Amia* and *Lepisosteus* have rounded tails. Quite possibly their caudal structure, emphasizing flexibility, is an adaptation to their modes of life and represents a sidetrack of the main evolutionary pathways in this respect. A more direct route toward the teleostean caudal structure may be provided by the pholidophoroids (Patterson 1968a). In these forms, as compared with *Amia* and *Lepisosteus,* forward thrust seems to have been emphasized, to some extent at the expense of flexibility.

In pholidophoroids (fig. 10B) the caudal fin is forked and externally symmetrical. Nevertheless, the body axis continues to extend well out into the dorsal portion of the tail. The skeletal support for the two lobes seems to have evolved differently (Patterson 1968a). The support to the lower lobe is still provided by hypurals which extend inward to separate, at least partly ossified centra. However, unlike *Amia* and *Lepisosteus,* there may be several rays per hypural. The upper lobe, on the other hand, has

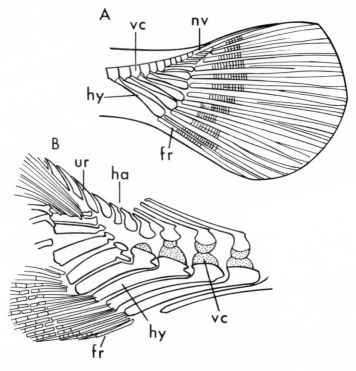

Figure 10. *A*, Diagram of the caudal fin and its skeleton in the holostean *Lepisosteus* (based on Goodrich 1909, fig. 62); *B*, caudal skeleton and part of the fin of the preteleostean *Pholidophorus* (based on Patterson 1968*a* fig. 1). *fr*, Fin ray; *ha*, hinge area; *hy*, hemal arch element; *nv*, notochord; *ur*, uroneural; and *vc*, vertebral centrum.

developed a rather specialized supporting structure. The centra with which its hypurals articulated were unossified (Patterson 1968*a*), and the axial support for the upper lobe must have been weak. Probably to compensate for this weakness, the bases of the upper caudal rays extend well in alongside, and at an angle to, their hypurals. Dorsal to the notochordal axis is a series of overlapping, shinglelike neural arch elements. Presumably, the rays to the upper caudal lobe, together with their underlying hypurals and dorsal neural arch elements, swung back and forth as a block with a sort of hinge in the axial skeleton at its base and behind the centra supporting the lower caudal lobe (Patterson 1968*a*). In short, the upper and lower caudal lobes of pholidophoroids seem to have had rather separate axes still arranged in tandem to one another.

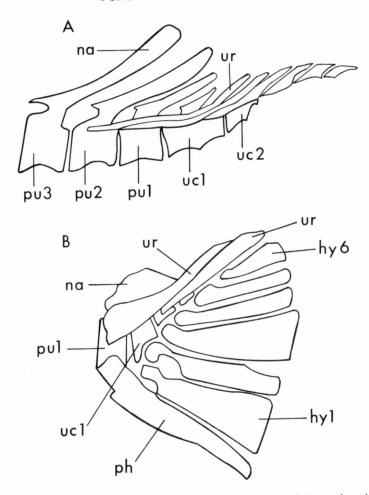

Figure 11. *A*, Posterior neural arch elements and centra of the early teleost, *Leptolepis* (based on Patterson 1968*a*, fig. 9A); *B*, caudal skeleton of juvenile *Albula* (based on Hollister 1936, fig. 23). *hy 1–6*, Hypurals; *na*, neural arch; *ph*, parahypural; *pu 1–3*, preural centra; *uc 1–2*, ural centra; and *ur*, uroneural.

Among teleosts the main evolutionary advance apparently was a union of these two axes into a single unit. This transformation occurred in several morphological steps. A first stage, represented by the earliest known teleosts, consisted of two parts. The axial support for the caudal skeleton was abbreviated by the fusion of the strengthened centra supporting the hypurals to the lower caudal lobe (fig. 11) and by further reduction of the axial support for the hypurals to the upper caudal lobe. At the same time, support for the upper caudal lobe was increased by the development of the pholidophoroid neural arch elements into elongate uroneurals (fig. 11). Notably, these rigid uroneurals extended across the old hinge area at the base of the pholidophoroid upper caudal lobe and on to the centra supporting the lower caudal lobe. Thus even the earliest known teleosts had a single axial unit supporting both caudal lobes.

In early teleosts several centra still supported the caudal skeleton (fig. 11). In higher teleosts, as a result of fusion and loss, there is only one, the so-called urostyle. Furthermore, the long uroneurals of the earlier teleosts have been somewhat retracted so that they overlie only the urostyle, with which they often fuse. There is also some loss of upper hypurals, with the result that the posterior edges of the few remaining hypurals together form a more or less continuous vertical surface. The upper caudal rays retract and movably articulate with this border, forming a movable hinge that replaces that of the old pholidophoroids at the base of the upper hypurals.

Further fusion of various types takes place in higher teleosts. Usually, because of the advantage of creating an upward or downward force at the rear of the body by differential timing of the swinging of the two caudal lobes, the hypural elements to the two lobes do not become fused into a single unit.

The evolution of caudal structure refers (with the exception of *Amia* and *Lepisosteus*) to the basal teleostean type of forked caudal fin. But such a fin shape is not always advantageous. As noted earlier, the forked caudal fin seems to be more effective where the fish creates a turbulent wake as it moves. The greater the speed, the greater the wake, and the more widely spread the lobes must be to extend beyond it. But the greater the speed, the more powerful the caudal thrust must be and the stiffer the caudal blades. This is all to the good for large fishes swimming rapidly through wide unobstructed spaces. But the caudal of such a fish as a tuna needs a powerful thrust before its structure can become effective, if only because there is no flexibility in its blades at a weaker thrust. There are, however, many fishes that live in congested areas, and these need to move about carefully and at low speed. For them a turbulent wake is no problem. They do, however, need flexibility within and between the rays. Such fishes have usually developed the rounded fin shape of *Amia* and *Lepisosteus,* with long flexible median rays.

A rounded caudal fin presumably could be developed from the ancestral forked type by merely lengthening the central rays and shortening the outer principal rays. This has happened, for example, in *Apogon waikiki*, a round-tailed member of a fork-tailed genus. However, the stresses on a rounded caudal are basically different from those on a forked tail and, if continued a sufficient number of generations, would result via natural selection, in a reorganization of caudal structure. Thus it is the outer principal rays of a forked tail which must be pushed from side to side during forward locomotion. The caudal skeleton and musculature (Nursall 1962a) are organized to accomplish this, and the central caudal rays are merely carried along with the outer rays. In round-tailed fishes, by contrast, the forces that move the tail back and forth are distributed throughout the base of the fin, but tend to be emphasized in the central area since this portion of the fin has the longest rays. As far as skeletal structure is concerned, two of the features that have developed time and again in round-tailed teleosts, such as cyprinodonts, gobies, and flatfishes, are (1) a change from a definite to an indefinite number of branched caudal rays, and (2) the tendency to strengthen the central portion of the caudal skeleton at the expense of its upper and lower portions. Thus, in round-tailed fishes one or more of the central hypural plates often become fused with the last centrum, whereas the uroneurals above and the parahypural, which supports lower caudal rays in fork-tailed forms, become detached from the rest of the caudal skeleton and dwindle to insignificance (see Monod 1968).

THE PAIRED FINS

The paired fins seem to have originated as lateral projections from the body. In most fast-swimming lower fishes the surfaces of these fins when extended are horizontal, and they serve as rudders controlling the vertical course of forward movement. Thus, if the leading edges of these fins are held higher than the trailing edges during forward motion, most of the passing water impinges against the bottom surface of the fin, forcing the fish upward. If such fins are forward of the center of gravity, as is true of the pectorals, the effect is to force the head upward in relation to the tail.

Three methods have been developed among fishes for changing the level at which they move through the water. One, found among many higher teleosts, is extension of the pelvic fins. When such fins are unfolded from the sides, their leading edges are limited to movement in an anteroventral direction by the nature

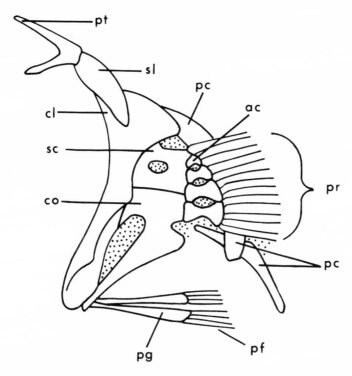

Figure 12. Left pectoral and pelvic girdles and fins of *Serranus* (based on Goodrich 1909, fig. 436). *ac,* Actinost; *cl,* cleithrum; *co,* coracoid; *pc,* postcleithrum; *pf,* pelvic ray; *pg,* pelvic girdle; *pr,* pectoral rays; *pt,* posttemporal; *sc,* scapula; and *sl,* supracleithrum.

of the articulation between the fin rays and the pelvic girdle. As a result, the leading edges of the extended pelvic fins are lower than their trailing edges, thus forcing the moving fish downward in the water (Harris 1938). Within limits, the farther the pelvics are extended and spread, the greater will be the downward force exerted. In such fins the edge of a single rigid bone, the pelvic girdle, determines and restricts the plane of pelvic fin expansion.

The other methods of changing the level at which the fish moves through the water depend on a swiveling of the fin axis. Such a swivel may have essentially a central axis, as it does in the pectoral of the lungfishes, the "chondrostean" *Polypterus,* and in certain teleosts, for example, salariin blennies, batrachoids, and lophiiform fishes (Monod 1960). The far more usual, and undoubtedly the original, teleostean type, is for the pectoral fin to swivel around the anteriormost (or uppermost) ray as an axis (fig. 12). The actinosts, progressively longer from top to bottom, provide the mechanism by means of which the fin base can be rotated about this axis. This type of swivel has the advantage that the anteriormost ray, which is fully exposed to the force of the passing water when the fin is extended, has a direct basal support and to some extent protects the more posterior rays with their indirect basal articulations.

The pectorals of early fishes extended from the ventrolateral angles of the body; that is, they were placed below the main axis of the body. Presumably, this location required that the pectorals be extended with the leading edge somewhat higher than the trailing edge just to offset the asymmetry of their position during forward movement. In any event, the pectorals of higher teleosts have moved up on the sides to a position essentially along or above the longitudinal axis (as in fig. 12). In the course of this development the bases have changed from an essentially horizontal to a primarily vertical alignment (fig. 12). With this change the pectorals have developed some new capabilities. One is the ability to maintain, by "fanning," a stationary position in the water. A second, used by many fishes that habitually rest on the bottom, is to clap partly extended pectorals sharply back against the sides to accelerate from a standing start.

Despite the change to a vertical base, the axis of rotation around the anteriormost (now the uppermost) ray is usually maintained, with the result that when the pectoral is extended the uppermost ray is swung out ahead of the lower. This in turn tends to push the anterior end of the fish upward.

In higher teleosts, however, the pelvics have moved forward to a position essentially below the pectorals, and any tendency to force the head up by extending the pectorals is counteracted by extending the pelvics at the same time. These four fins can, in fact, be extended synchronously in such a way as to form something like a "four-wheel" braking system (Harris 1938). The pectorals, however, remain the essential component in the system, and the pelvics frequently assume other functions than locomotion or are lost entirely. Only rarely, for example in some eel-like forms that move by undulation, are the pectoral fins lost.

Judging from the frequency with which the pelvic fins have been lost, they are the least important of fish fins. In all early fishes, they are located, when present, well behind the pectorals, and presumably, like the pectorals, they aid in controlling the (vertical) level at which the fish moves through the water. When, as in *Elops, Chanos, Salmo,* and other lower teleosts, the dorsal fin moves forward during development to function as a keel (see above), the pelvics may well take on an additional function. For when such fishes execute a turn, the dorsal keel minimizes side-slipping, but it controls only the dorsal rim of the body, while the ventral portion of the body tends to roll under and beyond the dorsal rim in the course of the turn. This could be prevented by extension of one or both pelvic fins directly below a dorsal fin used as a keel.

Circumstantial evidence supports this view of the function of pelvic fins. When, in higher teleosts, a spinous dorsal rudder is developed still farther forward (which, when in use, would cause the same tendency to roll), the pelvic fins move forward to a thoracic position. It is only after the pelvic fins have moved forward that the four-part braking system mentioned above can be effectively developed.

THE PELVIC GIRDLE AND THE EVOLUTION
OF FIN SPINES

Sewertzoff (1934) has shown that in the chondrostean *Acipenser* the broad-based pelvics have endoskeletal supports (the pelvic girdle) that form ontogenetically by the fusion of separate elements. In "holosteans" and the lower teleosts the pelvic girdle is made up of a single plate on each side, except for one or a few nodules at the base of the innermost pelvic rays. (Where there is more than one such nodule, the innermost is the longest.) This nodule arrangement appears to be the analog of the pectoral actinosts, permitting some rotation of the fin about the outermost ray as an axis. In higher teleosts these nodules are lost, and the pelvics can be extended or retracted only along an essentially single plane, as previously noted. It is perhaps this loss of ability to swivel about an axis that is ultimately responsible for the reduction in number of pelvic rays to six or fewer in almost all higher teleosts. (An exception is found in certain flatfishes, in which the many-rayed pelvic of one side forms, functionally, a forward extension of the anal fin.)

Perhaps the best place to take up the matter of teleostean fin spines is in connection with the pelvic girdle. Fish fins are primarily concerned with locomotion, but they serve other purposes as well. One that is common to many, indeed perhaps to most, higher teleosts is to provide a measure of defense—in the form of strong, sharp, strategically located fin spines.

From the point of view of defensive effectiveness, there seem to be three main requirements of fin spines. First, they must be strong and firm, but retractable. (Extended fin spines, however valuable they may be for defense, would present a considerable source of drag to forward motion.) Second, they must be so placed that they expand the perimeter of the fish to the maximum possible extent. Whether one fish will fit into another fish's mouth depends upon its maximum diameter, and fin spines that add to that diameter may make the difference between fitting and not fitting. If the fish is deep bodied, then spines protruding beyond the top and bottom surfaces at the point of maximum depth will be most effective. If the fish is more or less triangular in cross section, then spines extending out from the angles will be most effective. But if one border is protected and the opposite is not, then the undefended border is open to attack. It may be mentioned in this connection that the abdomen would seem to provide the single most vulnerable area, and fishes appear to have made a considerable effort to protect it.

The third requirement of fin spines for defensive efficiency is that they be firmly based. A firm spine on a flabby base would be of little use. Extending firmly based spines from the dorsal border of the fish would seem to present no difficulty because the endoskeletal supports for the dorsal rays can be anteroposteriorly expanded and extended inward even, if necessary, to an abutment against the vertebral column (see, for example, the cover illustration, based on *Antigonia*). Extending spines from the ventral or ventrolateral borders of the abdominal region has presented greater difficulty. Various means of accomplishing this have been tried by different fishes. Catfishes, which are unique in this respect among living fishes, have developed strong pectoral spines. The firm base for these spines is supplied by the pectoral girdles of the two sides, which have expanded and fused along the midventral line. Among higher teleosts in which the pectorals have moved up on the sides, pectoral spines can no longer effectively protect the abdominal area. Pelvic spines have been substituted. With pelvic spines, the principal difficulty would seem to have been to provide a firm support for them. The pelvic girdles, which in lower teleosts lie in the flesh over the abdomen, do not seem to have been adequate in themselves; in any event, strong pelvic spines never have been developed from such a base alone (except possibly in notacanthids). In sticklebacks the strong pelvic spines movably articulate with pelvic girdles that are greatly expanded as dermal plates. In other forms, such as the gray mullet, the pelvic girdles have developed an abutment against the tips of the postcleithra (Gosline 1962). However, the only generally adopted solution was not available until the pelvics had moved well forward. In most perciform fishes, for example, the pelvic girdles extend forward between, and are ligamentously attached to, the lower ends of the cleithra of the pectoral girdle (fig. 12).

Speculation about the evolution of teleostean fishes in general is perhaps permissible here. The perfection of fin spine equipment was essentially completed by the perciform stage of evolution. At and above this level a large number of slow-swimming or essentially sedentary forms of various types have evolved. Such fishes have reduced the emphasis on sustained speed as a means of escaping enemies. To compensate, they seem to rely to a greater extent on defenses of various sorts, fin spines being the principal one. In this they seem to have come full circle back to the old chondrostean-holostean system of defensive existence, though the fin spines of acanthopteran teleosts are very different structurally from the armored scales and dermal bones of the older forms.

THE PECTORAL GIRDLE AND THE
AXIAL MUSCULATURE TO THE HEAD

The pectoral girdle (fig. 12) of teleosts (Sewertzoff 1926) has two sources. The so-called primary girdle consists of the actinosts, scapula, coracoid, and sometimes mesocoracoid ossifications that replace cartilage (Starks 1930). The so-called secondary pectoral girdle of teleosts is made up of the dermal posttemporal, supracleithrum, and cleithrum, and the two postcleithra that are presumably of membranous origin. That the "secondary" pectoral girdle is one of the most ancient entities in fishes has been shown by Jarvik (1944). The particular ossifications that make up the "primary" girdle, by contrast, are of far later origin.

The actinosts of the primary pectoral girdle were apparently numerous in preteleostean actinopterygians, and each one must have been tipped by a separate nodule of cartilage (Gosline 1969), as the endoskeletal supports for the dorsal and anal fins still are. These actinosts articulated basally with a single ossification in the pholidophoroid *Ichthyokentema* (Griffith and Patterson 1963); this ossification in teleosts breaks up into scapula, coracoid, and mesocoracoid. The actinosts are reduced to four in all but a few teleosts, and the mesocoracoid bone disappears in higher forms.

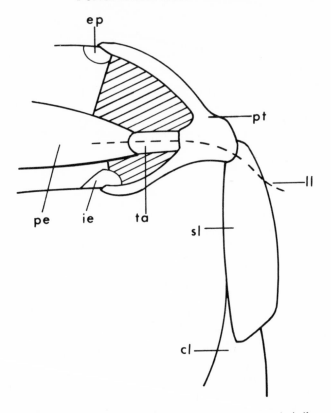

Figure 13. Diagram of the articulation between the pectoral girdle and skull, left side. *cl*, Cleithrum; *ep*, epiotic; *ie*, intercalar; *ll*, lateral line, its course from the pterotic to the body indicated by dashes; *pe*, pterotic; *pt*, posttemporal; *sl*, supracleithrum; and *ta*, tabular.

The primary pectoral girdle, which seems to have the single, but important, function of supporting the pectoral fin, is implanted basally on the cleithrum.

The secondary pectoral girdle serves a number of purposes. The two postcleithra (fig. 12), which extend back and down on the sides, seem to act somewhat as an anterior rib. The largest bone in the secondary girdle is the cleithrum, which meets its fellow on the midventral line. The heart lies between the anteroventral ends of the two cleithra. Posteriorly, the cleithrum supports the primary pectoral girdle, and in higher teleosts, by means of a movable ligamentous attachment, the pelvic girdle. The anterior surfaces of the cleithra form the posterior walls of the gill cavities; they constitute the structural partition between the gill cavity to the front and the abdominal cavity posteriorly.

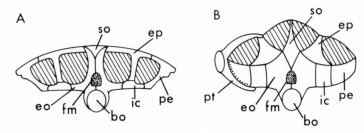

Figure 14. Diagram of the backs of skulls to show muscular attachments (the obliquely hatched areas). *A*, Skull of the *Albula* type with the fossae roofed by bone; *B*, skull of the percoid type without bony roofing for the musculature and with the supraoccipital crest developed. The posttemporal of the pectoral girdle is shown in position on the left side of *B*. *bo*, Basioccipital; *eo*, exoccipital; *ep*, epiotic; *fm*, foramen magnum; *ic*, intercalar; *pe*, pterotic; *pt*, posttemporal; and *so*, supraoccipital.

The upper portion of the pectoral girdle has had a complex origin. In holosteans and teleosteans the pectoral girdle is indirectly attached to the back of the cranium. In teleosts this attachment is like a double hinge that allows movement of the upper end of the cleithrum relative to the cranium in two planes. The lateral portion of the posttemporal, because of its two prongs extending anteromedially to attachments to the upper and lower surfaces of the cranium (figs. 13, 14*B*), can swing in and out around a central axis to a certain extent. The supracleithrum extends downward from the posttemporal, and its lower end can move fore and aft in relation to its articulation with the posttemporal (figs. 12, 13).

This two-plane hinge system between the skull and the upper end of the cleithrum also serves a quite different, but perhaps equally important, function in relation to the lateral-line system. The lateralis canals of the head are continuous with that of the body, and any lateral swinging or twisting of the head would tend to dislocate the lateral line where it crosses from the head onto the body. Since the head canals pass through the posttemporal and the upper portion of the supracleithrum (fig. 13) before continuing out on the body, the two-plane jointing system in those bones tends to alleviate tensions on the lateral-line canal in that area. In this respect, the posttemporal, because of its attachments to the head, moves primarily with the head, but its position is affected by what happens at its link with the supracleithrum. The supracleithrum, conversely, is primarily a bone covering the side of the body, but it is affected by movements of the head through its attachment to the posttemporal. Thus both bones buffer the effect of head movements on that part of the lateral-line system extending between the head and the body.

In lower actinopterygians there seems to have been little possibility of independent head movement. During the course of evolution, judging from the increasing specialization of muscular attachments to the back of the skull, ability to move the head has considerably increased. Indeed, in the teleost the change in these attachment surfaces has caused what is perhaps the major alteration in skull configuration. Since the location and development of these muscular attachments seem to be strongly influenced by the posttemporal-skull articulations, they will be discussed at this point. Throughout the course of the changes that have occurred, the posttemporal-skull articulations have remained relatively unaffected. Their functional significance to the fish is indicated by the fact that they remain as fixed points, with the body muscle extensions onto the skull developing on either side of them (fig. 14).

The importance of body muscle attachments in the formation of the cranium is indicated by the fact that the back of the fish skull, the so-called neocranium, is thought to be made up of vertebral elements that have been subsequently added to the original skull, the paleocranium. The number of vertebrae that have been added to the skull in this way differs in the various fish groups (see, for example, Ridewood 1904a; de Beer 1937). Regardless of the number of segments that have been added, one of the primary functions of the posterior face of the skull is to provide attachment for the body musculature. Whether the head is to be used as an anterior rudder in locomotion or is to be moved separately from the body in order to seize sidewise-darting prey, the ability to move the head is of first importance.

Initially, head movements in various directions were probably accomplished by contraction of particular portions of the body musculature attached to the rear of the skull. This has led to concentrations of particular portions of the musculature and to specialization of areas of attachment. If concentrations of musculature are to become attached to particular areas, this will tend to have one of two effects. Either the muscles will be concentrated into ligaments that need a firm source of attachment, or the areas of attachment will be expanded if it is possible. Surfaces for muscle attachment can be expanded either by the development of indentations into the surface or by the development of projections.

The supraoccipital at the top of the skull roof presumably arose as a surface for attachment of muscles which, on contraction, raised the head. In such a fish as *Chanos* the supraoccipital forms a posterior extension of the skull roof which splays out posteriorly into a series of ligaments (see Ridewood 1905*a,* fig. 140).

In many "holosteans" and lower teleosts (e.g., *Elops*), there is a deep concavity on either side of the posterior skull face, lateral to the epiotic and intercalar articulations of the posttemporal, into which the body muscles extend (fig. 14*A*). These concavities, the posttemporal fossae, presumably represent expansions of attachment surfaces for muscles which, when one contracted, swung the head to that side. In higher teleosts the roofs of the posttemporal fossae have disappeared and the body musculature often extends well forward over the skull roof on either side.

Another pair of concavities in the posterior face of the skull on either side of the supraoccipital, but medial to the epiotic and intercalar (fig. 14*A*) appear in such skulls as that of *Albula.* In higher fishes the roofs of these concavities have also disappeared and another pair of muscles extends forward on either side of the supraoccipital. When this happens, the surface areas for attachment of these muscles are often further increased by the development of a supraoccipital crest (fig. 14*B*). Thus in higher teleosts the upper surface of the back of the skull often contains three longitudinal crests of bone—the crest of the supraoccipital medially, and a frontal-parietal crest on either side. The lateral surfaces of all three serve for muscle attachment. In such fishes the configuration of the armor-plated, flattish skull roof of the early actinopterygians has become drastically transformed, and, among other differences, body musculature extends in over the surface of some of the bones that made up the original dermal covering.

THREE

Feeding and Respiration

From a morphological point of view, it would seem logical to follow an account of axial and fin structure with a description of the head skeleton. Functionally, however, axial and fin structures are concerned only with locomotion, whereas the head is concerned with several functions. Indeed, it carries out all those functions which, for various reasons, are advantageously located at the anterior end of the body. For purposes of presentation these functions will be divided into two categories: feeding and respiration, dealt with in this chapter, and sensory perception and coordination, in the next. Therefore, the head skeleton, usually considered as a unit, is discussed in various sections of the book. Because of this rather unorthodox treatment, it may be well, before proceeding, to compare briefly the morphological and functional approaches to the head skeleton.

If the head skeleton is treated as a morphological unit (e.g., Goodrich 1909, 1930; Gregory 1933; Devillers 1958; Bertmar 1959; Daget 1964), it is usually discussed according to the origin of its component parts. Thus, it is pointed out that the bony fish head is made up of bone of two types: endochondral bones, which more or less completely replace the earlier cartilaginous skeleton during ontogeny; and dermal bones, superficial to the endochondral bones and cartilaginous skeleton. All dermal bones originate in the dermis, but the endochondral bones have two sources, which provide a second basis for subdividing the head skeleton. The gill slits and gill arches supporting them form in the wall of the gut and are, ultimately, of endodermal origin. Thus, the endochondral bones that develop in the visceral arch system differ in source from those that make up the cranium (though Jarvik 1954, Bertmar 1959, and others have shown that certain cranial elements have, ultimately, a visceral-arch source). Finally, the cranium itself is often divided between the anterior paleocranium and a posterior neocranium, which consists of vertebral elements that have become fused to the back of the neocranium.

From the point of view of function, the paleocranium serves primarily as a seating for the brain, olfactory organ, eye, and internal ear (see chap. 4). The neocranium intermediates between the head and body of the fish by providing the articulation between the skull and vertebral column and a source for attachment on the cranium for the body musculature (see chap. 2). The bones of the visceral arch system are concerned with eating and respiration (see below). In the earliest fishes the dermal bones seem to have started out as an extension of the scaly armor over the head region. In modern teleosts the remaining dermal elements have been put to various other uses. Some bear teeth, some form the opercular apparatus, some contain lateral-line canals, and some have become associated with or fused to underlying endochondral bones to form surfaces for muscle attachments or bone articulations. Those bearing teeth and forming the opercular apparatus will be taken up in this chapter.

What happens to food after it reaches the oesophagus and to oxygen after it is taken up by the gills will be omitted from this book, not because these processes are unimportant, but because they are more closely related to physiology than to morphology. Thus, the present account will be restricted to the questions of how the food is brought to the oesophagus, and how water with its dissolved oxygen is passed to the gills.

In the basic teleostean system all of the food and almost all of the oxygen required for metabolism is acquired through the mouth, though a certain amount of respiration may still be carried on by the skin of the body (Fry 1957; Jakubowski 1958). The food is then passed along to the gut and the water is extruded through the gill openings on either side. Except in the case of air breathers, the oxygen required for respiration is extracted from the water before it is extruded. The oral cavity may be viewed as a sort of intake pipe with a filtering device on the outflow sides (fig. 15). Each filtering device is usually double; an inner (or medial) series of gill rakers (fig. 15E) screens out the larger material (i.e., food), and the remaining water then passes through a finer (peripheral) screen made up of gill filaments, where oxygen comes into close proximity with the blood and can be extracted.

As was noted in the first chapter, respiration seems to have arisen in the protovertebrates somewhat as an afterthought to eating. Oxygen was absorbed by extending vascularized surfaces (the gills) into the areas where excess water was being eliminated (the gill openings). So far as eating and respiration are concerned,

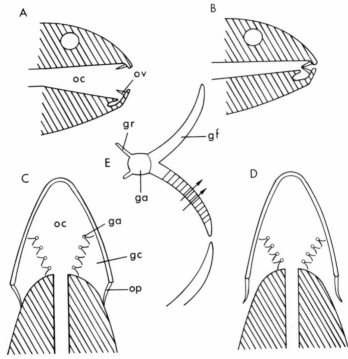

Figure 15. *A* and *B*, Diagrammatic vertical sections through the center of the mouth cavity. In *A* the mouth cavity is expanded; in *B*, contracted. *C* and *D*, Transverse sections through the mouth and gill cavities. In *C* both cavities are nearly expanded; in *D*, nearly contracted. *E*, Cross section of single gill arch, the direction of water movement indicated by arrows. *ga*, Gill arch; *gc*, gill cavity; *gf*, gill filament; *gr*, gill raker; *oc*, oral cavity; *op*, opercular valve; and *ov*, oral valve.

the whole subsequent evolution in fishes may be viewed in terms of increasing specialization and separation of functions. Not only does respiration become progressively independent of eating, but eating itself becomes divided into two components—biting and mastication—and the pumping system for obtaining a flow of water over the gills becomes increasingly complex. The development of these specializations will be traced in this chapter.

So long as protovertebrates were ciliary feeders maintaining a more or less constant flow of water into the mouth (see chap. 1), eating in itself probably provided a sufficiently continuous outflow over the gills for purposes of respiration. But as larger organisms became a source of food, eating became intermittent.

Metabolism, however, requires a more or less constant oxygen uptake. In lower teleosts an almost continuous, unidirectional flow of water across the gills is maintained (Hughes 1963) by the coordinated action of two pumping systems (Woskoboinikoff 1932): a pressure pump in the mouth cavity, the opening and closing of which is already involved in eating, and a pair of posterolateral suction pumps in the gill cavities external to the gills (fig. 15C, D).

Thus in lower teleosts, food and oxygen are obtained in part by a single mechanism, and in part by different but closely integrated systems. For purposes of presentation it seems best to start with an account of the mouth (which combines the functions of feeding and respiration), and follow with that of the gill cavities (concerned primarily with respiration).

SEIZURE OF FOOD ITEMS

The main line of evolutionary development of actinopterygian fishes seems to extend through a series of generalized carnivores (Schaeffer and Rosen 1961). The present account will be limited to such forms. As to herbivorous fishes, suffice it to say that these, with their numerous specializations for a plant diet (Jacobshagen 1911–1913; Suyehiro 1942; Al-Hussaini 1949; and others), have developed from various stages in teleostean evolution.

In the carnivores two related aspects of evolutionary development may be distinguished. One concerns the apparatus involved in the expansion and contraction of the oral cavity; the other has to do with grasping and mastication of prey.

So far as the grasping of prey is concerned, the early bony fishes differ from sharks principally in the presence of a coating of tooth-bearing dermal bones on the walls of the oral cavity. Presumably, a series of small, undifferentiated platelets (Jarvik 1954, p. 64 and figs. 27, 34; Nybelin 1968) have by fusion given rise to these bones (fig. 16). In early bony fishes any and all parts of the mouth were developed for seizing prey. From this generalized condition higher actinopterygians have tended more and more toward the development of a more specialized arrangement, with a biting apparatus around the front rim of the oral cavity, a masticating or triturating mechanism at the rear, and a progressive reduction of dentition in the central portion of the oral cavity.

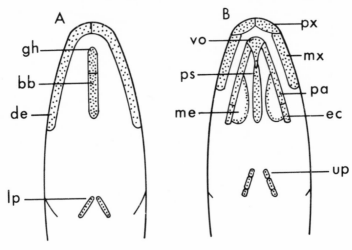

Figure 16. Maximum teleostean dentition. *A*, Floor of mouth; *B*, roof of mouth. *bb*, Basibranchial tooth plate; *de*, dentary; *ec*, ectopterygoid; *gh*, glossohyal tooth plate; *lp*, lower pharyngeal; *me*, mesopterygoid; *mx*, maxillary; *pa*, palatine; *ps*, parasphenoid; *px*, premaxillary; *up*, upper pharyngeal; and *vo*, prevomer.

THE UPPER JAW

The history of the transformation of the premaxillary and maxillary bones from roofing bones of the head into the functional upper jaw of teleosts begins with the freeing of the posterior end of the maxillary from the cheek. In "holosteans" (e.g., *Amia*) the posterior end of the maxillary has lost its attachment to the cheek and moves down with the mandible when the mouth is opened (fig. 17*B*). Though the principal advantage attained was doubtless the ability to close off a possible escape hatch for prey at the corners of the mouth, the maxillary also forms the primary, biting, upper jaw in many lower teleosts.

In the "holostean" *Amia* the anterior end of the maxillary is like a peg that extends into a hole in the side of the cranium, and the posterior part swings around this peg, while the premaxillary retains a rigid attachment to the cranium. Thus in *Amia* the premaxillaries remain toothed cranial bones, like the vomer. The history of the premaxillaries in the lower teleostean fishes is quite varied. In the argentinoids among the salmoniform fishes the premaxillaries are greatly reduced and toothless (Chapman 1942). In the eels the premaxillaries have become fused with the

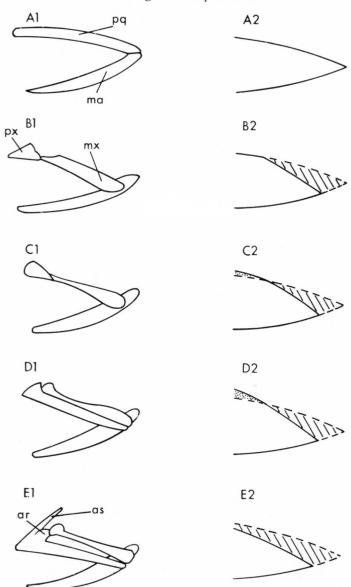

Figure 17. Jaws *(A1–E1)* and gape *(A2–E2)* with the jaws partly open in *A*, sharks; *B*, the holostean *Amia; C*, alepocephalids; *D*, myctophiform fishes; and *E*, percoids. In *A2–E2* the gape is shown as a solid line and its difference from the shark gape indicated by dashes or stippling. *ar*, Articular process of premaxillary; *as*, ascending process of premaxillary; *ma*, mandible; *mx*, maxillary; *pq*, palatoquadrate; and *px*, premaxillary.

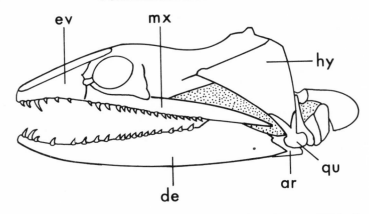

Figure 18. Head skeleton of *Gymnothorax* (based on Gregory 1933, fig. 82). *ar*, Articular; *de*, dentary; *ev*, premaxillary-ethmovomerine block; *hy*, hyomandibular; *mx*, maxillary; and *qu*, quadrate.

ethmovomerine portion of the cranium (fig. 18). The more usual condition among lower teleosts, for example, *Alepocephalus* and *Elops* (Gosline 1969), and the one from which the arrangement in all higher teleosts is derived, is for the anterior end of the maxillaries to wedge between the lateral portions of somewhat moveable premaxillaries and the cranium (figs. 17C, 19A2 and B2). When the mandible of such fishes is lowered, the posterior end of the maxillary swings down and its anterior end pushes forward the lateral portions of the premaxillaries. The result is to force the lower, toothed border of the premaxillaries somewhat outward and forward. This mechanism for moving the premaxillaries has been further developed in quite different ways in various lower teleostean groups, for example, the herring (fig. 19; see Kirkhoff 1958).

The functional significance of this change merits discussion. In the first place, loosening the premaxillaries from the cranium can only weaken the actual bite. For this reason, probably, the premaxillaries of terrestrial vertebrates, like those of holosteans, are rigidly incorporated into the skull. How, then, do teleosts compensate for this disadvantage?

Feeding methods among fishes can be grouped under three principal categories. One is to simply run down the prey and bite or seize it. This is the method used by sharks, eels, swordfishes, and all forms that bite off parts of sedentary organisms. For a fish that obtains its food in this way, the biting or grasping apparatus is of primary importance and determines the shape of the mouth

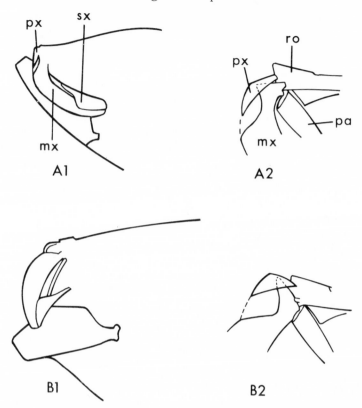

Figure 19. Mouth of *Clupea harengus* nearly closed *(A)*, and open *(B)*. In *A2* and *B2* the bones of the front of the upper jaw are shown. Based on Kirkhoff (1958). *mx*, Maxillary; *pa*, palatine; *px*, premaxillary; *ro*, rostral portion of cranium; and *sx*, supramaxillary.

opening. The jaws may be long (e.g., *Lepisosteus, Belone*) or short (e.g., *Serrasalmo*), but they must have a firm construction and emplacement, and powerful musculature for getting them shut firmly at the proper time. The requirements seem to be the same as those for most terrestrial vertebrates.

The other two methods of feeding are to swim through the water with the mouth open, as anchovies (Leong and O'Connell 1969) and pilchards do, or to suck in individual food items with the surrounding water, as pipefishes and angler fishes *(Antennarius)* do. Such feeding methods have rather different criteria of efficiency from those that apply in the case of fishes that simply run down their prey, and these differences are reflected in mouth structure. In both the straining and the suction methods of feedings, the strength of the bite loses significance, but the shape of the mouth opening becomes of primary importance. The mouth aperture in such fishes may be compared with the opening of a plankton net. A net with a round aperture would probably catch more organisms than one with deep slits extending back from the opening (Alexander 1967a). Early fishes had long, slitlike gapes, but at least the posterior ends of these slits are closed off in most holosteans and higher forms by movable maxillaries (fig. 17B). If, in contrast to slitting of the sides, the circumference of the mouth opening could somehow be expanded just as food items are approached, the percentage of items captured would probably be increased. The outward and forward movement of the teleostean premaxillary seems to accomplish this effect (figs. 17C, 19B).

Most fishes do not simply swim through the water straining out the food items that happen to lie in their paths. Rather, they select individual items for capture (Kirkhoff 1958; Hobson 1968). Furthermore, most teleosts do not bite off pieces but instead, engulf whole organisms. They do this in part by extending the jaws around the prey and in part by creating a negative pressure in the oral cavity that draws the prey and the surrounding water toward the mouth. Insofar as suction contributes to the capture of prey, the ability to *open* the mouth and the shape of that opening are of primary importance. Insofar as grasping contributes, the bite is of primary concern. The relative importance of these two factors varies greatly from fish to fish.

From the stage discussed above in which both the maxillary and premaxillary border the mouth, fishes have again and again extended the premaxillaries laterally below the maxillaries, effectively excluding them from the border of the gape (fig. 17D). When this happens the main bite becomes transferred from the maxillaries to the premaxillaries. The functional improvement accomplished by this change is not obvious (but see Alexander 1967a), though it is seen in a large number of fishes (e.g., the myctophiform and gadiform groups). Perhaps the exclusion of the maxillary from the gape is associated with some advantage in having all of the gape bordered above on each side by a single, continuous, bony rim.

The final stage, with many variants (van Dobben 1935), is the development of premaxillary protrusion. This also has occurred time and again in teleosts, but in most instances it seems to be predicated on the previous exclusion of the maxillaries from the gape by the premaxillaries. As Alexander (1967*a* and elsewhere) has shown, premaxillary protrusion can be adapted advantageously to numerous and varied situations. Indeed, it occurs in some half of all living teleosts. In general, fishes that have this mouth construction can accommodate the shape and size of the mouth opening much more appropriately to the shape of the item eaten than can fishes without premaxillary protrusion. Furthermore, it appears that teleosts can grasp prey at almost any degree of premaxillary protrusion (Alexander 1967*b*, and other papers).

The trend toward progressive specialization of the upper jaw apparatus at the front of the mouth is accompanied by a decrease in grasping dentition in the central portion of the oral cavity. Thus, with one peculiar exception among the Perciformes (Gosline 1968), parasphenoid teeth on the floor of the cranium (fig. 16*B*) do not occur in forms higher than the osteoglossiform and elopoid fishes. On the floor of the mouth (fig. 16*A*), the tooth-bearing plates on the mid-portions of the gill arch system (the basibranchials), though well developed in such lower teleosts as osmerids (Weitzman, 1967*a*), are lost in higher forms. The most significant reorganization, however, occurs in the suspensorium, which in lower teleosts, bears teeth on the palatines, ectopterygoids, and mesopterygoids (fig. 16*B*).

THE SUSPENSORIUM AND ASSOCIATED STRUCTURES

The actinopterygian suspensorium is made up of the upper portions of two gill arches plus dermal elements. The anterior part is derived from the palatoquadrate of the mandibular arch (figs. 20, 21), and its posterior part (the hyomandibular and symplectic), from the upper portion of the hyoid arch. Though these major components have remained the same throughout actinopterygian history, a whole series of changes has taken place.

In the earliest actinopterygians (i.e., the palaeoniscoids), which were long-jawed fishes, the lower jaw articulated with the suspensorium well behind the eye (fig. 22). The hyomandibular seems to have been a simple, separate strut extending from the skull down and back over the upper surface of the palatoquadrate. Judging from its position and orientation, it seems clear that the hyomandibular could not have played much of a role in jaw suspension. On the other hand the mandible articulated directly with the quadrate of the palatoquadrate arch (figs. 20, 21), and the dermal bones covering the surface of that arch formed perhaps

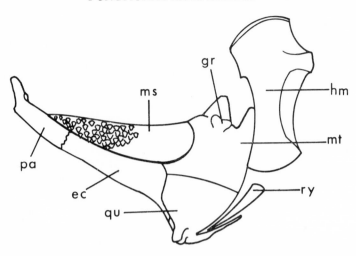

Figure 20. Suspensorium of the pholidophoroid *Ichthyokentema*, right side, medial view (based on Griffith and Patterson 1963, fig. 19). *ec*, Ectopterygoid; *gr*, groove into which a flange from the parasphenoid fits; *hm*, hyomandibular; *ms*, mesopterygoid; *mt*, metapterygoid; *pa*, palatine; *qu*, quadrate; and *ry*, symplectic.

the principal dentition of the roof of the mouth (fig. 16). It is therefore not surprising to find this palatoquadrate portion propped against the cranium at two points: anterior and posterior. Anteriorly in "holosteans," the palatine is propped against the ethmoid region of the skull. The posterior prop is made up of a lateral flange from the parasphenoid, which fits into a groove in the upper surface of the metapterygoid (fig. 20).

Almost all recent teleosts can expand their oral cavities laterally as well as vertically (see below). This, among other things, permits them to swallow larger prey than if their lower jaw articulations were separated by a rigidly fixed distance. The palaeoniscoids also apparently had this ability. In those fishes, however, the whole cheek region consisted of a firmly united covering of dermal bones (fig. 22), and when the lower-jaw articulations swung laterally, the cheek and circumorbital bones apparently swung laterally, too. So long as the jaw articulation was well behind the eye, the effect of lateral movement on the postorbital border was probably slight.

In the course of actinopterygian evolution the lower-jaw articulation has moved forward. Quite possibly this change, like the development of a movable maxillary, has been connected with the closing off of wide lateral escape-hatches for potential prey. In any event, the more forward position of the lower-jaw articulation

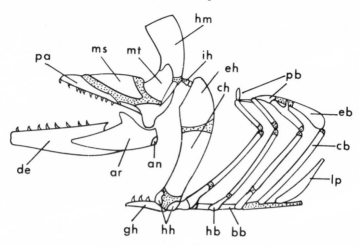

Figure 21. Bones of the teleostean visceral arch system (based on Goodrich 1930, fig. 436). *an*, Angular; *ar*, articular; *bb*, basibranchial; *cb*, cerato-branchial; *ch*, anterior ceratohyal; *de*, dentary; *eb*, epibranchial; *eh*, posterior ceratobranchial; *gh*, glossohyal; *hb*, hypobranchial; *hh*, hypohyal; *hm*, hyomandibular; *ih*, interhyal; *lp*, lower pharyngeal; *ms*, mesopterygoid; *mt*, metapterygoid; *pa*, palatine; and *pb*, pharyngobranchial.

has resulted in two major changes in the suspensorium and its associated structures. One is that the bones of the cheek region have separated into two quite independent series. In front is a ring of circumorbital bones around the eye. Behind, and in most higher teleosts completely separate from this circumorbital series, is the suspensorium with its dermal bones, including the preopercle. As a result, when the higher teleost expands its oral cavity laterally, the effect on the circumorbital series is only indirect, except in such forms as the sticklebacks and scorpaenids, which have redeveloped a connection between the circumorbital series and the suspensorium (Matsubara 1943).

A more important change has taken place in the construction of the suspensorium itself. In "holosteans," the suspensorium is still essentially in two sections (fig. 20): an anterior palatoquadrate part with two cranial articulations, and a posterior hyomandibular-symplectic part. But in the teleosts these sections become united (figs. 21, 23). The lower-jaw articulation, which has now moved forward to a position about below the hyomandibular-skull articulation, is propped entirely away from the skull by the hyomandibular and symplectic, to which the dermal preopercular has now been added as a supporting element. In all but a few of

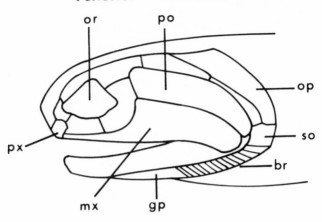

Figure 22. Bones of the side of the head of *Cheirolepis* (based on Watson 1925). *br*, Branchiostegal rays; *gp*, gular plate; *mx*, maxillary; *op*, opercle; *or*, orbit; *po*, preopercle; *px*, premaxillary; and *so*, subopercle.

the lower teleosts the parasphenoid-metapterygoid articulation has been lost, and in higher teleosts there are no teeth, or only minute ones, on the mesopterygoid.

Thus in teleosts the hyomandibular with its associated elements has taken over most of the propping function for the lower jaw. Sometimes, as in most eels (fig. 18), the anterior palatine-ethmoid prop has also been greatly reduced or lost. In such fishes lateral expansion of the mandibular articulations is still possible. Indeed in morays it is most important. However, it is also necessary that these articulations be fixed in their fore-and-aft position. This is accomplished in eels by extending longitudinally the articulation between the hyomandibular and the skull (fig. 18), so that the lower end of the hyomandibular is able to swing laterally but not forward or back.

The relationship between the anterior end of the suspensorium and premaxillary-maxillary movement is complex. Originally, the palatine seems to have extended forward as a simple strut, to end anteriorly between the maxillary externally and the rostral portion of the cranium medially. Where, as in *Amia*, the posterior end of the maxillary swings up and down around a peg extending in from the anterior end of the maxillary, the palatine has little to do with upper-jaw movement. But in higher teleosts, the anterior end of the palatine not only sends a prong out over a condyle in the maxillary head, but also has a ligament to the premaxillary which governs its course of protrusion.

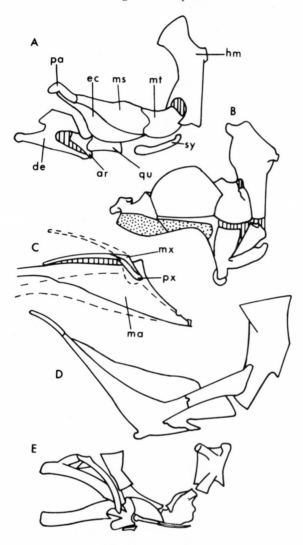

Figure 23. Suspensorium and/or jaws of A, *Chanos* (based on Ridewood 1905a); B, *Caproberyx* (based on Patterson 1964, fig. 71); C, *Dermogenys* (based on Alexander 1967*b* fig. 8b); D, *Hyporhamphus* (original); and E, *Aphyosemion* (based on Sethi 1960, fig. 50). In C, the dashed lines indicate the effect of slightly lowering the mandible. Parallel lines represent areas between bones; and stippling, teeth. *ar*, Articular; *de*, dentary; *ec*, ectoptery-goid; *hm*, hyomandibular; *ma*, mandible; *ms*, mesopterygoid; *mt*, meta-pterygoid; *mx*, maxillary; *pa*, palatine; *px*, premaxillary; *qu*, quadrate; and *sy*, symplectic.

Because of this added function, plus the importance of its forward prop against the skull in lower-jaw suspension, there is almost always a firm but movable (laterally rotatable) articulation between the anterior end of the suspensorium (the palatine) and the skull. This may be entirely at or near its anterior tip as in *Clupea* (Kirkhoff 1958) or *Cyclothone* (Günther and Deckert 1953). When this is the case, the mesethmoid may send out a stout anterolateral prong on each side to support the anterior end of the palatine, as in the fossil teleosts *Leptolepis* and *Diplomystus* (Patterson 1967*a*). A far more common situation in teleosts arises from the fact that the palatine usually extends longitudinally for a considerable distance under the rostral portion of the cranium. Then, the bottom of the cartilaginous flanges that border the orbit anteriorly extend out over it. The lateral ethmoids in teleosts come to extend down into this flange, and in higher teleosts they form an abutment not only for the palatines but for the lacrimal bones external to it. It is, incidentally, only when the lacrimal bones have such an abutment that they become spinous (the so-called serrate preorbitals).

PHARYNGEAL TEETH

In early fishes having the mouth more or less completely covered with tooth plates (Jarvik 1954) no specialized equipment was developed to pass food already in the mouth back into the oesophagus. But with the progressive emphasis on grasping jaws anteriorly placed, the functions of masticating the food and of passing it on into the gut have been taken over in large part by the posterior portions of the gill-arch system (Nelson 1967*b*). There, what is essentially a second pair of jaws has developed (Berghe 1928). Thus, the fifth ceratobranchials have become the tooth-bearing lower pharyngeals, biting against the tooth plates on the 2nd, 3rd, and 4th pharyngobranchials (fig. 16). The basic functions of this pharyngeal dentition in the lower teleosts are doubtless to seize the food in the oral cavity and to pass it along to the gut. In certain lower teleostean groups highly specialized pharyngeal jaws have been developed, notably among moray eels and cyprinoids. But, aside from the cyprinoids (Matthes 1963), the lower teleosts do not seem to use their pharyngeals for masticating food. For small food items at least, a number of lower teleosts (Nelson 1967*c*) have developed a separate system—the epibranchial organ. This organ is essentially an upward extension of the space behind the fourth gill arch, like a diverticulum, bordered fore and aft by the interdigitating edges of gill rakers. As the gill arch elements bearing these rakers move toward one another, any small food in the diverticula will be ground up. Higher fishes do not have epibranchial organs, but they may have triturating structures of other sorts.

The most important of these triturating mechanisms has developed as a further evolution of the pharyngeal apparatus. In the lower teleosts the pharyngeal teeth seem principally adapted for grasping (Nelson 1967*b*), as is suggested by the deep subtemporal fossae of lower teleosts (Ridewood 1904*a*; Patterson 1967*a*), into which the pharyngeal musculature extends. Higher teleosts do not have these fossae. Instead, as Dietz (1914), Holstvoogd (1965), and Nelson (1967*a,b*) have pointed out, the higher forms (but also *Amia*) differ from the lower teleosts in that they possess a pair of heavy muscles, the retractores arcuum branchialium, which extend between the upper pharyngeal bones and the vertebral column. Presumably, the development of this musculature is associated with the frequent use of the pharyngeal teeth as grinding organs in higher teleosts. The lowest of the many teleostean groups that have the lower pharyngeals fused is the Beloniformes. The culmination of this line of specialization is undoubtedly found in the parrotfishes, with their pharyngeal mill for crushing coral (see, for example, the illustrations in Schultz 1958).

EXPANSION AND CONTRACTION OF THE MOUTH CAVITY

With regard to the expansion and contraction of the mouth cavity, it may be well to start with a hypothetical consideration. If two flat boards are hinged together at one end, and the other, free ends are opened and closed under water, the water that comes in when the free ends are opened will pass back out the same way when they are closed. If anything is to be trapped between such boards, some place must be provided to hold the water when the boards are clapped back together again. In fishes this place is the mouth cavity with its posterior exits into the gill cavities (fig. 15). Actually, the upper jaw and the roof of the mouth, except in forms with a protrusile jaw, have very nearly the form of a board (fig. 15*A, B*), and fishes have been able to do little more than close off the corner exits with the movable maxillaries developed in the "holosteans" and inherited by teleosts. However, gnathostomes have developed a mechanism for lowering the floor and expanding the sides of the mouth cavity independently of the lower-jaw action. Thus when the jaws close, the water and whatever it contains stays in this expanded oral cavity and does not pass back out the front of the mouth. A pair of membranous valves just inside both jaws of many fishes (fig. 15A, B) is so arranged as to help prevent water from passing forward through the jaws (Gudger 1946). Once the jaws are closed, the floor of the mouth is raised and the lateral expansion contracted, forcing the trapped water out through the gills. Any food material contained in the water is strained out by the gill rakers and passed back into the oesophagus and thence to the stomach.

These various movements in the jaws and mouth cavity are made possible by a complex series of interlinked bones (fig. 24) and the muscles attached to them (van Dobben 1935). The complexity is increased by the fact that there are often two different ways of accomplishing the same movement. Coordination between different movements is brought about by the appropriate contraction of individual muscles at the proper time during a sequence of events (Ballintijn and Hughes 1965). This coordination is controlled by cranial nerves (Allis 1897).

Of all the movements in the mouth, closing the jaws is the simplest. This is accomplished by contraction of a large muscle, the adductor mandibulae, which extends from the inner surface of the lower jaw up and back to a broad insertion on the outer face of the suspensorium. It is a very important muscle indeed, since most of the nipping, grasping, and crushing of food depends on it. Both the size and the configuration of the adductor mandibulae vary greatly in teleosts (Vetter 1878; Dietz 1914; Takahasi 1925; Souché 1932; Eaton 1935; Rosen 1962; etc.). Thus, among fishes that crush molluscan food in the jaws (e.g., the eel *Echidna* or the blennioid *Anarhichas*), the muscle may be expanded above the suspensorium onto the sides of the cranium. If, as in pipefishes, the mouth is small and oblique, the adductor pulls back on the lower jaw to close it, but if, as in the bonefish *(Albula)*, the mouth is inferior and horizontal, the adductor must pull upward to close the lower jaw. Thus the configuration of not only the adductor but also that of its bony attachment surfaces vary with the shape, size, and placement of the mouth.

Opening of the lower jaw (and hence the mouth) is a far more complex matter. In the "holostean" *Amia*, lowering of the mandible appears to be entirely associated with, and dependent on, the

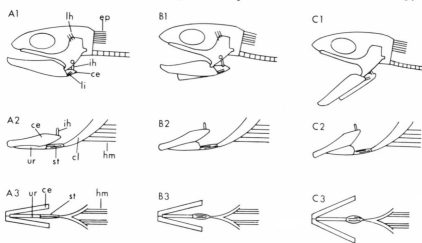

Figure 24. Diagrams to illustrate the mechanism for lowering the mandible in *Amia* (see text). In *Al–3*, the mouth is almost closed; in *Bl–3*, partly open; and in *Cl–3*, widely open. In *Al, Bl,* and *Cl,* the cranium, suspensorium, lower jaw, and only part of the underlying hyoid apparatus are shown from the side. In *A2, B2,* and *C2,* the changes in position of the hyoid bar are diagrammed from the side; in *A3, B3,* and *C3,* from below. *ce*, Ceratohyal; *cl*, cleithrum; *ep*, epaxial body musculature; *hm*, hypaxial musculature; *ih*, interhyal; *lh*, levator hyomandibularis muscle; *li*, ligament between angular and posterior ceratohyal; *st*, sternohyoideus muscle; and *ur*, urohyal.

lowering of the floor of the mouth. In higher teleosts, however, a second system has been developed that enables the fish to lower the mandible independently of the floor of the mouth.

In *Amia* there seem to be two ways by which lowering of the floor of the mouth may be initiated. In one method, contraction of the anterior portion of the body musculature on both sides raises the head at the same time that a backward pull is exerted on the cleithrum (fig. 24; Tchernavin 1948, 1953). (The epaxial musculature is attached in part to the rear of the skull above the vertebral axis, and its contraction pulls the head back and up in relation to that axis; contraction of the hypaxial musculature pulls the cleithrum back.) Anteriorly the cleithra are attached to the urohyal by the strong sternohyoideus muscle. Backward pull on the cleithra is therefore transmitted to the urohyal.

Alternatively, the cranium and cleithrum may be held in position by the body musculature, while the sternohyoideus muscle contracts. In this event, the urohyal is still pulled back. Some combination of these two alternatives probably represents the normal procedure in opening the mouth; when the mouth is only partially opened, contraction of the sternohyoideus probably predominates.

Anteriorly the urohyal is attached by a pair of short, strong ligaments to the anteroventral ends of the hyoid bars on either side. A backward pull on the urohyal is thus transmitted undiminished to a backward and downward pull on the front ends of the hyoid bars.

Within restricted limits, the hyoid bars are free to move backward and forward (fig. 24A2,B2) because their posterior ends are attached to the inside of the operculum by short, movable struts—the interhyals. However, the angular bone below the lower-jaw articulation is attached by another strong ligament to the outer face of the hyoid bar (fig. 24A1,B1,C1). Thus, when the front end of the hyoid bar is pulled backward and downward, the posterior end moves backward and the angular ligament attached to it pulls on the angular bone, opening the mandible (fig. 24B1,C1). Also, as the front of the hyoid bars is pulled downward, the ligamentous and membranous tissue between them and the front of the mandibles eventually becomes taut and pulls down on the anterior end of the mandibles.

This mechanism for opening the lower jaw is not only indirect, but it is so arranged that any opening of the mandible is preceded, if only momentarily, by a downward and backward movement of the floor of the mouth (which is underlain by the hyoid apparatus). This results in an expansion of the oral cavity and hence in suction of water into the mouth as the mandible is being lowered.

As noted in a previous section, most teleosts rely to some, often considerable, degree on the creation of a negative pressure to pull the prey and the water that surrounds it into the oral cavity. The effectiveness of suction in capturing prey depends in part on the suddenness with which it can be created. Perhaps it is in this connection that teleosts have developed a second, independent system (fig. 25) for opening the mouth to supplement the one already described. Here, a forward pull by contraction of the muscle to the top of the operculum causes the opercle to swing around the axis formed by the strut that extends back from the hyomandibular. This pulls the subopercle and interopercle backward. In turn, there has developed, between the interopercle and the back of the angular, a ligamentous attachment that pulls the

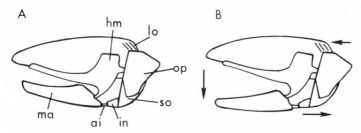

Figure 25. Alternate method of lowering the mandible developed in the Teleostei (see text). In *A*, the mouth is closed; in *B*, open. Arrows indicate the direction of movement of parts when the mandible is lowered. *ai*, Angular-interopercular ligament; *hm*, hyomandibular; *in*, interopercle; *lo*, levator operculi muscle; *ma*, mandible; *op*, opercle; and *so*, subopercle.

lower jaw downward. The extent to which the interopercular method of lowering the mandible is used independently of hyoid-arch retraction remains unknown, but on *a priori* grounds such independent action would seem to be advantageous, at least in nipping forms such as the parrotfishes.

So far, only the expansion of the oral cavity by a lowering of its floor has been discussed. However, as previously noted, even the early actinopterygians (see, for example, Nielsen 1942) seem to have been able to expand the posterior ends of the mandibles laterally. That is, the lower ends of the hyomandibular-quadrate strut (fig. 21) with its mandibular articulation could be swung wide, carrying the posterior ends of the maxillaries out with them.

In teleosts, there are two ways by which the lower ends of the suspensorium (i.e., the area of the mandibular articulation) can be expanded laterally. First, the muscle that extends from the outer surface of the hyomandibular upward to the cranium may be contracted. This has the effect of spreading not only the posterior parts of the lower jaw, but the back ends of the hyoid bars as well. Alternatively, if the urohyal is pulled back farther than the length of the interhyal, the posterior ends of the hyoid bars are forced apart (fig. 24*C3*).

The lateral expansion of the oral cavity may have originated as an adaptation for swallowing large prey, as noted previously, and is still so used today by such forms as the moray eels. However, it also serves two other purposes. One is to increase the amount of suction available to the mouth cavity. The other is in connection with respiration.

RESPIRATION

For respiration, the gill filaments have been so arranged (Hughes 1963) as to interdigitate into all portions of the water passing from the oral cavity to the opercular cavities (fig. 15C). If continuous respiration is to be attained, therefore, any suction in the mouth cavity must be accompanied by an even greater suction in the gill cavities. Actually, during normal respiration (as contrasted with the sometimes rapid and wide expansion of the mouth in eating) there is no great negative pressure in the mouth cavity, and fishes have developed a system to increase the suction in the gill chambers (Saunders 1961).

To visualize this mechanism, it is necessary to refer back to figure 15. The oral cavity is an anteromedian chamber and the gill cavities are posterolateral and ventral to it. In an oversimplified way it may be said that during normal respiration, while the oral cavity is expanding ventrally, the gill chambers are expanding laterally (Woskoboinikoff 1932). The gill chambers are covered posterolaterally by the operculum and ventrolaterally by the branchiostegal rays. Surrounding the outside of the operculum and branchiostegal rays is a flap of loose skin which is sucked tight against the underlying body when the gill chambers are being expanded (fig. 15C). During the expansion stage, therefore, the gill openings admit no water, though it is expressed by that route when the gill chambers contract (fig. 15D).

If the gill chambers are to provide greater suction than the mouth opening, they must expand at the same time (or only slightly later) than the oral cavity. In teleosts there are two ways by which the opercular cavities may be expanded. First, the operculum and suboperculum form a unit that articulates anteriorly with the hyomandibular (fig. 25); when the lower ends of the suspensoria are spread, the articulation between the hyomandibular and the opercle is carried outward, though to a lesser extent. This expands the gill chambers beneath. Second, the branchiostegals articulate basally with the hyoid bar. When the lower ends of the suspensoria are spread, the posterior parts of the hyoid bars open out with them. This moves the branchiostegal rays laterally, increasing the size of the gill chambers beneath. Thus any lateral expansion of the mouth cavity would seem to be accompanied by enlargement of the opercular cavities on either side. But even without this lateral expansion, depression of the floor of the mouth lowers the anterior ends of the hyoid bars and pushes the branchiostegal rays that articulate with them down and back. This in itself may enlarge the opercular cavities. In short, any enlargement of the mouth cavity would seem to expand the gill cavities almost synchronously.

Finally, in many fishes (Borcea 1907; Baglioni 1907) the outer ends of the branchiostegal rays may spread or fold together, somewhat as a fan, by the action of a series of muscles running among these rays. When the branchiostegals are spread, the opercular cavities beneath them are expanded; when they are folded, the cavities become smaller.

The typical teleost, then, has various, usually coordinated, methods of developing a backward flow of water across the gill filaments. Henschel (1939, 1941) has shown that if its mouth is held open a flatfish can maintain an adequate flow of water for respiration by the opercular cavity pumps alone, and that, conversely, if the gill openings are held open the fish can obtain adequate oxygen by the action of the oral-cavity pump alone. In addition, there are two rather different systems for expanding and contracting the opercular cavities. Most fishes use the two in coordination. But some (e.g., pipefishes: Leiner 1937, pp. 840–842) expand and contract only the operculi during respiration, whereas others (including many bottom-living forms: Baglioni 1907) rely almost entirely on branchiostegal ray movement as an opercular pumping system. In contrast to all of the forms discussed to this point, fishes like tunas and anchovies, which constantly swim forward with their mouths more or less open, would seem to have no real need for either an oral or a gill-chamber pump.

That the particular method used for pumping water over the gills varies with the mode of life of fishes is well known from the work of Baglioni (1907), Hughes (1960), and others. Here, it would seem more valuable to try to trace the evolutionary development of these systems. This can best be done by following the evolution of the branchiostegal rays.

EVOLUTION OF A BRANCHIOSTEGAL PUMPING SYSTEM

The opercle, subopercle, branchiostegal rays, and gular plates of the actinopterygian fishes probably originated as a single series of dermal elements protecting and forming a continuous rim for the gill opening (fig. 22). Woskoboinikoff (1932, p. 346) has pointed out that a movable cover for the gills may consist of large units over flat surfaces (the opercles laterally and the gular plates below), but that where the cover moves around a curved surface (from the ventral to the lateral plane of the body) it must be made up of smaller units (the branchiostegal rays). To what extent this continuous bony cover for the gill openings acted originally as a suction pump for the gill cavities is unknown. Already in the early palaeoniscoids, the opercle and subopercle had movable articulations with the hyomandibular (Nielsen 1942, pp. 181, 182), so that some expansion and contraction of the opercular portion of this gill cover may well have taken place. More probably, however, the lower portion of this continuous cover (the branchiostegal rays and gular plates) could have played at best a passive role in any expansion and contraction of the opercular cavities. In palaeoniscoids (fig. 22) the gular plates and branchiostegals formed a continuous series, and if they had any basal articulations at all, they have not been demonstrated.

In *Amia* (fig. 26) a number of changes that have taken place in the gill cover foreshadow the teleostean condition. The anterior branchiostegal rays extend under the gular plate (fig. 26*B*), and all but the first two articulate basally with the hyoid bar (Allis 1897, pp. 563, 564). The uppermost of the branchiostegal rays has become dislodged and has moved to a position at the base of the opercle where it has become the interopercle (fig. 26*A, C*). This bone, which has become an important component of the opercular functional system of higher teleosts, is in *Amia* transitional between the branchiostegal and opercular series. In position it is part of the opercular series, but basally it retains its ligamentous connection with the hyoid bar (fig. 26*C*), and in *Amia* it has not yet developed the teleostean ligamentous attachment to the angular bone of the lower jaw (Gosline 1969). The condition of the interopercle and the retention of a ligamentous attachment between the subopercle above it and the cartilage at the base of the hyomandibular (fig. 26*C*) suggest that the opercular and branchiostegal systems of *Amia* act together as a single functional unit.

Even the lowest of the living teleosts show the initial stages of division of the gill cover into two functional systems. Such fishes as *Alepocephalus, Elops,* and *Salmo* have lost the ligament between the subopercle and the hyomandibular and have developed a ligament between the interopercle and the angular (fig. 25), thus providing a second method of lowering the mandible (see above) that is unavailable to *Amia.* So far as a pumping system is

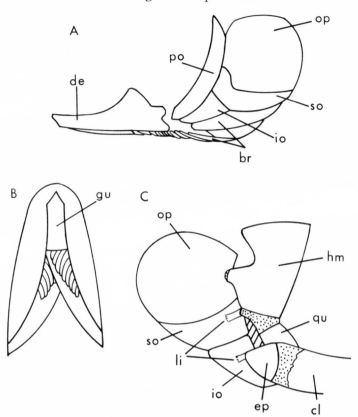

Figure 26. Branchiostegal rays and operculi of *Amia*. *A,* Lateral view of left side (based on Allis 1897). *B,* Bottom view (based on Woskoboinikoff 1932). *C,* Internal view of left opercular apparatus (based on Allis 1897). Stippling indicates cartilage; dashed lines, interspace. *br,* Branchiostegal rays; *cl,* anterior ceratohyal; *de,* dentary; *ep,* posterior ceratohyal; *gu,* gular plate; *hm,* hyomandibular; *io,* interopercle; *li,* ligaments; *op,* opercle; *po,* preopercle; *qu,* quadrate; and *so,* subopercle.

concerned, however, the numerous undifferentiated branchiostegal rays and the opercular apparatus still seem to form a single functional unit in lower teleosts (Ballintijn and Hughes 1965; Ballintijn 1969).

In the development of two separate pumping systems for the opercular cavity, the opercular portion has changed little from that of the lower teleosts; but the branchiostegal apparatus has developed into a partially separate functional unit. This branchiostegal pump, operating by expansion and contraction of the branchiostegal membranes, expands and contracts the lower portions of the gill cavities. When the branchiostegal rays are fanned out, the membranes between them expand to produce suction below. But when the posterior ends of the branchiostegals are folded together toward the isthmus below, they contract the cavity between the branchiostegal membrane and the isthmus, expelling the contained water.

In the lower teleosts a subcontinuous sheath of musculature extends from the hyoid bars between the branchiostegal rays and to the inner surface of the subopercle above. Apparently, contraction of this hyohyoideus musculature can only pull the branchiostegals together and toward the isthmus and the subopercle. Thus it appears that the hyohyoideus musculature is used only during the expiration phase of respiration (Ballintijn and Hughes 1965). Expansion of the part of the gill cavities beneath the branchiostegals is brought about by lowering the hyoid bars and is therefore directly associated with the expansion of the oral cavity (fig. 24B, C).

The evolution of a specialized branchiostegal pump seems to depend primarily on the development of a muscular system that will spread the branchiostegal fan as well as close it. Such a system occurs in the adductor hyoideus muscles of certain advanced teleosts, such as Trachinus (fig. 27). In these fishes the branchiostegal fan can be alternately spread by contraction of the adductor hyoideus and closed by contraction of the hyohyoideus, thus providing a pumping system for the gill cavity that may function quite independently from the opercular pump or that of the oral cavity.

Willem (1931) traced the differentiation of such a specialized branchiostegal pump in teleosts back to the cyprinoid fishes and Belone. In higher fishes it may almost completely replace the opercular apparatus as a suction pump for the gill cavities, as it does in many sand-dwelling perciform fishes (Baglioni 1907; Gosline 1968) and notably in the tetraodontiform fishes (Gabriel 1940; Willem 1947). In such fishes the branchiostegal pump may become enclosed superficially, so that its action is no longer observable from the exterior. At least in the tetraodontiform fishes the opercles and the branchiostegal rays seem to form two wholly separate systems with different functions: the opercles via the long interopercles are used for lowering the mandible (fig. 25), and the branchiostegal rays form a respiratory pump.

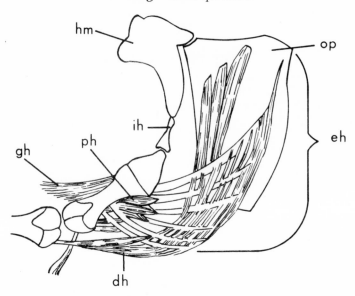

Figure 27. Branchiostegal musculature of *Trachinus*. An internal view of the right side with the hyoid bar, branchiostegal rays, hyomandibular, and operculum is shown; the anterior end of the left hyoid bar is folded out to the left (based on Borcea 1907, fig. 10). *dh,* Distal adductor hyohyoideus; *eh,* elevator hyohyoideus; *gh,* geniohyoideus; *hm,* hyomandibular; *ih,* interhyal; *op,* operculum; and *ph,* proximal adductor hyohyoideus.

The evolution of the branchiostegal pumping system traced above is not of course without exceptions. Certain fishes, for example, eels (Borcea 1907), have developed a quite different, essentially hydraulic, respiratory pump. Pipefishes, and to at least some extent the gobiesociform fishes, seem to have discarded a branchiostegal pumping system in favor of an opercular pump (Leiner 1937).

FOUR

Sense Organs, Brain, and Cranium

The sense organs and their centers of coordination and interpretation in the brain provide the means by which a fish perceives its environment. Fishes are free-swimming animals. The higher the speed attained, the greater the need for advance information concerning outlying areas. Such information, provided by distance perception, can then be used as a basis for setting the proper course of movement.

SENSE ORGANS

The major sense organs of fishes, and of vertebrates generally, are for distance perception. In this the vertebrates differ drastically from amphioxus, a relatively sedentary animal. (An analogous difference in sensory equipment seems to be that in the mollusks between squid and scallops.) Among vertebrates, the eye, ear, lateralis, and olfactory systems provide distance perception; at best they have only rudimentary antecedents in amphioxus. The essentially contact senses of touch and taste are comparatively unimportant to most fishes, though taste perception is highly developed in some (see Bardach and Case 1965).

It is a characteristic of vertebrates that, apparently unlike the squid, they use a complementary series of stimuli, perceived by various sense organs, to determine the nature of the surrounding environment. A fairly standard pattern of sensory equipment for receiving different environmental stimuli can be traced back to the first-known vertebrates and, except for the loss of the lateral-line system in terrestrial forms, it is carried through to man without fundamental change. The habitat to which this basic pattern of vertebrate sensory equipment is primarily adapted, and in which it presumably arose, is the well-lighted zone (Walls 1942, p. 208) of the aquatic environment. Nevertheless, the multiple nature of sensory perception in vertebrates has enabled them to invade habitats, such as lightless caves or the air, where one or another component of the basic sensory equipment is of little use.

Within the Teleostei, adoption of a particular mode of life frequently involves the reorientation of the components of sensory equipment, and/or change in their relative emphasis. Thus, forms that live close to the bottom may emphasize taste perception. Forms that live directly in contact with the bottom, tend to have their organs of distance perception on the upper parts of the body. Conversely, such surface-living forms as the beloniform fishes have laterally placed eyes, and the lateral line of the body extends along the lower sides. Nocturnal fishes and those that live in muddy or otherwise poorly lighted waters tend to compensate sensorially in various ways for the shortage of light. Rarely have fishes evolved wholly new sensory mechanisms; the most notable accomplishment in this respect is the development by certain nocturnal groups of the ability to perceive electrical stimuli (Lissman, 1961).

The successful adoption of any unusual mode of life depends on (1) the ability of the fish to perceive its surroundings adequately, and on (2) its ability to react appropriately. Sometimes, for example among remoras, the new mode of life involves primarily the development of specialized methods of action, with minimal or secondary changes in the sensory system. Anglerfishes of the genus *Antennarius* provide another example in this category. Often, however, some change in sensory perception makes the particular mode of life possible. Changes in sensory perception then form the prerequisite upon which numerous subsequent changes in other structures depend. Examples of this sort of evolution seem to be provided by the flatfishes (Norman 1934), with asymmetrical eyes, and the ophidioids (Gosline 1968), with their filamentous and presumably sensory pelvic rays.

An understanding of the sensory peculiarities of at least certain types of fishes is therefore important to any investigation of group origins and relationships. Unfortunately, the gross morphology of sense organs provides at best a rough indication of sensory perception, in part because of the complexity of the sense organs and sensory activity. As a result, casual observations on sense perception have little value, and satisfactorily controlled experimental evidence is difficult to obtain (see, for example, Tavolga and Wodinsky 1963). The functional morphologist tends to assume that there is a relationship between size and function. In dealing with locomotion, he is on relatively safe, well demonstrated ground in postulating that the power of a muscle increases with bulk. But the relationship between size and function in a sensory structure is more difficult to determine. In the first place, there is the problem in studying any sense organ of distinguishing between the quantity and the quality of stimuli perceived. Though the nature of this distinction has been worked out experimentally to some extent for vision and hearing in fishes, the implications for gross structure remain little known. Thus, the relationship between otolith size and hearing in the fishes that bear them seems never to have been investigated, and it is impossible to say whether species with larger otoliths hear better, differently, or both. The same difficulty applies to neuromasts, nasal organs, taste buds, and so forth. Thus the functional morphologist must tread warily in attempting to interpret sense-organ structure.

THE EYE

The simplest type of light receptor in fishes is the median, pineal organ, which is developed to quite different degrees in different groups. Its presumed functional significance has been dealt with by Breder and Rasquin (1950), Rivas (1953), and others.

The eye is a far more important sensory structure. Its basic features—cornea, lens, inverted retina, and eye muscles—are the same in all the vertebrates. The retina is unlike most other sensory structures in that it develops ontogenetically as an outpocketing of the brain. The eyes of fishes differ somewhat from those of terrestrial vertebrates in that the image of the external environment is focused on the retina almost entirely by the round, movable lens.

Teleosts have developed specializations for vision in various habitats, from above water level (e.g., *Anableps:* Walls 1942) to the deep sea (Munk 1966). Only those aspects of environmental adaptation associated with the size and movability of the orbit will be dealt with here, for these affect the entire structural organization of the head.

Vision depends on transmission to the brain of an image focused on the retina. The visual image of the environment received by the brain can be accurate only if it is divided among a large number of separate retinal impulses. Since, within fairly narrow limits, retinal cells have a minimum size, the retina itself must also attain a minimum absolute size before an accurate image can be transmitted by it. As Walls (1942, p. 171) pointed out, ". . . whereas with the other organs of the body it is relativity to each other that determines adequacy of size, the eye is essentially an optical instrument and obeys the laws of inter-organ proportioning only grudgingly, disobeying them entirely whenever, with impunity, it can."

The requirement that the retina reach a minimum absolute size before an accurate image can be transmitted to the brain has a profound effect on larval fishes. Since the early larvae are incapable of eating large prey, it is imperative that they be able to locate minute food items. Insofar as they do this by eye, as many of them seem to do, visual acuity would appear to be especially important just in the larval stage. The result, of course, is the early development and relatively tremendous size of the eyes in larval fishes.

The visual acuity necessary for larval existence seems to serve quite adequately for the later stages of a fish's life. Any increase in eye size as the larva becomes an adult fish is probably in large part for other reasons than to provide additional acuity. One of these is to increase the amount of light transmitted through the pupil and lens to the retina. And, indeed, fishes active in dim light frequently have large eyes (Marshall 1954). On the other hand, there are habitats in which no optical adjustment will improve vision. One is the completely lightless cave; another is turbid water. Fishes that live constantly in such environments frequently have small eyes or none at all (Eigenmann 1909; Moore 1950) and other sensory systems compensatingly emphasized (Schemmel 1967).

For one reason or another adult fishes vary greatly in eye size and position. Such differences affect not only the configuration of the cranium, but in some fishes that of the brain and lower jaw articulation as well. The eyes of large-eyed fishes may be either superior as in most bottom-living forms, such as *Draconetta,* or lateral in such surface-living fishes as the Beloniformes. In *Draconetta* (Gosline, in press) the two large, high-set eyes effectively pinch off the roof of the skull in the interorbital area; the frontals are restricted to the postorbital portion of the skull, and the preorbital part is entirely made up dorsally of the ethmoid bones. In the Beloniformes a broad flat frontal skull roof extends over the large, lateral eyes, but the suspensorium, which extends obliquely forward in *Draconetta,* is forced to extend down around the back of the low, large beloniform orbits. Probably an associated feature is the relatively posterior location of the mandibular-quadrate junction in the Beloniformes.

In large-eyed fishes the orbits of the two sides are separated from one another by a median membrane. The brain is restricted to the postorbital part of the head, and the olfactory nerves pass through the orbital cavities to reach the olfactory organ. In small-eyed fishes all of these features may change (Gosline

1963a). The orbits are delimited by bony sockets that may be separated from one another by a trough. The olfactory lobes may extend forward into this trough and, in a number of unrelated fishes, the nasal bulb of the brain may push forward in the trough to the base of the olfactory organ (Svetovidov 1953).

The amount of rotation possible to the eyeball seems to depend in part on the length of the eye muscles. In any event, some of the eye muscles of many teleosts have developed fore and aft excavations in the cranium known as myodomes (Goodrich 1930). The posterior of these myodomes may be of considerable length. When the cranium is high, a median basisphenoid bone usually separates the posterior eye muscles of the two orbits, but when the skull is low, as in the Syngnathiformes (Jungersen 1910; Gosline 1963a), the basisphenoid bone is frequently lacking.

ORGANS OF TASTE AND SMELL

Taste and smell are the two major chemical senses. Though it is rather difficult to distinguish between what these two senses perceive, the methods by which they operate are very different, as are the structures and the pathways by which their stimuli are carried to the brain (Herrick 1908).

Taste is essentially a contact sense. According to Herrick (1908) it originated as a method of determining the quality of items already in the mouth. But since taste receives and transmits stimuli from chemical substances dissolved in the water, there is no reason why taste organs of aquatic animals should not be located on other surfaces as well as in the mouth; and indeed they are in teleostean fishes. However, activation of the taste cells seems to depend on contact with the area of potential food; in any event these cells are often concentrated on structures which can be extended from the body as probes, for example, barbels and pelvic rays (Bardach and Case 1965). The various taste buds of the mouth and body surfaces are innervated by the trigeminus, facial, glossopharyngeal, and vagus nerves, and many of those on the body by a specialized ramus lateralis accessorius (or ramus recurrens) of the facial nerve (Teichman 1962).

The ramus lateralis accessorius appears to be a particularly variable part of the nervous system. Various configurations of this nerve in teleosts have been categorized under 16 patterns by Freihofer (1963). The functional significance of these different patterns has not been studied, but that they may have significance is suggested by the course of the branch to the pelvic fins.

Ordinarily this branch passes behind the pectorals, but when, as in the cods, brotulids, and zoarcids, the pelvics are far forward, the branch takes a more direct route across the pectoral base to the pelvics (Freihofer 1963; Gosline 1968).

The olfactory sense (Kleerekoper 1969) provides distance perception. The olfactory organs are restricted in position to the snout area. The sensory cells in these organs (Holl 1965), which in fishes usually take the form of a rosette, transmit their own stimuli directly to the olfactory bulb of the brain. As contrasted with taste organs, which are carried to the object to be tested, olfactory organs sample water which is brought to them. Fishes may sample the water passing over the olfactory organs for various purposes. "There is abundant experimental evidence that olfaction is important in the procurement of food, the recognition of sex, the discrimination between individuals of the same or of other species, in defense against potential predators, in parental behavior, and in orientation" (Kleerekoper 1967, p. 385). The uses to which the olfactory organ is put vary from group to group. Thus, in the cypriniform fishes injury to the skin releases a substance in the water which, when perceived by the olfactory organ of other members of the species in the vicinity, results in a defensive "fright" reaction (Pfeiffer 1963). Among many bathypelagic fishes, the olfactory organ of the male is greatly enlarged and presumably is used for finding a mate (Marshall 1967). Hasler (1957), Kleerekoper (1967), and others have suggested that the olfactory organ may be used in navigation during migrations.

Unfortunately, there is little known relationship between the way in which an olfactory organ is used or its sensitivity and the size or shape of the olfactory organ. Fishes with enlarged olfactory organs are known (Bardach, Winn, and Menzel 1959), or presumed (Marshall 1967), to make greater use of them than do fishes in which they are small. On the other hand, fishes that make no use of olfaction in locating food, for example, the pike (Pipping 1927), stickleback (Liermann 1933), and pipefish (Liermann 1933), often have reduced olfactory organs. However, those fishes for which the best discrimination between chemical substances has been as yet demonstrated experimentally (Hasler, 1957) do not seem to have enlarged or specialized nasal organs.

In at least some fishes, there seems to be a relationship, albeit of unknown nature, between the olfactory organ and the lateralis system. For example, in certain beloniform fishes one of the lateralis canals of the lacrimal may open into the depression from which the nasal tentacle projects (Miller 1945). In the moray genus *Anarchias* the posterior nostril and one of the pores of the supraorbital lateralis canal may exit from the same chamber (Schultz et al. 1953). Finally, in the Mastacembeliformes the anterior nostril and the supraorbital canal form parallel tubes extending to the anterior end of the fleshy trunk (Gosline 1968).

The olfactory rosette usually rises from the posteroventral floor of a nasal sac, which in turn communicates with the exterior by one or two openings in its roof. Though the nasal organ in teleosts is quite constant in position, it varies considerably in configuration and development. In a few fishes (e.g., the Beloniformes and tetraodontoids) there is no enclosed nasal sac, and the nasal organ consists of a sort of tentacle (Wiedersheim 1887). The sac, when present, like the olfactory rosette itself, may be variously represented. The olfactory rosette is frequently reduced to a strap-shaped organ (Liermann 1933; Gosline 1963a), and even within a single group of fishes, for example, the flatfishes (Norman 1934), it may vary markedly in configuration. Conversely, in such forms as the eels (Liermann 1933) and Grammistidae (Gosline 1960c), the nasal rosettes are much enlarged.

The olfactory rosette, when enclosed in a nasal sac is effectively protected, but the problem then arises of sampling the outside environment. A more or less constant flow of water over the nasal rosette is maintained in one of three main ways. Usually there are separate anterior and posterior nostrils. The posterior border of the anterior nostril is frequently rimmed by a funnel-shaped collar facing forward. As the fish moves, water passes down the funnel, over the nasal rosette, and out the posterior nostril. Such a method of sampling water is effective only when the fish swims.

A second method, developed in such forms as eels, is the induction of a flow, by ciliary action, from front to back over the olfactory organ. Such ciliary action may develop a constant, but hardly a rapid, flow of water over the olfactory epithelium; it would therefore be rather ineffective for rapidly swimming fishes. Furthermore, ciliary action can efficiently cause a flow of water only within narrowly enclosed spaces. Thus there is very little space between the expanded olfactory organ of eels (Liermann, 1933) and the nasal bone covering the nasal sac. With this type of mechanism for obtaining a flow of water, it does not much matter where the nostrils are. On a priori grounds, it would seem that fishes with tubular anterior nostrils must use ciliary action to keep water moving over the nasal epithelium.

A flow of water over the nasal epithelium is probably most commonly effected among teleosts by a pumping mechanism related to the upper jaw in such a way that water is sucked into the nasal rosette and then pumped out the posterior nostril. A number of higher teleosts, however, have only one nostril on each side of the head, and water is pumped in and out over the same route (Gosline 1968).

This pumping system depends on the expansion and contraction of the nasal sac itself, or, more usually, of diverticula extending from it. In teleosts three basic types of diverticula are involved, two of which are frequently operative in the same fish (Burne 1909).

Probably the most common is a diverticulum that extends down and back from the nasal sac just within the lacrimal bone. The anterior end of the lacrimal bone is ligamentously attached to the maxillary, so that the maxillary, when it swings down as the mouth opens, pulls the lacrimal bone down with it, expanding the lacrimal diverticulum below (Kirkhoff 1958).

In most lower teleosts (Derschied 1924), a second diverticulum extends up and back over the front of the orbit. This diverticulum is expanded and contracted by the jointed antorbital-supraorbital pump (Kirkhoff 1958; Gosline 1961), attached anteriorly to the maxillary. In higher teleosts this antorbital-supraorbital pump is frequently replaced by a diverticulum that extends medially behind the protrusile premaxillary pedicels. When the premaxillaries are protruded, these diverticula expand, sucking in water; when the premaxillaries are retracted, the diverticula are deflated (Gosline 1963*a*).

NEUROMAST ORGANS AND THEIR DERIVATIVES

In fishes three main sensory systems are based on neuromasts (Dijkgraaf 1963; but see also Szabo 1965): the perception of nearby objects by means of the water movement caused either by the object or by the fish itself, equilibrium, and hearing. In its presumably basic form as represented by pit organs, each neuromast has a series of fine, hairlike structures protruding beyond the body surface. Water flowing past these hairs in certain directions bends them, causing coded electrical stimuli that indicate the direction of flow to be transmitted to the brain. Originally, such neuromasts must have been located on the surface of the head and body, and many teleosts retain them there (see, for example, Disler 1960). Presumably, the extended hairs from such neuromasts would be bent by the fish's own swimming movements (but see Kuiper 1967). In any event, certain neuromasts have become partly enclosed within the tubes of the lateral-line canal system. Embryological evidence indicates that the inner ear with its semicircular canals represents a further invagination and specialization of a part of this lateralis system. In teleosts the inner ear and its semicircular canals are completely closed off from the external environment, and their neuromasts extend into a self-contained endolymphatic fluid. Whatever the course of evolutionary development, the lateral line, the semicircular canals, and the inner ear all extend back in vertebrate history as far as the fossil record can be traced.

The Lateral-Line System

The usefulness of a lateral-line system to fishes depends on the fact that water, unlike air, is nearly incompressible. Any movement in water displaces contiguous water particles to a considerable distance (the "near field" of Harris and van Bergeijk 1962). Fishes, by means of a neuromast system, are thus able to detect water displacement that occurs some distance away. Conversely, they can detect nearby stationary objects in the water if they themselves are moving (Dijkgraaf 1963; but see John 1957).

The basic manner in which the lateral-line system functions is fairly clear today, but the details remain to be worked out (for a preliminary attempt to relate lateral-line structure to ecological conditions, see Reno 1969). Perhaps the first problem is the functional relationship between the lateral-line canal organs and the superficial neuromasts (pit organs). Morphologically the superficial neuromasts seem to be quite variable in position and number. The lateral-line canal pattern, by contrast, is relatively stable throughout great groups of fishes (Stensiö 1947). It has been shown experimentally (e.g., Schwartz 1965) that the lateral-line system of the head is so arranged that the fish can perceive and discriminate between water movements coming from different directions. This, together with the relative constancy of the canal positions, suggests that, in teleosts at least, the neuromasts of the lateral-line canal are primary and that superficial neuromasts form a supplementary or perhaps a larval (Disler 1960; Iwai 1967) sensory system, which presumably accomplishes about the same thing.

Many slowly moving fishes living in quiet water increase the total amount of neuromast surfaces in one of three ways. One, frequent among oceanic fishes, is to lengthen the tail into a usually tapering filament and to continue the lateral line onto it. This method reaches its epitome among nemichthyid eels, where the lateral line of the sides is continued out to the tip of the extremely long, almost threadlike tail (Larsen, personal communication). Another system, exemplified by the oceanic macrourids, is to enlarge the lateral-line canals of the head into cavernous channels; at the bottom of each lies a greatly enlarged neuromast organ. In this regard, Marshall states (1965*b*, p. 308), ". . . it is clear from Pfüller's (1914) figures that each neuromast carries tens of thousands of sensory hair cells." Cavernous head canals occur not only in oceanic forms but in certain nocturnal freshwater fishes as well, for example *Acerina* (Jakubowski 1963), and also in the percopsiform fishes. In the third method of increasing neuromast surface, found in the cave-dwelling amblyopsids and many gobioids, rows, often numerous, of superficial sensory papillae have been substituted for lateral-line canals (see, for example, the illustrations in Eigenmann 1909). Judging from the figures of "neuromasts" given by Poulsen (1963), it may be concluded that some of them, at least, have been transformed into tactile organs.

The lateral-line canals themselves tend to be relatively constant throughout the fishes (Stensiö 1947). However, variations do occur—for example, in callionymids (Gosline, in press). In higher teleosts a minor but constant change is the substitution of a frontal commissure for the more anterior rostral commissure of ancestral forms. Presumably these two commissures are functional equivalents and the substitution has been made because the increasing upper jaw movement eliminated the feasibility of a commissure in the rostral region.

In most teleosts the neuromast organs on the floor of the lateralis canal alternate with pores through its roof to the exterior. However, the fluid in the interior of the canal may be continuous with that of the external environment in various other ways, or not at all. Not uncommonly a canal pore does not lead directly and broadly to the exterior, but divides into a series of arborescent branchlets with small terminal openings (Wohlfahrt 1937). Again (e.g., in *Albula*), the flesh that is pulled taut across the surface of the troughs making up the canal system of the head may have innumerable small holes (personal observation) instead of the usual primary pores. The lateral line of the body may also become arborescent (Makushok 1961). Finally, the neuromast organs in the canals of different fishes may have various shapes, as well as sizes.

There appears to be a basic relationship between the neuromasts and dermal bone formation. On the head, and in a somewhat modified way on the lateral-line scales of the body, each neuromast lies in the base of a bony ring. This ring is complete just above the neuromast, though the roof of the canal may be fleshy in intervening areas, and, indeed, the whole canal may be enclosed in membrane in such areas. The bony ring presumably protects the neuromast from damage or distortion. In what appears to be the simplest condition, for example, in the postorbital section of the circumorbital series or on the lateral-line scales of the body, each neuromast lies in its own separate ossification, which grows out from the neuromast area. From this apparently basal lateralis condition, modification may occur in either of two opposing directions. In certain eels (Trewavas 1932), parts of the canal system may be enclosed in a whole series of bony rings. In at least some suckers (Allis 1905), there appears to be a proliferation not only of bony rings but of neuromasts as well. The far more usual direction of evolution is toward the fusion of the bony bases underlying the neuromasts. Thus, in percoids the second circumorbital bone (that bearing the subocular shelf, where present) seems to be made up of what were originally the ossifications below two neuromasts, and the lacrimal bone of several.

The canal-bearing bones of the cranium doubtless represent, at least in part, fusions of ancient dermal lateralis ossifications. In the course of evolution, these bones have become variously modified. Thus, in higher teleosts the canal-bearing portions of the pterotic have become completely fused to an underlying endochondral portion. On the other hand, in certain fishes the canals of the head have come free from the canal-bearing ossifications that presumably formed around them. This phenomenon deserves some discussion.

The lateral-line canal system of teleosts is stimulated by water movement in the external world. Complete protection of the canal neuromasts would eliminate the possibility of detecting movement in the environment they are present to perceive. In any event, the lateral-line canals are usually located close to the body surface.

In chapter 2 it was pointed out that though dermal bones, as their name implies, usually lie just below the body surface, they are covered by musculature in some of the higher teleosts. The lateral-line canals have reacted in different ways to the overlapping of dermal bones by musculature. Two of these ways are exemplified by the lateralis commissures across the top of the head in the Carangidae. In carangids the body musculature extends far forward over the head on either side of a median frontal-supraoccipital crest. The extrascapular bones bearing the supratemporal commissure extend medially over the surface of this musculature. The lateral portions of the frontal commissure, however, are buried by it, although a canal of the frontal commissure extends up through the median crest to an opening just under the skin of the head surface. What sensory function the frontal commissure performs in the carangids and where the neuromasts lie in it remain unknown.

A more peculiar lateral line condition is that found, for example, in the Catostomidae (Allis 1905), Cyprinodontidae (Tchernavin 1949), and Callionymidae (Gosline, in press). Here, the lateral-line canals of the head may leave the bones that usually bear them and extend through the flesh overlying them.

The Ear

Teleosts have inherited from their ancestors an ear (Retzius 1881) consisting of three semicircular canals above, concerned primarily with equilibrium, and three otolith-bearing sacs, concerned primarily with hearing. Perception in the semicircular canals is attained through neuromasts that extend into the fluid of the canals (Dijkgraaf 1963). For the perception of sound, however, neuromasts form beds under the otoliths and receive their stimuli from vibrations in the otoliths set up by sound waves (i.e., pressure waves in the surrounding water).

The shape and size of the otoliths vary considerably from fish to fish (Frost 1930, and others), and often the auditory bulla containing the largest of them protrudes from the lower surface of the skull.

It may be, as van Bergeijk (1967) suggests, that the swim bladder, when present, is always used as a sound amplifier. Certainly many teleosts have developed some sort of direct or indirect connection between the swim bladder and the endolymphatic fluid of the ear. Direct connections have developed time and again in teleosts by the development of forward extensions of the swim bladder. Such connections may be a constant feature of large groups, for example, the Moridae (Svetovidov 1948), or they may be present in some members of a genus, for example, *Holocentrus* (Nelson 1955) but not in others. Wherever they occur, these connections seem to affect the shape and size of the otoliths, but what effect they have on hearing remains unknown. In the cypriniform fishes, which have a peculiar and complicated set of Weberian ossicles between the swim bladder and the endolymphatic fluid, both the range and acuity of hearing seem to be better than in other fishes tested (Dijkgraaf 1963).

THE BRAIN

The teleostean brain appears to be quite constant so far as the representation and relative position of its major components are concerned. Nevertheless, there is considerable difference in the relative sizes of its various parts. So far as is known, these variations seem to be related to the degree of development of the different sense organs. Thus, fishes that rely heavily on olfaction (e.g., eels) have enlarged olfactory lobes; those that have very large eyes (e.g., *Priacanthus*) have large optic lobes; whereas those with well-developed taste or lateralis systems have unusually large medullar areas or cerebella. One peculiar feature is the greatly enlarged "cerebellum" of the mormyrid (Franz 1911) and gymnotid (Castro 1961) fishes, undoubtedly related to the electric-field perception in these groups.

The evidence accumulated to date (e.g., Evans 1940; Bath 1962; Davis and Miller 1967; Svetovidov 1968) indicates a distinct relationship between the enlargement of particular brain parts, even within fish groups (e.g., cyprinids), and the method used for finding food. Again, the illustrations of brains of different tunas by Kishinouye (1923) or Tuge, Uchihashi, and Shimamure (1968) show a number of variations, presumably associated with differences of some sort in the mode of life.

THE CRANIUM

The teleostean cranium is the subject of a very extensive literature (e.g., Gregory 1933; Devillers 1958; Bertmar 1959; Daget 1964), most of it written from an ontogenetic or phylogenetic point of view. Only those functional aspects that have not already been treated (chap. 1) will be mentioned here.

The teleostean cranium, like that of any vertebrate, forms an integrated protecting and supporting framework for the various functions carried on at the anterior end of the animal. It provides a firm seating for the olfactory organ, eye, ear, brain, part of the lateralis system, etc. Since all of these structures are more or less enclosed in cranial cavities the cranium provides protection as well as a rigid emplacement for them. In addition, the cranium acts as a fulcrum from which various mechanical parts swing, and the nature of the articulations with these parts determines and delimits the planes of their movements. Finally, the cranium furnishes a surface of attachment for much of the musculature that causes their movement. The principal mechanically movable structures articulating with the cranium are the upper jaw, the suspensorium, the circumorbital series of bones, the vertebral column, and the pectoral girdle.

The importance and complexity of these functions severely limit the feasible alterations in cranial configuration. Such changes do occur in teleosts—for example, the two eyes on the same side of the head in adult flatfishes and the development of cavities in or crests on the skull (see chap. 1). At least equally frequent are changes in the nature of the structural material composing the adult cranium.

A continuous cartilaginous cranium seems to serve the sharks quite adequately. In the earliest bony fishes (see, for example, Nielsen 1942), the adult cranium appears to have ossified as one or two blocks. How or if growth of the cranium took place in such forms remains unknown. The "holosteans" (Rayner 1948) seem to be the first actinopterygians with skulls made up primarily of bones growing outward from separate centers of ossification.

In the course of fish evolution, the relative amounts of cartilage and bone in the adult skull have fluctuated considerably. At some point bone formation in the cranium seems to have become a selective as well as a quantitative process, with ossification developing in particular areas, for example, around the neuromast organs of modern teleosts (see above), rather than uniformly throughout the skull. Another example of selective ossification is provided by neotenic fishes (Gosline 1959) and many deep-sea fishes, in which the jaws and teeth become far more thoroughly mineralized than the rest of the skeleton. Gegenbaur (1878), in a study of the poorly ossified *Alepocephalus* cranium, came to the conclusion that endo- or perichondral bone formation tended to originate in certain specific regions and to spread concentrically. One such source, comprising the areas around persistent openings in the cranium, gives rise to the exoccipitals, prootics, and lateral ethmoids. Another series of ossification centers arises in areas of muscular or ligamentous attachments (the supraoccipital, epiotics, and intercalars). To these, two other categories may be added: (1) areas bordering movable articulations (the ethmoid, autosphenotic, autopterotic, and basioccipital), and (2) ossifications in the inner orbital walls (orbitosphenoids, pterosphenoids, and basisphe-noid—perhaps the lateral ethmoid and autosphenotic also belong here). The dermal bones of the fish cranium can easily be divided between the canal-bearing roofing elements (frontals and, origi-nally, parietals) and tooth-bearing elements in the mouth (vomer and, originally, parasphenoid).

It may be that bone formation as it occurs in certain modern fishes, such as *Alepocephalus*, follows somewhat different path-ways than it did in the early "holosteans," but the fact that essentially the same individual bones are found in both suggests that the ossification centers were the same. In any event, the individual skull bones of modern teleosts seem to develop ontogenetically in connection with certain specific functional roles. It is not as if the bones in themselves must make up the entire structural framework for the skull, for the cartilaginous cranium is already present, having preceded the bony cranium in ontogenetic development. Indeed, in the adults of many modern fishes, such as the trouts, the cartilaginous cranium is never completely replaced by bone. Rather, the bones would seem to be scattered here and there, in and over the cartilaginous cranium at critical points (see, for example, Norden, 1961 pl. 3).

Often, particularly in higher teleosts, the ossifications take over almost the entire supporting and protecting functions of the adult cranium. Here, the individual bones expand until they meet their neighbors, forming a continuously ossified cranial complex. Some bones, particularly among the dermal components, lose their original special function but continue to exist as members of this complex. The parasphenoid, which is toothless in most higher teleosts, is an example. Perhaps more instructive in this connection are the parietals. These bones were originally canal-bearing components of the skull roof. In most teleosts the lateral line no longer passes through the parietals. However, the parietals are generally retained as simple roofing elements. Again and again, however, the parietals have lost their autonomy and have become fused with one or another of the adjacent bones, as in catfishes or gobies (Gosline 1955). Indeed, in teleosts that have no lateralis canal in the parietal, it would seem unimportant whether a parietal center of ossification is present or not; what does matter is that ossification from some source spread over the parietal area.

CLASSIFICATION OF MODERN TELEOSTEAN FISHES

FIVE

Principles of Classification

Unless one accepts the dicta of numerical taxonomy, classification should attempt to express the genetic relationships of the forms classified. The determination of relationships is a zoological matter, but the way they are expressed involves human communication. A classification that does not indicate relationships is merely an inventory, but one that is incomprehensible serves no purpose at all.

With regard to zoology, the minimum requirement of any classification is that no taxon should include unrelated forms. For purposes of communication, a minimum standard would seem to be that no taxon be biologically undefinable.

Sometimes it is difficult to meet even these requirements. The problems of definability arise partly because of convergent characters, but more importantly in connection with efforts to separate lineages. In general, a classification based on lineage is preferable to one depicting collateral relationships, because it indicates more about evolutionary pathways. However, if any two lineages are traced back far enough, they will be found to originate among brothers who cannot be distinguished in biologically meaningful terms; that is, the brothers may not show the characteristics of the descendant lineages at all. In practice, one follows lineages back to a basal group and then switches from a father-son (vertical) to a fraternal (horizontal) classification for that basal group. This is done not only in the interest of definability but also because, zoologically, it is often impossible to tell which brother stands at the base of which lineage.

Extinction has shattered the evolutionary record. Both the phylogenetic and the definability requirements of classification are affected. As to definability, extinction creates the gaps that are seized upon by taxonomists to define taxa. As to relationships, any "phylogenetic" classification is merely a hypothetical reconstruction from such bits and pieces of evidence as happen to remain available. Phylogenetic hypotheses are also man-made

93

hypotheses and hence are subject to the foibles of the human mind as well as of the evolutionary record.

To summarize, any classification represents an amalgam of such disparate factors as the process of extinction, interpretation, and human communication. Remove any of these and the present system becomes unworkable.

Because of the nature of classification there are a number of aspects of biology to which it cannot be feasibly adapted. This is not to say that such aspects should not be expressed, but rather that other methods of expression seem preferable. Brundin (1966), for example, has shown that a knowledge of the relative ages of various lineages is essential for work in historical zoogeography. But for teleost fishes, an examination of the literature on fossil forms will provide more reliable information on this subject than any attempt to reclassify modern teleosts ever could.

Nor does there seem to be any valid reason why classification should be made an end in itself. To do so leads to preoccupation with the mechanics of classification and often results in the creation of superstructures that have rather tenuous attachments to their biological bases. A classification is at best an interim summary of available biological information, and, especially for any field in which knowledge is rapidly increasing, a minimum of formal superstructure would seem indicated.

The teleostean classification provided in this book is less an end in itself than a vehicle for discussing the interrelationships, so far as this author can interpret them, of the groups involved. What is aimed at here is a reasonable classification of modern teleostean fishes to provide a minimum, and insofar as possible a flexible, organizational framework for the investigation of teleostean evolution.

SIX

Lower Teleostean Groups

Included orders: Osteoglossiformes, Clupeiformes, Salmoniformes, Cypriniformes, Anguilliformes, and Notacanthiformes.

EVOLUTION AND RELATIONSHIPS

It seems well to bring together in the form of introductory statements certain general aspects of teleostean evolution. That for the "lower" teleosts will be followed by one for "intermediate" groups and another for the "higher" teleosts. Teleosts are divided in this way primarily for the sake of convenience. As a preliminary definition, the lower teleosts will here be understood as comprising those groups in which at least some members have the maxillary included in the gape; the higher teleosts are the Perciformes and their presumed derivatives; and the intermediate groups are the orders in between.

The lower teleosts extend back in the fossil record to the Jurassic. Their major diversification undoubtedly occurred in the Mesozoic, and some groups (e.g., the osteoglossiform and gonorhynchoid fishes) give every indication of being relict survivors. Though only the modern lower teleosts will be dealt with specifically, the fossil record is crucial to any attempt to interpret their relationships. Here it will be assumed (following Gosline 1965, and Patterson 1967a) that the teleostean fishes are monophyletic in origin and that the lower teleosts are interrelated forms representing the earliest major radiation from this origin.

For purposes of classification it is necessary to establish a boundary between the Teleostei and their "holostean" forerunners. Any decision as to where this boundary should be drawn will be arbitrary, depending in part on such nonzoological factors as gaps in the fossil record and consensus of opinion.

Attempts have been made to define the teleosts at some level on the evolutionary scale at which "holostean" characters—for example, lepiodosteid tubules in the scales and dermal bones (Berg

1940, p. 416)—have been lost. It is primarily on such a basis that the lower border of the Teleostei has sometimes been drawn between the extinct Leptolepidae and the living Elopidae (see Patterson 1967*a*). However, relict characteristics tend to be retained in a rather haphazard fashion among different groups and, at best, indicate directions in which the fishes that contain them have not evolved.

Among positive developments that distinguish the Teleostei from the "Holostei," the most drastic seems to be the reorganization of the caudal skeleton (see chap. 2). If this reorganization (Gosline 1965; Patterson 1967*a*) is used as a basis for defining the Teleostei, there are at least two stages that might be selected as a lower border for the group. One is that between *Amia* and *Lepisosteus* on the one hand and the extinct pholidophoroids on the other. This division would place the pholidophoroids among the teleosts.

The second stage—between the pholidophoroids and the teleosts, thus excluding the pholidophoroids—was advocated by Patterson (1968*a*) and will be adopted here, along with his definition of the Teleostei (p. 234): "Actinopterygian fishes in which the vertebral centra are perichordally ossified, the lower lobe of the caudal fin is primitively supported by two hypurals articulating with a single centrum, and in which the ural neural arches are modified into elongate uroneurals, the anterior uroneurals extending forward on to pre-ural centra."

Before proceeding, it seems well to examine briefly the implications of this decision.

That the pholidophoroids are forerunners of the Teleostei is agreed. In addition to general resemblances between the two groups, there is one very peculiar character, the subtemporal fossa with a narrow intercalar-prootic bridge across it, that was apparently developed within the pholidophoroids and has been carried over into a number of primitive teleosts before being lost again. Such a bridged fossa occurs in the pholidophoroid *Pholidophorus bechei,* in the fossil teleostean ichthyodectids, in *Thrissops, Allothrissops,* and *Leptolepis dubia,* and in the modern *Elops* and *Osteoglossum* (Patterson 1967*a*).

Excluding the pholidophoroids from the Teleostei has the great advantage to teleostean classification that it provides a fairly well known base (Griffith and Patterson 1963) from which to trace teleostean evolution. On the other hand, doing so throws the pholidophoroids into an already heterogeneous group generally

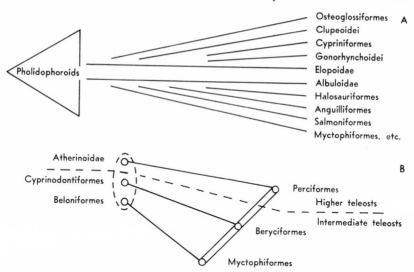

Figure 28. *A*, Oversimplified representation of possible relationships between modern lower teleostean groups. *B*, Two views regarding the relationships of the Beloniformes, Cyprinodontiformes, and Atherinoidae. The ellipse of dashed lines encloses the Atherinomorpha of Greenwood et al. 1965. The solid lines indicate, in oversimplified form, the postulates adopted in the present book.

aggregated under the name Holostei. It remains to be seen whether the pholidophoroids can be satisfactorily retrieved from this holostean wastebasket as part of a coherent "halecostome" subgroup of Holostei (see, for example, Arambourg and Bertin 1958), and what, if any, the relationships are between the "Halecostomi" and such forms as *Amia* and *Lepisosteus.*

Figure 28 may be used as a basis for a discussion of the various modern lower teleostean groups. The fossil evidence regarding the groups represented in the diagram will be dealt with first. An upper Cretaceous elopid, *Notelops,* very similar to the modern *Elops,* was described in considerable detail by Dunkle (1940), and Nybelin (1961) recorded an undescribed elopid from the Jurassic. Patterson (1967*a*) traced the clupeoids back to the Cretaceous *Diplomystus,* and the osteoglossiform stock, more tentatively, to near the Jurassic *Allothrissops.* In a number of features *Diplomystus* and *Allothrissops* approach the elopids more closely than do the present stocks of which these genera presumably represent forerunners, and Patterson concludes (1967*a*, p. 107) that the elopids, clupeoids, and Osteoglossiformes "seem to be a group of related lineages."

Though the gonorhynchoids are recorded from the Cretaceous (Andrews et al. 1967), the earlier forms are too poorly known to add to whatever evidence of presumed relationships can be obtained from the modern members. What has been said of the gonorhynchoids applies also to the albulids, Anguilliformes, and Notacanthiformes. The presently known fossil record of the Cypriniformes is even shorter and less enlightening.

Concepts regarding the Salmoniformes have been changing rapidly. Weitzman (1967a) added the stomiatoids to the order but pointed out that most, perhaps all, of the Cretaceous forms attributed to the stomiatoids were neither stomiatoid nor salmoniform. On the other hand, Goody (1968; 1969) has shown that the extinct Cretaceous fishes of the family Enchodontidae were probably specialized forerunners of the salmoniform stock. However, the Enchodontidae, so far as yet described, seem to show little evidence of merging between the Salmoniformes and the elopid-clupeoid-osteoglossiform group.

The Salmoniformes and Myctophiformes were merged by Greenwood et al. (1966) and by Weitzman (1967a). At the other extreme, the Myctophiformes has been separated out as an independent superorder Scopelomorpha by Rosen and Patterson (1969). In the present book the Myctophiformes will be considered as a separate order at the base of the "intermediate" teleostean groups.

For evidence of relationships between modern forms of lower teleostean groups, three character complexes seem to be of particular significance. Each of these will be treated in some detail, but first it should be noted that if teleosts had a monophyletic origin they all once had the same genetic background and hence had similar biological potentialities. Time and again, different groups have attained approximately the same specialized endpoints, but often by way of separate evolutionary routes. Thus, otherwise different teleosts that have developed fanglike teeth often have very similar jaw structure, and fishes with rounded tails may have similar caudal skeletons. The central sections of the evolutionary routes over which such groups traveled may provide a clearer picture of phylogenetic differentiation than either the earliest or the latest (convergent) portions.

Dorsal Fin Position. Many lower teleostean adults have a single dorsal fin more or less centrally located on the back. A dorsal fin

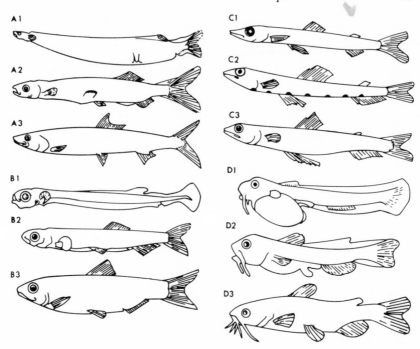

Figure 29. Three stages of development to show early, transitional, and final positions of the dorsal fin in *Elops* (A), 34, 29, and 450 mm; *Alosa* (B), 14, 23, and 52 mm; *Synodus* (C), 35, 40, and 57 mm; and *Ictalurus* (D), 10, 14 and 310 mm (all based on Mansueti and Hardy 1967).

in this position, for reasons dealt with in chapter 2, usually serves as a keel, and as such is useful only to relatively large, fast-swimming forms. The great majority of preteleostean actinopterygians have the dorsal fin more posteriorly placed (where it can be used as a rudder, as a stabilizer, or in forward locomotion), and the more forward position in lower teleosteans is presumably related to the greater swimming speed attainable by these fishes. However, larval and early juvenile stages of fishes do not have the bulk and cannot attain the forward speeds that would make a keel useful, whereas it would seem that they could make use of a dorsal fin in the more ancient, posterior position. In any event the early stages of such lower teleosts as the elopoids (fig. 29A), clupeoids (fig. 29B), and *Chanos* (Delsman 1926) have the dorsal fin more posteriorly placed than it is in the adult. Presumably, the increasingly forward position of the dorsal fin during growth is an ancestral teleostean attribute, represented today in such fishes as clupeoids and *Chanos*. From this type of development modern teleosts have presumably evolved in two quite different directions. One direction is represented by the modern elopids and albulids. In these forms, which have attenuated leptocephalous larvae (fig. 29 *A1*), the dorsal fin develops very far back and its forward migration to the final median postion is greatly exaggerated. Though the leptocephalous larvae of the Anguilliformes and Notacanthiformes do not have the posterior dorsal fin, there appear to be enough characteristics common to all leptocephali to suggest a common origin. The functional significance of a leptocephalous larva remains unknown, but it seems to represent a method by which an elongate, undulating larval form can make a successful living in the lighted surface waters of the sea. Such larvae apparently do not occur in deep water, nor, as might be expected, in fresh water. (Among higher teleosts, other specialized, planktonic larval forms developed, but again apparently as adaptations to existence in the surface waters of the sea, rarely if ever occurring elsewhere.)

Greenwood et al. (1966) emphasized the specialized leptocephalous larval stage in their teleostean classification by circumscribing in a separate superorder, Elopomorpha, all fishes that have this larval form. The difficulty is that, whereas some members of the Elopomorpha are represented by highly specialized adults (e.g., the Anguilliformes), the adult *Elops* is generally recognized as one of the most generalized (i.e., primitive) of teleosts (see, for example, Nybelin 1956, 1968). In the present classification, the elopoids, on the basis of adult characteristics, are combined into a single order with the gonorhynchoids and clupeoids (which do not have a leptocephalous larva). Presumably, in the course of time the elopoids have developed specialized (leptocephalous) larval forms but have retained the ancient adult traits, whereas the clupeoids and at least *Chanos* among the gonorhynchoids have retained the early teleostean type of larval development but have evolved into relatively specialized adults. If the above reasoning is correct, the taxonomic position assigned to the elopoids will depend merely upon whether one looks at the larva or the adult (a problem not unfamiliar to, for example, entomologists). Here, the adult is emphasized, because only the adult characteristics can be integrated with those of fossil forms. In addition, there is no present reason to believe that *Elops*, before it evolved its leptocephalous larva, did not stand near the base of the whole teleostean phylogeny.

In contrast to the foregoing groups, the cypriniform (fig. 29D), salmoniform, myctophiform (fig. 29C), and higher teleostean fishes (fig. 8) have the dorsal fin originating in its final, adult position. This would seem to represent a by-passing of the larval condition in which the dorsal fin originates posteriorly and moves forward (François 1956) over the back to a final forward position. It has been suggested in chapter 2 that the adipose fin of cypriniform, salmoniform, and myctophiform fishes represents a partial functional replacement for the posteriorly located dorsal of the larval elopoids, clupeoids, and *Chanos.*

If, as hypothesized here, the free-living larval stages characteristic of clupeoids are suppressed in salmoniform fishes and others, this change could take place in one of two ways. Starting with a clupeoid-sized egg, the rate of direct differentiation into an adult form could be speeded up, thereby reducing or eliminating the free-living, feeding, larval form and developing into an adult stage at a necessarily minute size. In the salmoniform fishes this developmental route has not been followed. Rather, the amount of yolk in the eggs of these fishes has been increased, permitting a prolonged dependence of the larval development on endogenous rather than external food sources. If this is what has occurred, the advantages and disadvantages of a minute, free-swimming larval form that must obtain its food from external sources will have been eliminated. The process of natural selection which before had operated during an early free-swimming stage, will then be transferred to the egg stage, with the result that at least a portion of the former larval development will be subjected to a quite different set of selective forces.

Though a specialized larval form seems to be an adaptation for life in the surface waters of tropical seas, there are other habitats in which such larvae appear to have proved disadvantageous. Thus Marshall (1953) for fishes and Thorson (1950) for invertebrates have shown that in very cold and very deep seas the size of eggs tends to be increased and the free-living pelagic larval stages to be suppressed. Rass (1941) has gone even farther in postulating that the size of the fish egg is inversely related to the temperature of the water in which it is laid. Marshall (1953) and Thorson (1950) relate the suppression of larval stages to the scarcity of suitable food for free-swimming larval stages in very cold or very deep waters. It may be significant in this connection that the salmoniform fishes are limited to the colder waters of the world and that they are perhaps the only lower teleostean group with members that spend their whole lives in deep oceanic waters. The Cypriniformes comprise mostly tropical freshwater fishes, but here again the absence of a suitable food supply for free-living larvae may have led to their suppression.

Caudal Skeleton. In the caudal skeleton the upturned notochord forms the earliest axis, and the centra partially replace it during ontogeny. Among teleosts two features have perhaps a predominant influence on the elements of the caudal skeleton. The lesser is the nerve cord, which extends above the notochord and its centrum replacements to a more or less enlarged urophysis (see, for example, Fridberg and Bern 1968) enclosed by the caudal skeleton itself, neural arch derivatives protecting the urophysis laterally and dorsally. More importantly, the caudal skeleton supports the caudal fin, which is the chief source of forward locomotion in most teleosts (chap. 2). In nearly all primitive teleosts and in most higher ones, the caudal fin is forked, and the major forward thrust is created by the uppermost and lowermost principal caudal rays. It is the way in which these rays are supported by the caudal skeleton that seems to be most significant for the classification of lower teleostean groups.

Patterson (1968*a*) has shown that in the earliest teleosts as many as five of the neural arch elements of the posteriormost centra in the vertebral column become transformed into elongate, paired, strap-shaped elements—the uroneurals (fig. 11*A*). The anteriormost uroneurals extend forward on either side of the neural arches of the more anterior centra in the caudal skeleton. The relationship between the uroneurals and the remaining centra and their neural arches differs considerably in the various teleostean groups. In *Elops* (fig. 11*A*) the uroneurals extend far forward but never fuse with the centra, and the neural arch of ural centrum 1 remains cartilaginous until late in the life of the indivual. The arrangement in *Albula* (fig. 11*B*) is essentially the same, but there is a further fusion and shortening of the uroneurals, and the neural arch of ural centrum 1 (fig. 11*B*, *na*) ossifies much earlier in ontogenetic development.

From a caudal skeleton like that of *Elops*, the clupeoid condition was presumably derived. There, except in *Denticeps*, the uroneurals fuse anteriorly with the last preural centrum, so that the upturned strut in the clupeoid tail is made up primarily of uroneurals rather than centra, as Regan (1910*b*) pointed out. This upturned strut of the clupeoids was given the special name *pleurostyle* by Monod (1967, 1968) to distinguish it from the upturned caudal centra making up the usual teleostean urostyle. In fishes that have a pleurostyle, the neural arch element of ural centrum 1 seems to have been reduced or to have disappeared completely.

Among lower teleosts a pleurostyle of the type described above is typical of clupeoids, gonorhynchoids, and the Cypriniformes (Monod 1967, 1968). It seems to be an early specialization serving as protection for the urophysis and as support for the upper portion of the upper caudal fin lobe. In the course of the fusion of caudal skeleton elements that is common to the evolution of all teleostean fishes, a pleurostyle-like element develops in various other groups, but it does not seem to be as basic to those groups as it does to the clupeoids, gonorhynchoids, and Cypriniformes.

Perhaps in relation to this pleurostylar development, the same three groups exhibit peculiarities in the lower parts of the caudal skeletons. Thus, in the clupeoids, gonorhynchoids, and Cypriniformes, the parahypural and 2nd hypural often fuse basally with centrum elements, whereas the 1st hypural tends to lose its basal articulation (Gosline 1961).

The evolution of the caudal skeleton of the Salmoniformes and Myctophiformes seems to have followed a quite different course—one that could easily have originated in the condition found in *Albula*. A single, enlarged, anterior pair of uroneurals fuses with the enlarged but dislocated neural arch element (fig. 11B) of the (apparently) 1st ural centrum (except in alepocephaloids and esocoids, in which the neural arch element is reduced or absent). The resulting fusion gives rise to a convex crest on the anterior uroneurals, and the combined structure has been called a *stegural* by Monod (1967, 1968) and by Patterson (1968b). Only later in caudal-skeleton evolution does the stegural become fused with the centrum elements of the caudal skeleton. In the lower parts of the caudal skeleton of fishes with a stegural, hypural 1 usually has at least as strong a basal articulation with centra as do the parahypural and hypural 2. In this respect also these fishes differ from the clupeoids, gonorhynchoids, and Cypriniformes. As Patterson (1968b) has shown, the stegural type of caudal skeleton characterizes both fossil and recent forms of higher teleosts.

There seem, therefore, to be two main types of caudal skeleton: (1) a pleurostylar type represented by most clupeoids, gonorhynchoids, and Cypriniformes, and possibly foreshadowed by *Elops;*

and (2) a stegural type characteristic of most Salmoniformes, Myctophiformes, and higher teleosts. What seems to be still a third type occurs in most Osteoglossiformes (Gosline 1961; Greenwood 1966), but it will not be considered here (see order Osteoglossiformes). If the pleurostylar and stegural types actually represent separate lineages, the adipose fin of the Cypriniformes must represent a development independent from that of the Salmoniformes, Myctophiformes, and Percopsiformes. Two lines of evidence support the thesis, which is here accepted, of two separate origins for the adipose fin. First, there is some slight evidence (Weisel 1968) that the adipose fins of the Cypriniformes and Salmoniformes are structurally different. Second, the morphology of the ribs and skull of the Cypriniformes (Greenwood, et al. 1966) again suggests a relationship with the gonorhynchoids rather than with the Salmoniformes.

Finally, there is the matter of the relationship between elopoids and albuloids. Both have a well-developed leptocephalous larva, but Ridewood (1904a) long ago suggested that the other resemblances between the two groups consist primarily of primitive characters held in common by both. Little information has since been added (see Gosline 1965) that would gainsay this opinion. The caudal skeletons of the two groups might suggest that the elopoids represent forerunners of the clupeoids, and the albuloids those of the salmonoids, but this phylogeny is dubious. In any event, the split between the two groups goes deep, as is indicated in figure 28.

Upper Jaw Structure. The lower teleosts were provisionally defined as comprising those orders in which at least some members had the maxillary included in the gape. That this character *per se* has little biological or phylogenetic significance is sufficiently shown by the fact that many members of the lower teleostean orders, for example, almost all catfishes, have the maxillaries excluded from the gape, whereas certain intermediate teleosts, for example, the larval stages of some myctophiform fishes (Berry 1964) and the adults of some fossil myctophiform fishes (Rosen and Patterson 1969) and berycoids (Patterson 1967b), have the maxillary included. The exclusion of the maxillary, however, is a rough indicator of a major evolutionary change in jaw apparatus. For an understanding of this development it is necessary to refer to certain aspects of the history of the teleostean suspensorium described in chapter 3.

Basically, in the intermediate and higher teleosts a prong from the upper portion of the forward end of the palatine extends laterally over the anterior (medial) part of the maxillary (fig. 23B). Because the suspensorium acts as a single movable unit, the tip of this palatine prong swings upward when the lower portion of the two suspensoria are spread apart, which happens whenever the oral cavity is laterally expanded (chap. 3). Since the palatine prong extends over the anterior end of the maxillary (i.e., the maxillary area that ordinarily lies behind the premaxillaries), movement in the palatine prong affects both the premaxillary and the maxillary. In short, in the intermediate and higher teleosts the palatine becomes a component of the complex mechanism for moving the front of the upper jaw. Though this mechanism becomes modified in various ways (see, for example, van Dobben 1935), the ability to move the premaxillaries and maxillaries separately from the cranium is never again lost.

In the lower teleostean groups the mouth structure is quite different. Except in a very few salmonoids (Gosline, Marshall, and Mead 1966), there is never an anterior strut extending laterally from the palatine over the maxillaries. Typically, the palatine extends forward to wedge between the maxillary laterally and the cranium medially. Spreading of the lower portions of the suspensorium in such fishes can at best push the maxillaries laterally to only a slight extent. Various jaw modifications occur in lower teleosts, including the development of protrusile upper jaws (Alexander 1966; Thys van den Audenaerde 1961), but the basic type of palatine-associated upper-jaw movement found in the intermediate and higher teleosts never develops. The premaxillaries may be lost completely, as in some argentinoids (Cohen 1964) and apparently in giganturids (Walters 1964), or they may revert to a more or less firm attachment to the cranium as in eels (fig. 18) and erythrinine characins. Again, the forward, palatopterygoid part of the suspensorium may become reduced by the fusion or loss of bony elements, as in osteoglossiform fishes, eels (fig. 18), and some characins; or, conversely, it may bear greatly enlarged teeth, as in the giganturids. In almost all lower teleosts, however, the upper jaw and the suspensorium act as independent or only slightly associated functional elements. That this should be so is hardly unexpected, for the suspensoria are gill-arch structures, whereas the teleostean premaxillaries and maxillaries originated as dermal bones of the cranial roof (fig. 22).

In the following accounts the three basal groups of the old

isospondylous fishes—Osteoglossiformes, Clupeiformes, Salmoniformes—are dealt with first, followed by the more specialized and presumably derivative Cypriniformes, Anguilliformes, and Notacanthiformes. The order Myctophiformes is placed as the first of the intermediate teleostean groups discussed in chapter 7.

1. Order OSTEOGLOSSIFORMES*

Suborder Notopteroidei
  Superfamily Hiodontoidae
    Family Hiodontidae
  Superfamily Notopteroidae
    Family Notopteridae
Suborder Osteoglossoidei
  Superfamily Osteoglossoidae
    Family Osteoglossidae
  Superfamily Pantodontoidae
    Family Pantodontidae
Suborder Mormyroidei
    Families Mormyridae, Gymnarchidae

The following diagnosis of living Osteoglossiformes is based primarily on Greenwood (1963): Nasal capsule rigid, without a mobile antorbital-supraorbital pumping device, the supraorbital bone absent or fused with the frontal. Maxillary without pedicels or supramaxillary. Palatine ending anteriorly in a simple point, without a well-developed maxillary-palatine articular facet. Parasphenoid ending well forward of the posterior limit of the basioccipital (except in *Scleropages*), usually toothed, sometimes with a lateral process for the support of the endopterygoid. Vertebral parapophyses well developed, ankylosed with the centra. No epipleural intermuscular bones (Patterson 1967c). Dorsal fin behind the center of the body except in tapering forms. Caudal fin with 16 or fewer branched rays.

Though the fossil record of modern osteoglossiform fishes, as of other freshwater forms, is quite poor, a number of lines of evidence suggest that the Osteoglossiformes are very ancient teleosteans. Patterson (1967c) postulated that the extinct Mesozoic Plethodontidae, Protobramidae, and possibly Ichthyodectidae

---

*For a general discussion of the problems of osteoglossiform classification and zoogeography, see Nelson (1969b).

belong to the order, and, as previously noted, the Jurassic *Allothrissops* has been suggested as a possible early forerunner of the osteoglossiform group (Greenwood and Patterson 1967; Patterson 1967*a*), though the basis for this suggestion has not been explained.

An osteoglossoid, *Scleropages*, is the only true freshwater teleost in Australia today. Aside, perhaps, from the mormyroids, the modern osteoglossiform fishes of other continents are represented sporadically by a relatively few diverse and apparently relict species. (Since the distribution of the far more abundant cypriniform fishes overlaps that of the Osteoglossiformes, except in Australia, it may well be that the Cypriniformes have replaced the osteoglossiform fishes in most habitats.)

The various, living osteoglossiform fishes display a mosaic of ancient teleostean traits. These have been well summarized in Greenwood et al. (1966), and only three character complexes will be mentioned here.

In the course of teleostean evolution, the bite has become progressively concentrated between the jaws at the front of the mouth (Nelson 1968; see also chap. 3). In this regard the Osteoglossiformes show a stage of arrested development, and the fusion of the bones at the front of the pointed suspensorium in these fishes represents evolution in a different direction. Not only are teeth usually retained on the parasphenoid on the center of the mouth roof, but a flange from the parasphenoid sometimes supports the toothed endopterygoid. Parasphenoid teeth develop in other living teleosts only among the elopoids and certain percoids (Gosline 1968), which, perhaps significantly, are also freshwater forms. A parasphenoid support for the endopterygoid occurs among other living teleosts only in some alepocephaloids (Gosline 1969). Both traits, however, are found commonly in Mesozoic teleosts.

The osteoglossiform caudal skeleton appears to have evolved from the primitive type found in *Hiodon* in a direction somewhat different from that taken by other lower teleostean groups. Instead of fusing with the ural centrum to form a pleurostyle (see introduction to this chapter), as, for example, in clupeoids, or of fusing with a neural arch element to form a stegural, the uroneurals of Osteoglossiformes tend to become progressively reduced and eventually to be lost entirely. While this change is occurring, the support for the upper caudal lobe becomes more and more concentrated in an enlarged upper hypural which fuses basally with a centrum. This unusual course of caudal skeleton evolution may be traced in a typological series from *Hiodon* and †*Eohiodon* (Cavender 1966) through †*Singida* (Greenwood and Patterson 1967, †*Phareodus* (Cavender 1966), and †*Proto-brama* (Patterson 1967c) to that found in modern osteoglossoids and mormyroids (Greenwood 1966; Taverne 1967; Monod 1968). There seems to be a rather strong implication that the type of caudal skeleton found in the modern osteoglossoids evolved as a support for a rounded caudal fin. Three lines of evidence are involved. First, the main support of the caudal fin has shifted to a more central position than in *Hiodon, Elops, Clupea,* etc. Second, in Osteoglossiformes the dorsal fin seems never to have moved forward on the body (except in tapering and presumably undulating forms) for use as a keel and, in other lower teleosts, a posterior dorsal position is often associated with a rounded tail. Finally, the same basic type of caudal skeleton evolution as occurs in the Osteoglossiformes is found again in other round-tailed forms (Monod 1968, fig. 18 III). If the osteoglossoid caudal skeleton indeed evolved in rounded-tailed forms, then the forked tail of the mormyroids is a secondary redevelopment.

Another character that sets the Osteoglossiformes apart from all other modern lower teleosts is the absence of an antorbital-supraorbital system for pumping water over the olfactory epithelium (Gosline 1961, 1965). Whether the Osteoglossiformes never had one or lost it secondarily remains unknown. In any event, this and a host of other osteoglossiform characters suggest that the group diverged very early from the main teleostean stock and seem to justify fully the recognition of a separate order Osteoglossiformes.

The interrelationships between the very diverse survivors of this group are not clear. Many show considerable specialization, and they may be grouped in various ways depending on which morphological character is emphasized. Usually, the mormyroids have been considered as a separate, derivative order (e.g., Greenwood et al. 1966), but, on the basis of a study of the gill arches, Nelson (1968) suggested recently that the mormyroids may be more closely related to certain of the Osteoglossiformes than the various forms included in that group *(sensu stricto)* are to each other. If, to select another character complex from several possibilities, the caudal skeleton is examined, that of *Hiodon* shows a wholly different and more primitive level of organization from that of other osteoglossiform fishes (Gosline 1961; Greenwood 1966; Taverne 1967). Under the circumstances, the subordinal classification of the Osteoglossiformes adopted here is no more than a provisional compromise that may well prove a poor indicator of the actual lineages represented within the order.

Suborder NOTOPTEROIDEI

This suborder, as generally recognized, contains two very different living families: the Hiodontidae of North America and the Notopteridae of the African and Oriental faunal regions. In a number of respects, for example, the caudal skeleton (see above) and gill-arch structure (Nelson 1968), *Hiodon* is among the most "primitive" of living teleosts. By contrast the notopterids, especially perhaps in body form and fin structure, are rather specialized. The principal reason for placing the two families in a single suborder is that they are unique among living fishes in the nature of the connection between the swim bladder and the ear, in that anterior prongs of the swim bladder pass forward lateral to the skull (Greenwood 1963). However, Ridewood (1904*b*) was unimpressed with this feature as an indicator of relationship, and, as Greenwood (1963) pointed out, the detail of the swim bladder-ear connection in the two groups is quite different. Dehadrai (1962) has shown that two Indian species of *Notopterus* use their swim bladders as accessory air-breathing organs.

Suborder OSTEOGLOSSOIDEI

The Osteoglossoidei also comprise two families of quite different fishes. Of the two, the Osteoglossidae, with a few genera of moderate-sized to very large fishes distributed over the southern continents and in the Oriental-Australian region, is much nearer to the ancestral stock. Indeed, the osteoglossids are among the few living teleosts in which such features as a basipterygoid process on the parasphenoid, a bridged subtemporal fossa, and parasphenoid teeth are retained. The Pantodontidae, with a single genus of small African fishes, seem to be highly specialized derivatives of the Osteoglossidae (Greenwood and Thomson 1960), in which the pectorals have apparently become adapted for aerial locomotion and the gas bladder for use as an air-breathing structure (Nysten 1962).

Suborder MORMYROIDEI

Unlike the other osteoglossiform suborders, the mormyroids are represented today by a fair number of species, all African. All are nocturnal, and, like their unrelated gymnotoid counterparts, all have developed the ability to produce an electric field by means of which they are able to locate nearby objects (Lissman and Machin 1958). This specialization is associated not only with the development of electric-field-producing organs on the tail (in the Mormyridae), but also with the development of peculiar lateral-line receptors (Szabo 1965), an enlarged lobe overlying the cerebellum of the brain (Franz 1911; Lissman 1963), and indeed with specializations of all parts of the head and body (Ridewood 1904b). Despite these peculiarities, the relationship between the mormyroids and the other two osteoglossiform suborders has long been recognized. Indeed, the basic osteological patterns of mormyroids and osteoglossoids are sufficiently similar that there is much to recommend Nelson's (1968) suggestion that the Osteoglossiformes be divided into two primary divisions: the notopteroids on the one hand and the osteoglossoids plus mormyroids on the other. In the elongated body form, the gymnarchids differ from the mormyrids somewhat as, among the Notopteroidei, the notopterids do from the hiodontids. However, in other features (Ridewood 1904b; Nelson 1968), the distinctions between gymnarchids and mormyrids are relatively minor.

2. Order CLUPEIFORMES

Suborder Elopoidei
  Superfamily Elopoidae
    Family Elopidae
  Superfamily Albuloidae
    Family Albulidae
Suborder Clupeoidei
  Superfamily Denticipitoidae
    Family Denticipitidae
  Superfamily Clupeoidae
    Families Dussumieriidae, Clupeidae, Engraulidae
Suborder Gonorhynchoidei
  Superfamily Gonorhynchoidae
    Family Gonorhynchidae
  Superfamily Chanoidae
    Family Chanidae
  Superfamily Knerioidae
    Family Kneriidae
  Superfamily Phractolaemoidae
    Family Phractolaemidae

The fishes of this order, which comprise those families of the Isospondyli of Regan (1929) and Gosline (1960*a*) that remain after the osteoglossoid and alepocephaloid-salmonoid-stomiotoid stocks have been removed, are much too diverse to allow any unexceptionable diagnosis. The clupeiform fishes tend to be silvery, fork-tailed, surface-living forms. None of them has an adipose fin, and the single dorsal fin is usually centrally located on the back, a position attained by forward change in position during ontogeny (François 1956). The maxillary extends well behind the somewhat movable premaxillary. Ribs and intermuscular bones are extensively developed. The caudal skeleton is variously developed, but the uroneurals are never lost, nor, except incipiently in albulids, is a compound stegural element developed (Monod 1967, 1968; Patterson 1968*b*).

In older classifications, for example, that of Regan (1929), the isospondylous fishes constituted the great basal group of teleostean fishes. Increase in knowledge of lower teleostean lineages has led to the splintering of the Isospondyli. Thus Greenwood et al. (1966), emphasizing lineage concepts, divided its members among four different superorders. This emphasis on father-son relationships obscures the fact that the early members of the four superorders were undoubtedly closely related fishes; it results in placing such generalized adult forms as *Elops* with the highly specialized eels, and such other early teleostean stocks as the extinct Leptolepidae become unassignable (except to still another superorder). Here, a compromise classification is adopted, and the isospondylous fishes are divided among three orders: Osteoglossiformes, Clupeiformes, and Salmoniformes. The difference between the present classification and that of Greenwood et al. (1966) is not zoological; it merely represents a difference of opinion as to the best means of integrating zoological knowledge into a classification.

The retention in this book of the central core of the old isospondylous groups as an order Clupeiformes is provisional, however. There are several ways in which its components could be reallocated, but the justification and advantage of any one way of doing so does not appear to be adequately established at the present time. Retaining the Clupeiformes as a central isospondylous unit (fig. 28) has at least the advantage, as compared with the classification of Greenwood et al. (1966), of stressing the ancestral teleostean morphology of the adult *Elops*. Further, the Clupeiformes, as here recognized, may prove to be at least as coherent a group as the Osteoglossiformes or Salmoniformes.

The four modern isospondylous groups—Elopidae, Albulidae, Clupeoidei, and Gonorhynchoidei—provisionally retained here in the order Clupeiformes are clearly the descendants of an ancient teleostean proliferation. Adult elopids do not seem to have changed much since the Jurassic and could, indeed, serve as typological ancestors for almost all modern teleosts. The postulate of a relationship between *Elops* and the in many ways more peculiar but also ancient *Albula* rests primarily on the specialized leptocephalous-like larval form common to both genera. As to the clupeoids, they have recently been traced back to the Cretaceous *Diplomystus* by Patterson (1967a). Though *Diplomystus* seems to lack features that indicate a specific relationship with *Elops*, its generalized protoclupeoid characteristics appear to place it closer to the elopids than to the Osteoglossiformes or Salmoniformes. A relationship between the clupeoids and the gonorhynchoids is suggested by the pleurostylar caudal skeleton (Monod 1967, 1968) found only in these two groups and the Cypriniformes.

Suborder ELOPOIDEI

The elopoids and albuloids are provisionally included in the suborder Elopoidei. Among the characters they hold in common (Gosline 1965) are the leptocephalous-like larval form, the multiple valves in the conus arteriosus, the gular ossification, the separate dermo- and autopalatine elements, and the parasphenoid teeth. All except the leptocephalous-like larval form occur in "holosteans" and are found in few other modern teleosts (see Nybelin 1956, 1968).

Nevertheless, the differences between elopids and albulids also seem to extend far back into the fossil record, and they at least suggest major taxonomic separation. The elopids are surface-living forms with a connection between the swim bladder and the ear. The albulid adults are bottom feeders without such a connection, and the members of one genus, *Pterothrissus*, inhabit rather deep water. In view of a number of elopid-albulid differences, the albulids seem to have diverged from the ancestral teleostean type in the direction suggested by figure 28. The bridged subtemporal fossa of *Elops* (Patterson 1967a) is lacking in albulids. The superficially located ethmoidal commissure of *Elops* (Nybelin 1956) has become a deep channel through the ethmoid ossification in *Pterothrissus* (Gosline 1961), foreshadowing the condition in eels (Allis 1903). The albulid caudal skeleton, as already noted, has evolved in the direction of the salmoniform-myctophiform type, not that of the clupeoids and gonorhynchoids.

Suborder CLUPEOIDEI

The modern clupeoid fishes appear to constitute one of the more distinctive and easily definable fish groups. The cranium, lateral-line system, caudal skeleton, intermuscular bones, and scales all seem to provide diagnostic characters. Of these, Greenwood (1968, p. 262) has recently emphasized the following: "(i) The presence of intracranial swim bladder diverticula encased in bony bullae developed in association with either the prootic and pterotic bones, or the prootic alone; the prootic bulla is intimately associated with the utricular recess. (ii) An intracranial space, the *recessus lateralis,* into which open the major cephalic laterosensory canals as well as the temporal canal; the recessus is separated by a membranous fenestra from the perilymphatic spaces of the ear (see Wohlfahrt, 1936). (iii) The caudal fin skeleton."

All clupeoids apparently feed near the surface. Indeed, Aleev (1963) has shown that the sharply keeled, silvery abdomen, a very ancient clupeoid trait (Patterson 1967a), is an adaptation for life in well-lighted surface waters. There, the clupeoids may be plankton feeders, or, as in *Chirocentrus,* a very ancient clupeoid type (Patterson 1967a), they may be voracious carnivores. Patterson (1967a) has traced the clupeoid stock back to the Cretaceous *Diplomystus,* a generalized form resembling in a number of respects the more primitive osteoglossiform-elopoid type.

Among the modern clupeoids, the dussumieriid-clupeid-engraulid stock appears to be closely knit, the small African *Denticeps* representing an aberrant, partly primitive form (Greenwood 1968).

Suborder GONORHYNCHOIDEI

This suborder includes today a small number of diverse, presumably relict species united especially by a proliferation of rib structures (Greenwood et al. 1966) and peculiarities associated with the mouth. In all species, the rami of the lower jaw are short. This not only results in a small mouth, but is more or less closely related functionally to the anterior quadrate position of the suspensorium (fig. 23A), to the reduced number of branchiostegal rays, and to the attachment of the gill covers to the throat (Gosline 1967).

Greenwood et al. (1966) placed the gonorhynchoids in the same lineage with the Salmoniformes. As already mentioned, the caudal skeleton and complex rib structure suggest a clupeoid rather than a salmoniform relationship. Other gonorhynchoid features that point in the same direction are the smoothly rounded vaulting of the posterior portion of the cranium, the lack of an adipose fin, and the fact that the dorsal fin, at least of *Chanos,* assumes a more forward position over the body during growth (Delsman 1926). These similarities suggest a common origin with the clupeoid fishes and, except for the lack of an adipose fin, with the Cypriniformes as well. This is not to say that the modern gonorhynchoids gave rise to the clupeoids and Cypriniformes, or vice versa, for all three groups have become specialized in different ways. The peculiarities associated with the jaw of the gonorhynchoids have already been mentioned. In the caudal skeleton the modern gonorhynchoids, though similar to the clupeoids and Cypriniformes in pleurostylar development (see discussion of lower teleostean groups), differ from them in having a single epural which tends to be attached basally to a neural arch arising from the last preural centrum (Monod 1968, pp. 70–71, 133–136, 199).

The main categories of Gonorhynchoidei are provisionally considered here as superfamilies. Of these, the superfamily Chanoidae (Ridewood 1905*a*) appears to be the most generalized. The Gonorhynchoidae (Ridewood 1905*c*) has a most peculiar, rounded basibranchial tooth plate as one of a series of notable features. The remaining Gonorhynchoidei are African freshwater forms. One genus, *Phractolaemus,* has an upwardly protrusile mouth (Thys van den Audenaerde 1961). The remaining members have usually been divided into three families—Cromeriidae (d'Au͘ benton 1961), Grasseichthyidae, and Kneriidae—but Greenwood et al. (1966) have combined them into a single family.

3. Order SALMONIFORMES*

Suborder Alepocephaloidei
    Families Alepocephalidae, Searsidae, Bathylaconidae, Leptochilichthyidae, and Bathyprionidae

*Two papers bearing on salmoniform classification have been received too late to be integrated into the text of the present work: Goody 1969, and McDowall 1969. Suffice it to say here that Goody, in including certain Cretaceous groups in the Salmoniformes, considerably broadens the concept of that group, and that McDowall's paper provides a much more thorough osteological background for galaxioid classification and relationships than has hitherto been available and provides an excellent discussion of the basal groups of modern salmoniform fishes.

Suborder Giganturoidei
    Family Giganturidae
Suborder Argentinoidei
    Families Argentinidae, Bathylagidae, and Opisthoproctidae
Suborder Stomiatoidei
    Superfamily Gonostomatoidae
    Families Gonostomatidae and Sternoptychidae
    Superfamily Stomiatoidae
    Families Stomiatidae and Chauliodontidae
    Superfamily Astronesthoidae
    Families Astronesthidae, Melanostomiatidae, Idiacanthidae, and Malacosteidae
Suborder Salmonoidei
    Families Salmonidae, Osmeridae, Plecoglossidae, Salangidae, Retropinnidae, Aplochitonidae, and Galaxiidae
Suborder Esocoidei
    Superfamily Esocoidae
    Family Esocidae
    Superfamily Umbroidae
    Family Umbridae
Incertae sedis: Families Rosauridae and Macristiidae

The Salmoniformes comprise fishes in which, aside from a few Southern Hemisphere forms (Stokell 1941), the maxillary is included in the gape and the palatine has no anterolateral projection extending over the maxillary. The swim bladder of modern forms has no connection of any sort with the ear (but see Goody 1968). The dorsal fin originates in its final, adult position, and an adipose fin is frequently present. In the caudal skeleton, the anterior uroneural usually fuses with a neural arch element to form a stegural. Except for relatively deep water forms, the modern Salmoniformes do not occur in tropical regions today.

The modern salmoniform fishes are well represented throughout the colder waters of the world, except in Antarctica. In many of these waters they predominate. Whether cold water has led to the development of salmoniform characteristics or whether the salmoniform characteristics are a preadaptation to such an environment remains unknown. That the cold-water habitat affects salmoniform physiology is clear (see, for example, Fry 1957); it may also have something to do with the ontogeny (see introduction to this chapter) and with the tendency for the adult skeleton to retain an unusually high proportion of cartilage. Perhaps the high cartilage retention is related in turn to the simplification of bony structure in the Salmoniformes as compared, for example, to the Clupeiformes. Thus, in the Salmoniformes a number of ancestral dermal ossifications have been lost, for example, rostral ossicles, gular plate, and fulcral scales; the skull has become simplified by the loss of subtemporal fossae and, usually, of roofed posttemporal fossae; and the excessive rib proliferation in the Clupeiformes has been reduced.'

The known fossil record of modern salmoniform groups does not extend back beyond the Tertiary. Though there are a number of supposed Mesozoic stomiatoids (Andrews et al. 1967), Weitzman (1967a) has shown that these are either misidentifications or are, at most, only doubtfully stomiatoid. Goody (1968), however, included the extinct Cretaceous Enchodontidae in the Salmoniformes on the basis of the head skeleton.

In most features the Salmoniformes seem to represent a streamlining of the early, complex teleosts in the direction of the Myctophiformes and higher teleosts. Thus, on the head the ethmoidal commissure of the lateral line system and the subtemporal fossa are lacking. The roof of the posttemporal fossa has been lost in high-headed forms and reduced (perhaps secondarily redeveloped) in such flatheaded members as *Esox*. Parasphenoid dentition has been lost, and a parasphenoid supporting strut for the endopterygoid is found only in certain alepocephaloids (Gosline 1969). Epibranchial organs are absent except in certain alepocephaloids (Gosline 1969). A connection between the swim bladder and the ear is lacking, except possibly in the extinct *Enchodus* (Goody 1968). On the body the dorsal fin develops in the adult position, and in the caudal skeleton the single anterior pair of uroneurals fuses with a neural arch element to form the stegural type of structure common to most higher teleosts. As a possible unifying theory for most of these changes it might be suggested that, whereas such fishes as *Elops* and *Chanos* reduce the weight of the old holostean body by decreasing the weight of the individual bones (most of which they retain), the Salmoniformes reduce body weight by replacing bone by cartilage (see, for example, Gegenbaur 1878), with consequent simplification of bony structure (see chap. 1).

Many of the features which differentiate the Salmoniformes from other lower teleosts are also found in the Myctophiformes. Indeed the Salmoniformes and Myctophiformes seem to have arisen from the same basal teleostean stock. In other respects, however, these two great groups appear to have moved apart (Gosline, Marshall, and Mead 1966). The major difference in upper-jaw structure has already been noted (see introduction to this chapter). The myctophiform fishes, unlike the Salmoniformes, seem to have arisen from bottom-resting forms, and perhaps the consolidation of the pelvic fin base and the often more anterior pelvic placement, the development of a lateralis commissure in the interorbital area, and the retention of caudal fulcral scales in the more generalized forms (Patterson 1968*b*) may be functionally associated with this ancestral habit.

If the salmoniform fishes form a coherent though diverse group of modern fishes, the question of the phylogenetic relationships of its components remains open. Not only have the different modern groups become specialized in different ways but, probably in a negative relationship to specialization, the characters that would seem to represent the ancestral form are variously retained. Some examples of the phylogenetic dilemma that results will suffice. The extinct Mesozoic Enchodontidae (Goody 1968) apparently were already specialized, at least in the matter of enlarged dentition on the forward border of the suspensorium, but they may have retained a connection between swim bladder and ear. The modern giganturids also show enlargement of the dentition on the rim of the suspensorium, but whether they developed this independently of the enchodontids remains unknown. Though the argentinoids are similar to the giganturids in the reduction of the premaxillaries, they have evolved in the opposite direction, developing small mouths with reduced dentition, a reduced number of branchiostegal rays, etc. However, *Argentina* (Gosline 1960*a*) seems to be the only existing salmoniform fish in which the anterior uroneurals have not fused with a neural arch to form a compound stegural. The alepocephaloids, like most argentinoids and the giganturids, are fishes of the relatively deep sea. But, unlike the giganturids and argentinoids, at least certain of the alepocephaloids have retained mouth structures not found else-where among salmoniform fishes: a parasphenoid support for the suspensorium and an epibranchial organ (Gosline 1969). On the other hand, alepocephaloids lack the adipose fin which is characteristic of most other salmoniform groups. In brief, the various salmoniform fishes, like those in the order Osteoglossi-formes, provide excellent examples of mosaic evolution, each group being a separate mosaic.

Here, six suborders are provisionally recognized. Four of these are quite distinct from one another, but all members inhabit the (mostly) deeper waters of the oceans. The suborder of the freshwater esocoids is also distinct. The remaining freshwater and inshore Salmoniformes are lumped together into the suborder Salmonoidei—admittedly an awkward group.

Suborder ALEPOCEPHALOIDEI

Judging only from morphology, for a fossil record is unknown, it is suggested that the alepocephaloids were among the first teleosts to adopt a deep-water existence. This was made possible, apparently, by even further simplification of the already stream-lined basic salmoniform structure (see above), for example, by losing the swim bladder completely. As a result, of course, the difficulty of attaining neutral buoyancy is increased, a problem which seems to have been solved at least in part by the reduced mineralization of bony elements (Gegenbaur 1878; Denton and Marshall 1958). Though other specializations for deep-water life also occur, such as the development of light organs by some species, one or another alepocephaloid retains ancestral teleostean traits that other salmoniform fishes have lost, for example, the basipterygoid process and an epibranchial organ (Gosline 1969). Their generalized ancestral traits combined with specializations for deep-water existence make it difficult to determine their relationships with any assurance. They are here placed with the Salmoniformes primarily because of general resemblances, such as a more or less direct development from a large egg.

Nielsen and Larsen (1968) have shown recently that the Bathylaconidae, a family for which even the ordinal allocation was previously in doubt, belong among the alepocephaloids. Indeed, they appear to be rather generalized representatives of this stock.

Suborder GIGANTUROIDEI

The giganturids are a small group of highly specialized, deep-sea fishes with an unstable systematic history (summarized by Walters 1961; McAllister 1968). Among their peculiarities are telescopic eyes (Brauer 1908) and the presence of a large otolith in the utriculus (Bierbaum 1914). The giganturids are often assigned a separate order (e.g., Walters 1964), but the peculiar upper jaw structure with the premaxillaries lacking, the small maxillaries included in the gape, and the large teeth on the palatopterygoid strongly suggest the Salmoniformes, most notably the extinct Enchodontidae (Goody 1968).

Suborder **ARGENTINOIDEI**

This group of oceanic fishes has the premaxillaries reduced or absent and the maxillaries toothless. There are no supramaxillaries. The mouth is of moderate to small size and the branchiostegal rays are few (2 to 6). The eyes are large and sometimes tubular. Cohen (1964), followed here, recognized three families.

Suborder **STOMIATOIDEI**

The stomiatoids are a heterogeneous group of mostly black, bathypelagic fishes with a peculiar swim-bladder structure (Marshall 1960) and usually two (sometimes one or three) rows of serially arranged light organs along the lower sides. The premaxillaries are well developed and may even be protrusile, and the more generalized forms frequently have two supramaxillaries (Morrow 1964). The stomiatoids differ significantly from other salmoniform groups in the serial arrangement of the photophores (always present though sometimes small), which approaches the analogous myctophid configuration.

Morrow (1964), following Parr (1930b) divided the suborder into three groups: the Heterophotodermi, with the families Gonostomatidae and Sternoptychidae; Lepidophotodermi, with the families Chauliodontidae and Stomiatidae; and Gymnophotodermi, with the families Astronesthidae, Melanostomiatidae, Idiacanthidae, and Malacosteidae. In a recent study on the osteology and relationships of the Astronesthidae, Weitzman (1967b) followed the classification of Greenwood et al. (1966), which provided formal superfamily recognition for the three groups of Morrow and of Parr. This arrangement is adopted here.

Suborder **SALMONOIDEI**

The suborder Salmonoidei as here recognized is a group of highly diverse inshore and freshwater salmoniform fishes. Though the included families no doubt should be divided into superfamily groupings, inadequate knowledge of the Salangidae and the Southern Hemisphere forms (McDowall 1969) would seem to make any formal superfamily classification premature at the present time. Informally, the members may be divided between Southern and Northern Hemisphere forms. The diverse forms from the Southern Hemisphere seem to be most closely related to the northern osmerids (Gosline 1960a; Weitzman 1967a), though more than one group may be represented. The Northern Hemisphere osmeroids are represented by four quite distinct families:

Salangidae, Plecoglossidae, Osmeridae (see Weitzman 1967*a*), and Salmonidae (Norden 1961).

Suborder ESOCOIDEI

The members of this suborder are united by the presence of separate proethmoid bones anterolateral to the frontals. They are also united in the posteriorly placed dorsal fin, the lack of an adipose fin, and the toothless maxillary without supramaxillaries. The osteology and classification of the group has been dealt with by, among others, Starks (1904*a*), Chapman (1934), and Berg (1936, 1940), and most recently by Cavender (1969), whose suggestions concerning family relationships are followed here.

INCERTAE SEDIS

Family Rosauridae (Tucker 1954). This family is based on a single specimen 8.4 mm long. It is assigned to the Salmoniformes because it is an oceanic fish with the maxillary included in the gape and with an adipose fin.

Family Macristiidae. This family is known from three specimens; one was dried (Regan 1911*f*) and is now apparently lost, and the other two were larvae (Marshall 1961; Berry and Robins 1967). Marshall (1961) suggested that *Macristium* is an extant representative of the extinct Ctenothrissiformes. Patterson (1964, p. 243) stated: "I feel that the evidence presented so far is not sufficient to justify the inclusion of *Macristium* in the Ctenothrissidae." The fin structure of *Macristium* is certainly closer to that of ctenothrissids than to that of the salmoniform fishes. Because it has the maxillary included in the gape it would fit in either group, and only a more detailed knowledge of the adult upper jaw articulation could provide a decision on the matter.

4. Order CYPRINIFORMES

Suborder Siluroidei
> Families Diplomystidae, Ictaluridae, Bagridae, Cranoglanididae, Siluridae, Schilbeidae, Pangasiidae, Amblycipitidae, Amphiliidae, Akysidae, Sisoridae, Clariidae, Heteropneustidae, Chacidae, Olyridae, Malopteruridae, Mochochidae, Ariidae, Doradidae, Auchenipteridae, Aspredinidae, Plotosidae, Pimelodidae, Ageneiosidae, Hypophthalmidae, Helogeneidae, Cetopsidae, Trichomycteridae, Callichthyidae, Loricariidae, and Astroblepidae

Suborder Cyprinoidei
  Superfamily Characoidae
    Family Characidae (sensu lato)
  Superfamily Gymnotoidae
    Families Gymnotidae, Electrophoridae, Apteronotidae, and Rhamphichthyidae
  Superfamily Cyprinoidae
    Families Cyprinidae, Gyrinocheilidae, Psilorhynchidae, Catostomidae, Homalopteridae, and Cobitidae

This vast order of primarily freshwater fishes is based primarily on the presence in all its members of a series of bony Weberian ossicles between the swim bladder and the ear. Though these ossicles are sufficient to strongly suggest a monophyletic origin for the Cypriniformes, two other characteristics reinforce the same conclusion. One is the ability, apparently constant throughout the Cypriniformes (Pfeiffer 1963), of a fish under stress to excrete a substance *(Schreckstoff)* that serves as a warning to nearby members of the same species. Second, the caudal skeleton of all Cypriniformes except the tapering-tailed gymnotids contains a fused pleurostyle (see introduction to this chapter).

The cypriniform fossil record does not extend below the Tertiary and indicates very little about the origin of the group. However, Eocene records demonstrate that the Cypriniformes had by then attained approximately their present diversity and distribution, strongly suggesting a Mesozoic origin. The presence of the cypriniform family Characidae in both Africa and South America (Regan 1922) points to an origin previous to the separation of those two continents, which, according to present views of continental drift, did not occur later than the Cretaceous.

The relationships of the Cypriniformes have been a matter of some controversy (for two views on this matter that are not discussed here see Sagemehl 1885, and Bertmar 1959). The adipose fin of characins and catfishes resembles that of the salmoniform-myctophiform lineage, but for reasons that have in part been already stated (see introduction to this chapter) it is here provisionally postulated that the adipose fin has evolved independently in these two groups. In most other features the Cypriniformes more closely resemble the Clupeiforms, notably the gonorhynchoids. Though there is no real evidence regarding the origin of the Weberian apparatus, Greenwood et al. (1966) argued that it could most easily have been developed from forms which have the abundant anterior ribs and intermuscular bones of the gonorhynchoids. Again, the well-developed posttemporal fossae and vaulted cranial roof of many characins (Sagemehl 1885; Weitzman 1962) suggest *Chanos* and the elopoids—certainly not the salmoniform fishes. In the caudal skeleton of the Cypriniformes, the pleurostyle is that of gonorhynchoids and clupeoids. Gonorhynchoids and cypriniform fishes also hold in common the skin glands producing alarm substances (Pfeiffer 1967). In at least some cyprinoids there are also subtemporal fossae (Sagemehl 1891), but these may well have originated independently of the subtemporal fossae of elopoids, osteoglossiform fishes, etc. (Patterson 1967a).

The conclusion tentatively reached here, primarily on the basis of the caudal morphology of modern forms (Monod 1968), is that the clupeoids, gonorhynchoids, and Cypriniformes represent three basally related lineages, the last two being quite possibly the closer. All three groups are now so specialized along different lines that it is impossible to derive any one from any other, and any postulate of relationship between the three must be based on the concept of an ancestral Mesozoic stock.

The general account of the cypriniform fishes given in Greenwood et al. (1966) is excellent. Here, only certain problems of cypriniform classification will be discussed. It is generally agreed that the order should be divided into two sections, one containing the catfishes and the other the cyprinoid-characin-gymnotid group. The catfishes are primarily nocturnal (Lissman 1961), and their many morphological peculiarities may be interpreted as adaptations for a nocturnal existence (see Alexander 1965). Among the cyprinoid-characin-gymnotid group, the gymnotids are the only nocturnal members (Lissman 1961) of an otherwise primarily diurnal group. It is generally agreed that the gymnotids represent a secondary line of specialization from the characins, and it is perhaps odd that they should have arisen in an area (South America) that was presumably already infested with nocturnal catfishes. Possibly the explanation lies in the fact that the gymnotids, by developing an electric field system for perceiving objects (Lissman 1963) have been able to find a niche that the catfishes were unable to occupy (though there is an electric catfish).

Throughout the tropical and temperate regions of the world except Australia the catfishes and the characin-cyprinoid group preempt much of the freshwater habitat so far as fishes are concerned. Yet there are basic differences in the distribution patterns of the two groups. The catfishes are divided into numerous families, some restricted to one faunal region and some to another, with the partly marine Ariidae circumtropical. The characins and cyprinoids, however, are—or were until fairly recent invasions (Regan 1922)—divided between the southern continent characins (Africa and South America) and the northern continent cyprinoids (North America and Eurasia). The characins, though they are an obviously ancient, abundant, and diverse group, especially in South America, do not seem to have developed discrete subgroups, as the catfishes have. Thus there is no present agreement on the number of families that should be recognized among the characins, and they are often lumped together under a single family, as is done here. As a result, in South America, where there are about equal numbers of characin and catfish species, one family of characins is recognized and about 14 of catfishes. The significance of this difference is not clear.

Suborder SILUROIDEI

The interrelationships of the various catfish families have been the subject of considerable discussion but little general agreement. Part of the difficulty stems from the fact that most workers have had representatives from only one or a few areas of the world available for investigation. The family Diplomystidae is usually placed at the head of the list, primarily because of its normal, toothed maxillary. Indeed, Berg (1940, p. 447) separated the Diplomystidae as a separate superfamily from all the other catfishes. However, Hoedeman (1960, fig. 23) showed that *Hoplosternum*, a number of the Callichthyidae that is usually placed among the most specialized families, has not only a normally developed maxillary, but a supramaxillary as well.

Suborder CYPRINOIDEI

Whatever the relationships between the Characoidae and the Cyprinoidae may be, the modern characins retain a number of ancestral features that all Cyprinoidae have lost, for example, the oral dentition and the adipose fin. Indeed, the cyprinids and their allies seem to have developed one of the most specialized feeding mechanisms that exists in teleosts. The protrusile upper jaw (Alexander 1966) is only one component of this mechanism. A branchiostegal pumping system (Willem 1931) and a pharyngeal grinding mill are others. Probably the subtemporal fossa of cyprinoids (Sagemehl 1891) has arisen in connection with the musculature associated with the pharyngeal mill and is not the homologue of the subtemporal fossa of such lower teleosts as *Elops* (see introduction to this chapter). Among the characins, on the other hand, such forms as *Erythrinus* contain so many apparently atavistic characters that Sagemehl (1885; see also Weitzman 1964) thought the characins were derived from the holostean *Amia*.

5. Order ANGUILLIFORMES

Suborder Anguilloidei
> Families Anguillidae, Moringuidae, Myrocongridae, Xenocongridae, Muraenidae, Heterenchelyidae, Dysomminidae, Muraenesocidae, Neenchelyidae, Nettastomidae, Nessorhamphidae, Congridae, Ophichthidae, Todasidae, Synaphorbranchidae, Simenchelyidae, Dysommidae, Derichthyidae, Macrocephenchelyidae, Serrivomeridae, Nemichthyidae, Cyemidae, and Aotidae

Suborder Saccopharyngoidei
> Families Saccopharyngidae, Eurypharyngidae, and Monagnathidae

Diagnosis: The two premaxillaries, the vomer, and the ethmoid united into a single bone. Maxillaries movable, bordering the gape, toothed. Suspensorium consisting only of a hyomandibular, quadrate, and usually a forwardly projecting pterygoquadrate strut. Gill openings far back, often restricted, the gill cavities surrounded by circular muscles (Borcea 1907; Tchernavin 1947). Pectoral girdle not attached to the skull; the posttemporal bone missing. Body elongate, with numerous vertebrae. Pelvic fins absent in modern forms. Scales in a herring-bone pattern, present only along the lateral line, or totally absent. Eggs passing into the body cavity and to the exterior by a pore. A leptocephalous larval stage.

All eels are highly specialized, to the extent that the saccopharyngoids have sometimes, for example, Tchernavin (1947), been removed from the bony fishes altogether. Nevertheless, the arguments of Böhlke (1966) and others for a relationship between the saccopharyngoids and anguilloids seem not only sound, but can easily be amplified, as has been done to some extent in the preceding diagnosis.

The primary specialization of the adult anguilliform fishes seem to be for wedging themselves through small openings (Gosline 1960*b*). The head is very solidly constructed. The premaxillaries are fused into the cranium and the forward end of the suspensorium is reduced or eliminated. The gills (and gill openings) are displaced posteriorly (Nelson 1966) and the fish forces water over them by swallowing water rather than by the usual expansion and contraction of the gill covers, which are reduced. Scales are never overlapping. The elongate body can usually be forced through any opening an eel can push its head through. Furthermore, an eel can back out of any hole it gets stuck in.

From this basic type of existence, certain eels have adopted either of two further modes of life. One is burrowing in loose bottom. The other is a midwater existence. Most bathypelagic eels seem to have made use of the elongate body as a method of extending the lateralis system, and at least some of the saccopharyngoids have added a light organ to the tail. (One bathypelagic eel *(Cyema)*, however, has become short bodied.) The second basic eel characteristic that has perhaps preadapted eels for an oceanic existence is the elongate jaw structure with simplified suspensorium. Still another attribute that may bear on the development of oceanic midwater types is the larval history. All eels have leptocephalous larvae that live in oceanic surface waters. However, leptocephali seem to do very well there and may attain a length of as much as six feet. If they are that successful, it would seem that they might profitably develop sexual maturity and spawn. Perhaps in this connection it may be noted that the mature bathypelagic nemichthyids have jaws that seem poorly adapted for eating.

As to relationships, the leptocephalous larval forms of the anguilliform and elopoid fishes are so similar that a relationship between the two groups is strongly suggested. The lateralis commissure in the rostral region of eels (Allis 1903) also suggests the ethmoidal commissure, and perhaps also the lateralis canals in the premaxillaries, of *Pterothrissus* (Gosline 1961). Less diagnostic but indicating a low teleostean origin not incompatible with *Albula* and *Pterothrissus* is the caudal skeleton of eels. In at least *Anguilla* the last preural and the first ural centra (*tv* and *pt*$_1$ of Gosline 1963*a*, fig. 7) apparently remain as separate entities.

Though it does not negate a relationship between eels and elopoid fishes, one difference is at least curious. The teeth of elopoids and often of eels extend well back medially on the roof of the mouth. In elopoids the posterior portion of this dentition is on the parasphenoid. But in eels, as in the unrelated *Esox,* it is the vomerine area that extends backward and bears the posterior teeth. The elopoid condition is the ancestral one, and the posterior extention of the vomerine teeth seems to be a secondary condition, functionally equivalent to the earlier parasphenoid dentition.

In two features the eels seem to have advanced beyond the lower teleostean condition, namely, in the presence in most eels of a frontal commissure of the lateralis system with a median pore (Allis 1903), and in the development of retractor muscles for the pharyngeal apparatus (Nelson 1967*a*).

Suborder ANGUILLOIDEI

Given "wedging" as the basic mode of life, various eel groups have followed out this line of specialization to various degrees. The question that arises in determining the interrelationships between eel families is basically that of determining how many different times these lines of specialization have developed. Regan (1912*c*) divided modern eels into two groups of families: one with the frontals paired and one with the frontals fused. Trewavas (1932) showed that two oceanic families—the Nemichthyidae and Cyemidae—bridge Regan's groupings in having the frontals usually united anteriorly but not posteriorly. Bertin and Arambourg (1958), in line with previous work by the senior author, recognized a separate suborder (Nemichthyoidei) for the families Serrivomeridae, Nemichthyidae, and Cyemidae. Referring only peripherally to these "nemichthyoids," Nelson (1966), on the basis of gill–arch structure, divided Regan's families with the frontals fused into two lineages. Unfortunately, the foundation of eel classification is not sufficiently sound to support much peripheral reorganization. The generally recognized eel families are merely listed here. The great proliferation of families, many of which were originally based on one or a few specimens, is gradually being reduced.

Suborder SACCOPHARYNGOIDEI

For reasons that are not entirely clear, large-mouthed fishes have developed repeatedly in the bathypelagic regions. The upper jaw of such fishes may have developed in either of two quite different ways: by the premaxillary–maxillary series, as occurs for example in eels and *Malacosteus* (Günther and Deckert 1959), or, more rarely, by the palatopterygoid series, as apparently occurs in giganturids (Walters 1964). The end result in either circumstance may be quite similar. A large number of saccopharyngoid features other than the jaws (e.g., the gill openings) suggest a relationship to the eels, in which case the upper jaw bone would certainly be a maxillary. It is therefore disconcerting when such authors as Tchernavin (1947, pp. 311, 331) insist that the upper jaw of the saccopharyngoids extends posteriorly *medial* to the quadrate-mandibular articulation. This would suggest a palatopterygoid jaw like that of the giganturids, unless the posterior end of a maxillary has somehow become displaced from its usual external position.

That the saccopharyngoids have leptocephalous larvae has been demonstrated by a number of authors, most recently Orton (1963). Apparently the tremendous elongation of the jaws does not occur until transformation.

6. Order **NOTACANTHIFORMES**

Suborder Halosauroidei
    Family Halosauridae
Suborder Notacanthoidei
    Families Lipogenyidae, Notacanthidae

Any diagnosis of this order is handicapped by the lack of information regarding the osteology of the group (though this will presumably be rectified by McDowell in a forthcoming volume of *Fishes of the Western North Atlantic*). The notacanthiform fishes are moderate to deep-water, bottom-living, marine forms with many-rayed, abdominal pelvic fins and the maxillaries sometimes included in the gape. The body tapers posteriorly. A long anal fin extends to the tail and a shorter dorsal fin is more anteriorly placed. The swim bladder is of anguilliform type (Marshall 1962*b*), and there is a leptocephalous-like larva (Mead 1965).

The fossil record of these fishes extends back to the Cretaceous.

Marshall (1962*b*) pointed out a number of similarities, notably in the swim bladder, between the Notacanthiformes and Anguilliformes. Nevertheless, there are enough differences, including those of the fossil records, to suggest that the two groups have long been separate. A certain number of features, for example, the supraorbital lateralis canal bones of the head of halosaurids (Gosline 1961), would suggest that the Notacanthiformes and Anguilliformes evolved independently from the albuloid stock near *Pterothrissus*.

Berg (1940) separated the two main sections of the Notacanthiformes into independent orders. Marshall (1962b), however, has shown that this separation was based mainly on erroneous statements in the literature concerning opercular structure, and that the two groups are, in fact, related.

Suborder HALOSAUROIDEI

These fishes and the Beloniformes are the only teleosts in which the lateralis system on the body extends along the full length of the lateroventral surface. In the halosaurs the lateral line extends forward below the pectoral fins and presumably has no connection with the lateralis system of the head. The larval *Aldrovandia* (Mead 1965) is the only leptocephalous-type larva so far known (the larval form of notacanthids has not been recorded) in which the dorsal fin is far forward on the body.

Suborder NOTACANTHOIDEI

In notacanthoids the lateral line follows its usual course well up on the sides. The group is peculiar in having made, so to speak, an evolutionary trial run with fin spines (Marshall 1962b). Notacanthoid spines are soft-ray derivatives. In some notacanthoids they appear as a series of separate elements anterior to the dorsal; in others they are clumped into the front of the dorsal. In some there may be as many as three spines in each pelvic, a character unique among teleosts.

SEVEN

Intermediate Teleostean Groups

Included orders: Myctophiformes, Cetomimiformes, Beloniformes, Percopsiformes, Gadiformes, Cyprinodontiformes, Syngnathiformes, Beryciformes, Lampridiformes, and Zeiformes.

INTERRELATIONSHIPS

In a phylogenetic sense the term "intermediate" for the teleostean orders included in this category is probably misleading. What is meant is that in certain respects these orders have passed beyond the "lower" teleostean level of structural organization but have not attained that of the perciform fishes and their derivatives. Phylogenetically, it is postulated here that all of the intermediate teleostean groups have been derived from a single stock most closely represented among known forms by the extinct Ctenothrissiformes and the basal Myctophiformes, for example, *Aulopus.* This stock is a very old one, and it may indeed represent one of the earliest lines of teleostean adaptive radiation. If this proves to be true, the use of the term "intermediate" to distinguish this stock from other "lower" teleostean lines of radiation is inappropriate from the point of view of phylogeny.

The orders here included among the "intermediate teleostean groups" may be divided into two categories. One contains the Myctophiformes, Percopsiformes, and Beryciformes, all of which are recorded from the Cretaceous (Patterson 1964, 1968*b*; Rosen and Patterson 1969). The basal members of all three orders are generalized, benthic carnivores. Presumably the Perciformes and other "higher" teleostean groups have evolved over a pathway that has led through, or very close to, the basal Myctophiformes and on up through the Beryciformes. Some of the structural changes that have occurred in the course of this evolution are as follows:

Attachment of the Body Musculature to the Head (see chap. 2). The roof of the posttemporal fossa is lost in forms higher than the myctophiform fishes, but a supraoccipital crest on the dorsal surface of the head becomes strongly developed as a surface for body-muscle attachment, at least in high-headed forms. Probably an associated character is the extension of the supraoccipital forward between the parietals.

Upper-Jaw Construction. The premaxillaries are always movably attached to the cranium. In modern adult forms they exclude the maxillaries from the gape. Various types of jaw protrusion have been tried. In the more highly evolved forms, an essentially perciform type has developed, in that the premaxillary ascending processes ride over a medially ridged ethmovomerine area. However, intermediate teleostean groups with this type of jaw protrusion (Syngnathiformes, Beryciformes, and perhaps Gadiformes) have the premaxillary ascending processes roofed above by nasal bones that are rigidly united to the cranium; the Perciformes usually have no bony roofs over the ascending premaxillary processes.

Lateral-Line System of the Head. Probably in association with the development of increasingly moveable premaxillaries, the ethmoidal commissure has been lost. It seems to be functionally replaced by a commissure in the interorbital region. More posteriorly, the supratemporal commissure is incomplete, and the tabular bones that bear it are usually separated from the cranium by a layer of muscle.

Circumorbital Bones. Various changes develop in the circumorbital bones. Probably again in association with the development of increasingly movable premaxillaries, the antorbital-supraorbital olfactory pump is lost (see chap. 4). There is no supraorbital bone in forms higher than the Myctophiformes, where it is usually rigidly attached to the cranium, and a separate antorbital is finally lost in the Beryciformes. The laminar expansions of the postorbital members of the circumorbital series are lost (though what is perhaps a modification of this expansion occurs in the Syngnathiformes). On the other hand, a subocular shelf develops.

Branchiostegal Rays. Above the Myctophiformes and Beloniformes the branchiostegal rays are, with few exceptions, reduced in number to eight or fewer (Hubbs 1920). Furthermore, a specialization in the musculature to the rays makes the branchiostegal apparatus into a semi-independent portion of the opercular respiratory pump (see chap. 3).

Pharyngeal Apparatus. Longitudinal muscles are developed between the pharyngobranchials and the anterior vertebrae (Holstvoogd 1965; Nelson 1967*b*), providing the pharyngeal teeth with the possibility of a triturating or grinding function as well as a grasping function. In association with this, the pharyngeal tooth plates may become united or fused.

Swim Bladder. In the adult the connection between the swim bladder and the gut is lost, and a method of secreting and excreting gas through the walls of the swim bladder is substituted (Jones and Marshall 1953).

The Vertebral Column and Associated Structures. There is a gradual differentiation and reduction in the number of vertebrae until in berycoids the basal percoid number of 24 or 25 (10 abdominal and 14 or 15 caudal) is reached. Epineural intermuscular bones are last found in some beryciform fishes. Epipleurals continue to originate on the first vertebra, but pleural ribs disappear from the first two.

Fins. Various, probably associated changes take place in the fins and their supporting structure. The pectoral is always above the ventral rim of the body; it has a more or less vertical axis and no mesocoracoid arch. The pelvic fins, though they may be abdominal in some elongate forms, tend to move forward. Where the pelvic girdle provides a more or less firm support either via an abutment against the tip of the postcleithrum or from an enlarged dermal plate, a pelvic spine often occurs. However, intermediate teleosts, unlike most Perciformes, never seem to have developed a direct articulation between pelvic girdle and cleithra. The dorsal fin tends to originate well forward and may approach the typical percoid condition, preceded by one to three predorsal bones. As the dorsal origin moves forward, it may become divided into an anterior spinous portion and a posterior soft portion. The adipose fin is lost above the Percopsiformes. Only the forked caudal fin with (16 or) 17 branched rays and its supporting skeleton remain essentially unchanged in all the basal members of the myctophiform-percopsiform-beryciform series (Patterson 1968*b*).

The second category of orders included here among the intermediate teleostean groups comprises very diverse, specialized fishes—the orders Cetomimiformes, Beloniformes, Cyprinodontiformes, Gadiformes, Syngnathiformes, Lampridiformes, and Zeiformes. None of them is known from the Cretaceous. Though some may eventually prove to have Mesozoic records, the adoption of a peculiar mode of life in more recent times may have led to rapid as well as drastic changes in morphology. In any event, all of the known members of some of these groups are so specialized that it is often difficult to determine their derivations.

Under the circumstances, differences of opinion regarding their relationships are not surprising.

The controversies regarding particular groups can best be dealt with in the discussion of the group concerned. Here only a matter of general approach will be taken up. Greenwood, et al. (1966) combined within their Atherinomorpha, Gadiformes, and Paracanthopterygii (see also Rosen and Patterson 1969) fishes which the present author considers unrelated. The hoary question that arises with each of these three groups is how to distinguish between similarities that indicate a common inheritance and those that have arisen through convergent evolution among unrelated forms. All three of these groups, as usual when the question of convergence arises, include forms that have adopted rather specialized modes of life. In such cases the present author, in attempting to distinguish between convergence and inheritance, would start from the following assumptions: (1) that two or more groups adopting a similar mode of life can be expected to show adaptive similarities; (2) that such adaptations may be the result either of similar inheritance, or of convergence; and (3) that no decision between these two possibilities can be made on the basis of such similarities, regardless of whether there are one or a hundred of them.

If the above assumptions are correct, the only way to get at the question whether two or more groups which have similar modes of life are or are not related is by investigating the pathway or pathways over which they have evolved. To determine such pathways, it seems necessary to erect one or more working hypotheses concerning the derivation of the groups under investigation. In the instance of the Atherinomorpha of Greenwood et al. (1966), the present author has assumed that origin from any lower teleostean group is unlikely, and that the atherinomorph fishes must have evolved from one or more points along a base line that extends roughly from the primitive Myctophiformes to the generalized percoids (fig. 28B). If this is assumed, the characters to be investigated in determining the pathway (or pathways) of atherinomorph development are those most closely approximating some point (or points) along this base line. If the more generalized members of the Atherinomorpha (using the above criteria to determine what is "generalized") point toward different origins, as the present author thinks they do, then convergence seems indicated.

Because the present views on this and other matters more or less coincide wtih those of many earlier echthyologists, it is perhaps not surprising that the classification of intermediate teleostean orders adopted here is hardly novel. Thus the limits and contents as here defined of the Myctophiformes (Scopeliformes, Iniomi), Beloniformes, Gadiformes (Anacanthini), Beryciformes, Lampridiformes, and Zeiformes are essentially traditional. Those of the Percopsiformes follow McAllister (1968) and Rosen and Patterson (1969); of the Cyprinodontiformes, Rosen (1962); and of the Syngnathiformes, Jordan (1923). The Cetomimiformes as recognized here is admittedly a catch-all group of oceanic forms of unknown relationships.

7. Order **MYCTOPHIFORMES**

Group 1. Families Aulopidae, Harpadontidae, Synodontidae, Ipnopidae, and Bathypteroidae

Group 2. Families Evermannellidae and Scopelarchidae

Group 3. Families Chlorophthalmidae, Neoscopelidae, Myctophidae, and Scopelosauridae

Group 4. Families Paralepidae, Omosudidae, Alepisauridae, and Anotopteridae

The differences between the Myctophiformes and the Salmoniformes have been discussed in the introduction to chapter 6. Because of the great diversity within the Myctophiformes, the ordinal diagnosis cannot be very definitive:

Maxillary excluded from the gape in the adults of modern forms, but this is not true of at least some fossil members of the group (Rosen and Patterson 1969). Premaxillaries not protrusile. Mouth moderate to large; all members of the order apparently carnivorous. Anterior ceratohyal without a fenestra. Branchiostegal rays 6 to 26, all aciniform with little differentiation within the series. No true fin spines, though the dorsal fin rays of *Alepisaurus,* at least, have little segmentation (personal observation). Pectoral fin base above the ventral rim of the body. No mesocoracoid arch. Vertebrae numerous, 39 or more; ribs, epipleurals, and epineurals from the anteriormost vertebra. An adipose fin present. Caudal forked, with 17 branched rays; caudal skeleton with a stegural element (Patterson 1968*b*). Swim bladder, when present, without an oesophageal duct, and with a characteristic series of structures associated with the secretion of gas (Marshall 1960).

Various forms of the Myctophiformes have been recorded from the Cretaceous. One of them, *Nematonotus* (Rosen and Patterson 1969), appears to be quite similar to the modern *Aulopus* (Regan 1911*a*). In the caudal skeleton (Patterson 1968*b*), the fin configuration, and the rigid attachment of the supraorbital bone to the cranium, the aulopids resemble the extinct ctenothrissids (Patterson 1964), and there seems to be no reason why a common ancestor for the two groups should not be postulated.

With the exception of certain synodontids and *Harpadon*, which penetrate brackish water, all of the modern members of the Myctophiformes are marine, mostly oceanic.

The interrelationships of the various groups within the order are not clear. Marshall (1955) divided it into two sections, the myctophoids and alepisauroids. One difficulty with this division is that the poorly known *Scopelosaurus* has certain characteristics intermediate between the two groups. But in other features, such as the maxillary structure (Berry 1964), *Scopelosaurus* appears to be a very primitive myctophiform type. As indicated above, *Aulopus* is another primitive myctophiform fish, though it may well have developed certain specializations for a bottom-living existence, for example, the loss of the swim bladder.

Because of the questionable position of *Scopelosaurus* as well as other difficulties, the order Myctophiformes is here merely divided into four provisional groups of families. For a discussion of the group made up of the Evermannellidae and Scopelarchidae, see Parr (1929), who derived it from the *Aulopus*-like forms. The reasons for separating such bottom-living fishes as the Aulopidae from the mostly pelagic Chlorophthalmidae and related forms are given in Gosline, Marshall, and Mead (1966), McAllister (1968), and Rosen and Patterson (1969).

8. Order CETOMIMIFORMES

Group 1. Pelvics jugular; dorsal fin well forward
Family Ateleopidae
Group 2. Pelvics jugular or absent; dorsal fin posterior
Families Miripinnidae, Eutaeniophoridae, Megalomyc-teridae, and Cetomimidae
Group 3. Pelvics subabdominal
Families Kasidoridae, Gibberichthyidae, Barbourisiidae, and Rondelettiidae

Greenwood et al. (1966) are followed here in using the ordinal name Cetomimiformes as an umbrella for an assemblage of peculiar and poorly known oceanic fishes. The order will no doubt prove to be of composite origin, as Parr (1929) indicated long ago. Because all families in the order have the maxillary excluded from the gape, and because many have a supramaxillary, more than five soft pelvic rays, etc., all apparently may be classed as intermediate teleosts. As to more precise allocations, only a few tentative suggestions concerning possible relationships and interrelationships can be made on the basis of present knowledge.

The ateleopids, like the ophidioids and some gadids, have developed filamentous, anteriorly placed pelvic fins (probably for probing the bottom for food) and a downwardly protrusile mouth. The cranium of *Ateleopus* is largely cartilaginous, without ossified epiotics, intercalars, orbitosphenoid, pleurosphenoids, or basisphenoid; and the pectoral actinosts are replaced by a cartilaginous plate (Regan 1911*a*). Despite these peculiarities Regan (1911*a*) placed the Ateleopidae among the myctophiform fishes. Other authors, however, have suggested relationships with such various groups as the ophidiids, macrourids, and myripinnids (for summary, see McAllister 1968). Still more recently, Rosen and Patterson (1969) suggested an affinity between ateleopids and lampridiform fishes.

The second group of families here included in the Cetomimiformes is perhaps in itself a composite. The Miripinnidae and Eutaeniophoridae are known only from immature fishes some two inches long or less (Bertelsen and Marshall 1956, 1958). These two families differ from one another in various characters and are quite possibly unrelated. Both may represent larval or paedomorphic forms, though a 39.5-mm specimen of *Miripinna* appears to have a rather well ossified skull (Bertelsen and Marshall 1956, fig. 2). The megalomycterids, which have greatly enlarged olfactory organs (Myers and Freihofer 1966), may prove to be male cetomimids (Marshall 1967). *Cetomimus* itself has been shown (Parr 1929) to have strong osteological affinities with myctophiform fishes.

In the third group, the family Kasidoridae is based entirely on specimens less than an inch in length taken from the surface waters over deep sea (Robins and de Sylva 1965; Robins 1966; Thorp 1969). Possibly *Kasidoron* is the larval form of one of the other members of this same group. Of these, *Rondelettia* is a beryciform derivative (Parr 1929), and *Gibberichthys* (Parr 1933,

1934) seems to be an intermediate between *Rondelettia* and the more normal type of beryciform fish. *Barbourisia*, however, is intermediate in its known characters between *Rondelettia* and *Cetomimus* (Harry 1952); thus, whereas cetomimids have 51 to 52 vertebrae and *Rondelettia* 27, *Barbourisia* has 42 (Abe, Marumo, and Kawaguchi 1965). Though the internal structure of *Barbourisia* is unknown, it is here provisionally placed with *Rondelettia* primarily because of the well-developed, subabdominal pelvics. Aside from *Barbourisia*, there seems no reason to think that all of the members of the present group are not beryciform derivatives, possible related to the Melamphaidae and Stephanoberycidae.

9. Order **BELONIFORMES**

Suborder Scomberesocoidei
    Families Scomberesocidae, Belonidae
Suborder Exocoetoidei
    Families Exocoetidae, Hemiramphidae

All nonpaedomorphic beloniform fishes have two features which, in combination, separate them from other teleosts. The nasal organ consists of a tentacle that protrudes from the base of a concavity, and the lateral line extends along the abdomen below the pectoral base. Other, less peculiar characteristics are the following: posttemporal usually simple; basisphenoid generally present; no orbitosphenoid, intercalar, or mesocoracoid; lower pharyngeals fused; branchiostegal rays 6 to 15; vertebrae 35 to 97 (Collette 1966); caudal with never more than 13 branched rays and, except in paedomorphic forms, forked, with the lower lobe the longer; parahypural with a well-developed hypurapophysis (Nursall 1963), attached basally to a ural centrum or fused with the hypural plate.

The order Beloniformes comprises fishes that have become highly specialized for existence at the surface of the water. Indeed, its specializations are so extensive that any convincing evidence concerning its origin and relationships have been obscured. Various authors have suggested quite different interpretations (see, for example, Allis 1909; Boulenger 1904; Regan 1911c; Hubbs 1920). In 1964 Rosen placed the beloniform, cyprinodontiform, and atherinoid fishes in the order Atheriniformes, pointing out numerous similarities between the three groups. Foster (1967) has added to the list. The present author is of the opinion that the three groups are unrelated and that the undoubted resemblances between them are associated with the adoption by all three of a mode of life at the water surface (fig. 28B). Here, only the question of beloniform-cyprinodontiform relationships will be discussed; the atherinoids, in the author's opinion, belong with the higher teleostean groups and will be dealt with in that chapter.

Within the Beloniformes there has been a considerable amount of adaptive radiation (Nichols and Breder 1928). To determine the type of fish from which this radiation started, it seems advisable to investigate characteristics held in common by at least some members of all four existing families. Such an investigation suggests that the ancestral fish was quite different from a cyprinodont. The central tendency among beloniform fishes would seem to be represented by a rather large, strongly swimming fish with a forked tail in which the lower lobe is longer than the upper and supplied with a rather specialized musculature (Grenholm 1923). This peculiar caudal structure is undoubtedly associated with the beloniform habit of skipping or gliding over the water surface. The cyprinodonts, in contrast, are usually small, hence rather weakly swimming fishes, generally with rounded tails, which never skip or glide over the water surface. All beloniform fishes have a nasal tentacle, and in all but the paedomorphic forms the lateral line extends along the ventral rim of the body; cyprinodonts show neither of these specializations. The beloniform fishes are large-eyed and usually have a basisphenoid; the cyprinodonts tend to be small-eyed and always lack a basisphenoid. The jaws and associated structures are quite different in the two groups. In both, as might be expected of fishes living near the water surface, the mouth opening is more upturned than is usual in fishes, but this upward tilt has evolved in different ways. In cyprinodonts (fig. 23E), the mandibular articulation has moved forward relative to the cranium, thrusting the lower jaw forward also, and the two jaws retain their relative sizes. In the beloniform fishes the mandible is long, with its quadrate articulation well back (fig. 23C, D); the upper jaw is much shorter, and its posterior end is attached by membranes relatively far forward along the mandible. The result of this beloniform jaw construction is that when the mandible is slightly depressed the anterior portions of the premaxillaries are forced sharply upward (fig. 23C). Two other major differences between the cyprinodonts and the beloniform fishes are probably associated with their jaw structure. In the beloniform fishes, as is usual in teleosts, it is the maxillary that is ligamentously attached to the outside of the mandible; in the cyprinodonts, it is the premaxillary (Gosline 1963a; Alexander 1967c). In all beloniform fishes except the paedomorphic forms the branchiostegal rays are relatively numerous (8 to 15); in the cyprinodonts they are relatively few (4 to 7).

One last difference is perhaps associated with all of those previously discussed: the Beloniformes are basically marine fishes whereas the Cyprinodontiformes are primarily freshwater forms. The central beloniform tendacies toward relatively large size, skittering habit, etc., would seem more appropriate to open clear water areas than to the relatively restricted, often turbid freshwater environment. Members of two beloniform families have taken up a freshwater existence, but this has been clearly a secondary development. The freshwater members of the order are all reduced in size, and *Belonion* (Collette 1966) is represented by minute, paedomorphic fishes. Though these approach the cyprinodonts more closely than do the marine forms, they retain certain diagnostic features that immediately distinguish them from all cyprinodonts—for example, the nasal tentacle, the large, laterally placed eye, the relatively anterior upper jaw, and the parahypural fused into the hypural plate. Because these features are beloniform specializations either lacking or differently represented in cyprinodonts, it seems highly improbable that the Cyprinodontiformes have been derived from the riverine beloniform fishes.

To summarize, it seems to the present author that the Beloniformes have no genetic relationship to the Cyprinodontiformes, and he agrees with Regan (1911c) that the order constitutes "an isolated group" without close relatives among living fishes. As to derivation, the branchiostegal ray structure, at least, suggests an origin among the intermediate teleosts no higher than the Myctophiformes.

Within the Beloniformes, a series of transitional forms bridges the major gaps. Thus *Oxyporhamphus* is intermediate between the flyingfishes (Exocotidae) and the halfbeaks (Hemiramphidae), and the juvenile forms of some flyingfishes have an elongate lower jaw like the halfbeaks (Parin 1961). Among belonids the genus *Belonion* at least superficially resembles the halfbeaks. The belonids and scomberesocids have always been associated, and it may be that paedomorphic scomberesocids, some still to be described (see Collette 1966), will further break down the differences between these two families. In view of what has been said, the validity of dividing the Beloniformes between the two generally accepted suborders (Scomberesocoidei and Exocoetoidei) is open to question.

10. Order **PERCOPSIFORMES**

Suborder Percopsoidei
    Family Percopsidae
Suborder Aphredoderoidei
    Families Aphredoderidae and Amblyopsidae

This classification and much of the following diagnosis are based on Rosen and Patterson (1969).

Maxillary toothless, excluded from the gape; no supramaxillary. Premaxillary with a separate ascending head and articular process. Eyes small to rudimentary, the orbits widely separated from one another by skull bones which form a trough bearing the olfactory nerves or tracts (Gosline 1963*a*). No orbitosphenoid or basisphenoid. Parietals separated by the supraoccipital. Intercalar large. Exoccipital condyles distinct from that of the basioccipital. Lacrimal with an ascending process that extends upward in front of the lateral ethmoids. Opercle spinous or sharp pointed. Basibranchial teeth present. Branchiostegals 6, arranged in typical acanthopteran pattern. No epineurals. Caudal fin with 16 branched rays. Upper hypurals fused basally to a centrum element. Dorsal and anal spinous. Pelvics without a true spine and with 0 to 8 soft rays.

The only known Mesozoic member of the Percopsiformes, *Sphenocephalus,* is a marine, European form (Rosen and Patterson 1969). All Tertiary and Recent members of the order are from the fresh waters of North America. Two of these, *Percopsis* and *Columbia*, are the only living spiny-rayed fish with an adipose fin.

The amblyopsids, presumably derived from an *Aphredoderus*-like form, are fishes of swamps, springs, and caves. They have received considerable attention (see, for example, Eigenmann 1909; Poulsen 1963). Among amplyopsid features associated with a cave environment is first and foremost the degeneration of the eye. Related to this feature is the filling in of the interorbital region by the skull bones, for example, by the pleurosphenoids in *Chologaster* (Gosline 1963*a*). The lateral-line organs, contained in part in cavernous channels in the head in *Aphredoderus*, have become external in amblyopsids (see Eigenmann 1909). The dorsal and anal fins of amblyopsids are farther back on the body, and their spines are less well developed than in *Aphredoderus*. In the adults of *Aphredoderus* and amblyopsids the anus and urogenital openings are far forward; however, *Aphredoderus* is said to build nests, whereas at least some amblyopsids incubate the eggs in their gill chambers.

11. Order GADIFORMES

Families Melanonidae, Gadidae, Moridae, Merlucciidae, Bregmacerotidae, Muraenolepidae, and Macrouridae

The following diagnosis is based on Marshall (1965*b*):

The premaxillaries, which are sometimes protrusible, exclude the maxillaries from the gape. No orbitosphenoid or basisphenoid. Saccular portion of ear enlarged, partly covered by the large intercalar (opisthotic?), which bears the glossopharyngeal foramen. Branchiostegal rays 5 to 8, of acanthopteran configuration (Hubbs 1920; McAllister 1968). Olfactory bulbs usually more or less distant from the forebrain. A branch of the ramus lateralis accessorius nerve passes across the pectoral base. No epineurals; first two vertebrae without pleural or epipleural ribs. No true spines in the fins. Pelvic fins, if present, thoracic or jugular, with as many as 17 rays. Caudal skeleton usually with the last centrum fused to the base of an upper hypural.

The Gadiformes have been assigned to quite different positions by various authors. At one extreme, Goodrich (1909) placed them at the very end of the teleostean series; at the other, Regan (1912*a*) suggested that they may have arisen from generalized myctophiform fishes, such as *Aulopus*. Eaton (1935), Rosen (1962), and Gosline (1963*a*) have hypothesized a relationship between the Gadiformes and the Percopsiformes, notably *Percopsis*. Rosen and Patterson (1969) have recently compared the two groups in considerable detail, arriving at the conclusion (p. 437) that "the Gadiformes are very closely related to the Percopsiformes, and originated from a Cretaceous fish resembling *Sphenocephalus*". Though the closeness of the percopsiform-gadiform relationship is perhaps overemphasized, there seems no reason to doubt that the two groups are derived from a single basal stock. However, the inclusion by Rosen and Patterson (1969, following

Greenwood et al. 1966), of the ophidioid and zoarcid fishes in the order Gadiformes is a different matter. The present author (who summarized his views on the subject in 1968) believes that the ophidioids and zoarcids are percoid derivatives and hence have only a distant relationship with the Gadiformes. That the zoarcids should be removed from close proximity to such an indisputably percoid offshoot as *Bathymaster* and assigned to the Gadiformes can only be viewed with astonishment. As to the ophidioids, their resemblances to the Gadiformes have not passed unnoticed (e. g., Regan 1903). In the opinion of the present author these resemblances are associated with the habit, characteristic of both groups, of probing the bottom for food by means of pelvic rays bearing taste organs (see Bardach and Case 1965).

According to Marshall (1965*b*, p. 300), whose family classification of the Gadiformes is adopted here, ". . . *Melanonus* seems to be the most primitive genus in the order." Unfortunately, no account of the osteology of *Melanonus* is available. By contrast, the family Gadidae has received more attention from anatomists than almost any other family of fishes (see, for example, Svetovidov 1948).

12. Order **CYPRINODONTIFORMES**

Suborder Adrianichthyoidei
    Families Oryziatidae, Adrianichthyidae, and Horaichthyidae
Suborder Cyprinodontoidei
    Families Cyprinodontidae, Goodeidae, Jenynsiidae, Anablepidae, and Poeciliidae

It is impossible to write a succinct diagnosis of the Cyprinodontiformes that will immediately distinguish them from all other fishes. Though they are a highly specialized group, their osteological peculiarities consist primarily of losses and fusions which occur also in other groups, particularly among small fishes (Te Winkel 1935). Another difficulty in characterizing the order is that no one, with the possible exeption of Sethi (1960), has reviewed the osteology of more than a small proportion of the various cyprinodont types; it is therefore probable that many of the characters listed below will prove to have exceptions.

Nostrils two on each side of head, leading into a nasal sac which contains the olfactory organ (Gosline 1963*a*). Maxillaries toothless, excluded from the gape, with an anterior process extending forward behind the medial portions of the premaxillaries. Except possibly in the Adrianichthyidae the premaxillaries have a direct, and the maxillaries an indirect, ligamentous attachment to the mandible (Rosen 1962; Alexander 1967c). Mandibular-quadrate articulation well forward, ahead of the middle of the suspensorium (fig. 23E); symplectic large. Branchiostegal rays 7 or fewer, with a typical acanthopteran configuration. Ethmoid ossification small or absent (except in Adrianichthyidae and Horaichthyidae), flat above; an enlarged rostral cartilage to which the anterior ends of the maxillaries are attached (Alexander 1967c). Parietals, if present, separated by the supraoccipital. No supramaxillary, orbitosphenoid, basisphenoid, intercalar, or tabular bones. Circumorbital series incomplete, represented only by a lacrimal anteriorly and a dermosphenotic posteriorly. Postcleithra absent or scalelike. Pleural and epipleural ribs present; no epineurals. Caudal fin usually rounded, sometimes slightly emarginate but never forked, with a highly variable number of branched rays. Upper hypurals fused to the last vertebral centrum, as are the lower, except, apparently, in *Xenopoecilus* (Rosen 1964, fig. 21C, D); parahypural never fused with hypurals. A single dorsal fin. Pelvics, if present, abdominal, without a spine and with up to 9 rays. Lateral line on head incomplete, disrupted on body. Swim bladder without a duct to the oesophagus.

The fishes included here under the order Cyprinodontiformes are among the best known of all teleosts to experimental zoologists and aquarists. Nevertheless their relationships have perplexed taxonomists.

Basically, cyprinodonts are fishes of transitional and/or evanescent estuarine and freshwater environments, and have become the dominant teleosts only in those major freshwater habitats that have not been generally accessible to other groups. Cyprinodonts have reached a number of these habitats (e.g., Lake Titicaca in South America, and the Mexican highlands) apparently because of their adeptness in surviving in unstable environments. Part of this adeptness would seem to have arisen in association with small size and a varied repertoire of reproductive capacities, such as viviparity and hermaphroditism (Harrington 1961).

A wide variety of relationships has been postulated for the cyprinodonts. For example, Starks (1904a) placed them in his order Haplomi between the esocoids and the amblyopsoids, whereas Rosen (1964) assigned them to his order Atheriniformes between the beloniform and atherinoid fishes. The present author (1963a), following Regan (1911e) and others, tentatively associated the cyprinodonts with the amblyopsoids. However, the amblyopsoids seem to be more clearly related to the Percopsiformes than to the cyprinodonts, and are now transferred to that order (McAllister 1968). The cyprinodont fishes are here provisionally recognized as a separate order.

Starks' (1904b) decision to place the cyprinodonts with the esocoids was probably influenced by a general resemblance between cyprinodonts and *Umbra*. However, a whole series of characters suggest a higher level of organization: the maxillary excluded from the gape, ribs commencing from the third vertebra in at least some cyprinodonts (Rosen 1964) and not attached to separate ossicles wedged into the centra, the lack of separate ural centra in the caudal skeleton, etc.

Some of the problems associated with a postulate that cyprinodonts originated among the Beloniformes have already been dealt with in the discussion of that order.

At least since the time of Regan (1911e) the cyprinodonts have generally been associated with the amblyopsoids. However, the relationship, if it exists, is not a close one. Thus the premaxillary of cyprinodonts (Rosen 1962) is ligamentously attached to the lower jaw (see also Alexander 1967c), and the maxillary may or may not move downward and forward with it when the mandible is lowered (Gosline 1963a). In the amblyopsoids, percopsoids, and Beloniformes, as in most teleosts, it is the maxillary, not the premaxillary, that is ligamentously attached to the mandible, and such movement as occurs in the premaxillary is secondarily brought about by lowering the maxillary. This premaxillary-mandible attachment in the cyprinodonts seems to have developed within the group probably as one method of protruding the premaxillary in a more upwardly directed plane than usually occurs in fishes. Premaxillary protrusion in the beloniform *Parexocoetus* (see Parin 1961, fig. 28) and apparently in atherinids (see Schultz 1948, pls. 1,2; also Alexander 1967c, fig. 3) is brought about by the more usual method of having the premaxillaries forced forward by the maxillaries.

There are, however, a number of similarities between cyprinodonts and amblyopsoids, or at least with the percopsiform-gadiform assemblage. The most obvious peculiarity held in common by amblyopsoids and cyprinodonts is the fact that at the corner of the mouth the lower lip folds over the upper, giving the superficial impression that the upper jaw is enclosed by the lower. The significance, if any, of this peculiarity remains unknown. The skull throughout the whole cyprinodontiform-percopsiform-gadopsiform group is relatively low, with small orbits, and it lacks both orbitosphenoid and basisphenoid. At least one curious feature of the caudal skeleton is held in common by the adrianichthyoids (Rosen 1964, figs. 21B-D) and the gadiform fishes. This is the free, splintlike bone between the hemal spines of the last two preural vertebrae (the element labelled Y in Monod's 1968 figures 571–574 and 576).

The pros and cons of a possible relationship between the cyprinodonts and atherinoid fishes (including the phallostethids) have been discussed by Hubbs (1944), Gosline (1963a), Rosen (1964), and others. The relationship among the Atherinidae, Mugilidae, and Sphyraenidae has been questioned only by Rosen (1964) and will not be questioned here. The atherinid pelvic fins have a spine and 5 soft rays, and the forked caudal fin has 15 branched rays as in the perciform fishes generally. (The phallostethoid fishes, aside from the loss of pelvics, have been shown by Hubbs [1944] to have essentially the fin structure of the atherinids. In any event the phallostethids are much too specialized to have given rise to the cyprinodonts or any other group.) The cyprinodonts have no pelvic spine and as many as 9 soft pelvic rays; in the basal Adrianichthyidae there are 6 or 7. Dorsal spines, if present, do not form a separate fin.

Though attempts to associate the cyprinodonts with any given group seem inconclusive, the possibility remains of attempting to narrow down the level of teleostean organization from which they may have evolved.

There seems to be no reason to believe that the cyprinodonts have evolved independently from any of the lower teleostean orders. On the other hand, their abdominal, spineless, but often many-rayed pelvics indicate an origin in some group below the perciform (including atherinid) level of organization, and suggest that the cyprinodonts belong to the intermediate teleostean groups—where they have generally been placed. Hubbs (1920) long ago noted the acanthopteran nature of the cyprinodont branchiostegal apparatus. Rosen (1964) has shown that the adrianichthyoids have the first pleural ribs on the third vertebra—another, and functionally independent, acanthopteran character. In sum, these characters seem to indicate a cyprinodont origin at about the percopsiform level of teleostean organization, which is, again, about where cyprinodonts have usually been placed. The interrelationships of the various cyprinodont groups is also unclear. The cyprinodonts have long been divided between the oviparous Cyprinodontoidae and the viviparous Poecilioidae. Hubbs (1924), however, suggested that the viviparity of the Poecilioidae has developed several times from different oviparous forms, and therefore Sethi (1960) recommended that the old division between oviparous and viviparous cyprinodonts be at least provisionally abandoned.

In 1964 Rosen (whose classification is followed here) erected a new superfamily Adrianichthyoidea for the families Oryziatidae, Adrianichthyidae and Horaichthyidae. In certain respects, such as the origin of the first pleural rib on the third vertebra in adrianichthyids and oryziatids, this group would seem to be more generalized than other cyprinodonts for which the character has been investigated. On the other hand, in the loss of a prevomer and metapterygoid, it would seem to be more specialized than the circumtropical aplocheilines, which Sethi (1960) considered the most primitive members of the order.

13. Order **SYNGNATHIFORMES**

Suborder Syngnathoidei
  Superfamily Aulostomoidae
    Families Aulostomidae, Fistulariidae, Macrorhamphosidae, and Centriscidae
  Superfamily Syngnathoidae
    Families Solenostomidae, Syngnathidae
Suborder Indostomoidei
    Family Indostomidae
Suborder Gasterosteoidei
    Families Aulorhynchidae, Gasterosteidae

Diagnosis: Mouth small, at the end of a more or less tubular snout, the mandibular-quadrate articulation ahead of the orbit. Probably in association with the jaw configuration (Gosline 1967), the number of branchiostegal rays is reduced (1 to 5), and the branchiostegals play no role in the opercular respiratory pump. No supramaxillary, orbitosphenoid, or basisphenoid. The postcleithrum reduced to a single bone or absent. There may be an anterior spinous dorsal, but in any event the soft dorsal fin is over or even behind the anal. Abdominal or subthoracic pelvics with a spine and up to 6 branched rays *(Solenostomus)*; the pelvic bones never directly attached to the cleithra. The caudal fin sometimes indented, usually rounded, never deeply forked; the hypurals, and usually the parahypural, fused with the last centrum to form a hypural plate. There is a tendency throughout the group, least developed in *Aulostomus* and *Fistularia*, for the dermal elements on the body to form plates or rings.

The inclusion of the Syngnathoidei and Gasterosteoidei in the same order is provisional. It rests in part on the statements that *Indostomus* is, in some respects at least, intermediate between the two groups (Bolin 1936; see, however, Bannister 1970, whose detailed work on the structure and relationships of *Indostomus* was received too late for integration into the present text).

If *Indostomus* and poorly known fossil forms are excluded from consideration, the syngnathoids and gasterosteoids show certain trends of evolutionary specialization in common. Both groups consist of usually slow-moving fishes in which the caudal fins play a subordinate role in locomotion; probably in relation to this the forms are variously camouflaged, and plated and/or spined. Nevertheless, within this general trend there are several consistent differences between the two groups. One is in the method of capturing prey. The syngnathoids for the most part stalk theirs and, when close enough, create a pipette-like suction that draws the prey into the mouth. The gasterosteoids, by contrast, have nipping jaws, with the upper jaw protrusile (Alexander 1967*b*). Among the syngnathoids, circumorbital bones, except for a lacrimal, are missing; in the gasterosteoids the circumorbital bones are continued as a strut that overlaps the preopercle. In the syngathoids the anterior vertebrae are rigidly united; in gasterosteoids they are not.

Both of the major groups of the Syngnathiformes are so specialized as to provide little evidence of their possible origins. Spines may be present in the dorsal and pelvic fins of both groups, and *Solenostomus* appears to have a separate, anterior spinous dorsal. Unless these spines have developed independently, both would appear to have had acanthopteran origins and there is nothing to indicate that they did not. The abdominal or subthoracic pelvics without a pelvic-cleithral articulation suggest a preperciform origin. Jungersen (1908) suggested a scorpaenoid relationship for the gasterosteoids, probably because of the suborbital stay, but the origin of this suborbital stay was different in the two groups. The protrusile upper jaw roofed by a nasal bone rigidly united to the cranium and the enlarged dermal pelvic plate of gasterosteoids recalls more closely the Beryciformes. In sum, such indications as there are of origin for both the gasterosteoids and syngathoids suggest one or two origins in the percopsiform-beryciform area.

14. Order **BERYCIFORMES**

Families Polymixiidae, Caristiidae, Berycidae, Trachichthyidae, Diretmidae, Monocentridae, Anomalopidae, Holocentridae, Anoplogasteridae, Stephanoberycidae, and Melamphaidae

The order Beryciformes contains a great mass of diverse fishes. Though the osteology of certain of the beryciform fishes, both recent and fossil (Patterson 1964,1967b, 1968b), has been worked out in detail, a number of the modern groups are represented by oceanic forms that are rare in collections. The internal structure of some of these forms is almost unknown, and it seems premature to try to assign them to any formal suborders within the Beryciformes. The following diagnosis is necessarily restricted to the better-known forms.

Parietals separated by the supraoccipital, which often forms a crest on the dorsal surface of the skull. Nasals large, more or less rigidly attached to the cranium. Supraorbital lateralis canals with a frontal commissure and a parietal branch. Premaxillaries protrusile, with a well-developed ascending process and an articular process. Maxillary excluded from the gape in modern forms, usually with one or two supramaxillaries. Suspensorium with a full complement of separate ossifications; the palatine functionally associated with the premaxillary protrusion. Orbitosphenoid and a Y-shaped basisphenoid usually present. Intercalar well developed, sometimes forming part of the wall of an enlarged otic bulla containing a large otolith. Exoccipitals broadly meeting one another below the foramen magnum, the two exoccipitals together with the basioccipital condyles forming a single, subtriangular surface of articulation for the first vertebra. Opercle usually scaled, frequently with a spiny border. Pars jugularis of the trigemino-facialis chamber with three openings (Patterson 1964). Branchiostegal rays 9 or fewer. Circumorbital bones usually with a subocular shelf. Lower pharyngeals separate. Vertebrae 23 (9 + 14) or more, usually fewer than 30. Pleural ribs from the third vertebra, epipleurals from the first; epineurals sometimes present. A spinous anterior portion of the dorsal fin usually present; anal fin frequently with 4 spines. Pelvics with or without a spine and with up to 13 branched rays. Caudal fin usually forked, with 16 or 17 branched rays; caudal skeleton with a well-developed stegural element and with two ural centra, the second not fused with hypurals. Swim bladder without a duct to the oesophagus.

In the Cretaceous there was already considerable diversification within the order Beryciformes (Patterson 1964, 1967b). It is very difficult to coordinate the classification of modern forms with those of the Cretaceous, especially since, as noted, the osteology of some of the modern forms is almost unknown.

Patterson (1964; see also Rosen and Patterson 1969) divided Cretaceous forms into three suborders: Polymixioidei, Dinopterygoidei, and Berycoidei. Of these the extinct Dinopterygoidei seems to be somewhat intermediate between the other two, and need not be discussed further. In 1967 Patterson described a Cretaceous member of the Berycoidei (Gnathoberyx) in which the maxillary was not only included in the gape, but toothed. In the Polymixioidei the toothless maxillary is always excluded from the gape. In other features, however, the polymixioids seem to resemble the lower teleosts more than the berycoids. For example, the polymixioids have no true pelvic spine but do have epineural bones. At least in Polymixia (the only modern polymixioid), the acoustico-lateralis system is relatively little developed as compared with that of berycoids; neither the lateralis canals nor the auditory bulla are expanded.

As for the modern, oceanic, beryciform fishes, the Caristiidae are usually included in this order (e.g., Maul 1954), but Greenwood et al. (1966) place it in the Perciformes. Regan (1911b) erected a separate order for the Melamphaidae and Stephanoberycidae, but Patterson (1967b, fig. 11) included the Melamphaidae in the suborder Berycoidei. Parr (1929) demonstrated the beryciform affinities of Rondelettia, here provisionally placed in the Cetomimiformes, and it may prove that the whole of Group 3 here placed under that order should be transferred to the Beryciformes. Still another genus of uncertain affinities is Trachyberyx (Mead and Maul 1958).

15. Order LAMPRIDIFORMES

Suborder Lampridoidei
    Family Lampridae
Suborder Veliferoidei
    Family Veliferidae
Suborder Trachipteroidei
    Families Radiicephalidae, Lophotidae, Trachipteridae, and
        Regalecidae
Suborder Stylophoroidei
    Family Stylophoridae

Regan (1907, 1924) placed together in a single order a number of very different oceanic fishes in which the maxillary heads, instead of being ligamentously attached to the ethmoid and palatine, slide in and out with the highly protrusile premaxillaries. In some members there is an orbitosphenoid, and the thoracic pelvics may have from 0 to 17 soft rays.

The family Lampridae contains a single large, moon-shaped species; the trachypteroids and stylophoroids are long and ribbon shaped. All members of these three groups are highly specialized. Only the veliferoids are rather "normal" fishes. Regan (1907), Patterson (1964), and McAllister (1968) have suggested a beryciform relationship for the order.

16. Order ZEIFORMES

Families Zeidae, Grammicolepidae, Caproidae, and Antigoni-
idae

These families of deep-bodied, frequently more or less armor-plated, oceanic fishes would probably be considered perciform derivatives except that some of them have as many as 9 pelvic soft rays. Their peculiarities are not such as to preclude a perciform derivation: the first vertebra is firmly united to the skull; the anal is preceded by a more or less separate fin of 1 to 4 spines; and the caudal has only 10 to 13 principal rays.

The traditional families accepted here are somewhat different from those recognized by Greenwood et al. (1966), who probably incorporated in their study the results of as yet unpublished work on the group by G. S. Myers. Otherwise the zeiform classification has remained almost undisturbed since the time of Regan (1910*a*).

EIGHT

Higher Teleostean Groups

Included orders: Perciformes, Pleuronectiformes, Scorpaeniformes, Gobiesociformes, Tetraodontiformes, Echeneiformes, Mastacembeliformes, Synbranchiformes, Icosteiformes, Pegasiformes, and Lophiiformes

EVOLUTION AND RELATIONSHIPS

The problems of determining the relationships of higher teleostean groups are of a somewhat different nature from those in the lower, or even the intermediate, teleostean orders. The higher teleosts represent the last great proliferation among fishes. In the course of this adaptive radiation, the new taxa have doubtless replaced many earlier forms, but they have not themselves been replaced and most of them are represented by fishes living today. Thus the living higher teleostean groups probably represent a fair cross section of the radiation that has occurred; they are not, as are other groups, the possibly biased sample that has managed to survive competition from more recently evolved forms. However, the very adequacy of the higher teleostean representation presents its own problems (see below).

The higher teleostean groups are here defined as those orders which are at, or have passed through, the percoid level of structural organization. However, certain not-quite percoid groups are still in existence, and as a result the line between the higher of the intermediate teleosts and the base of the higher teleosts is of necessity an arbitrary one drawn through a morphological transition zone. Following the lead of Regan (1913a) and others, this dividing line is usually set, as it is here, at that point at which no living member of an order retains more than 5 soft rays in the pelvic fins. *Channa (Ophicephalus)*, which often has 6 soft pelvic rays, and the Pleuronectiformes, with as many as 13 (in *Ammotretis*), are included in the higher teleosts, but an extenuation for this procedure lies in the fact that *Channa* probably, and

150

the Pleuronectiformes almost certainly, have secondarily redeveloped an increased number of soft pelvic rays. On the other hand, the Zeiformes, according to this division, fall among the intermediate teleostean groups. The arbitrariness of all this is adequately demonstrated by the fact that if the few existing zeiform fishes having more than 5 soft pelvic rays had happened to become extinct, the Zeiformes would not be classed as intermediate, but as higher teleosts.

The reduction in pelvic ray number is not, of course, the only feature characterizing the percoid level of structural organization. There is a whole syndrome of such features. However, the components of this syndrome have not evolved at exactly the same rates, and each of them would provide a slightly different interpretation of which fish groups to include among the basal percoids. It merely happens that the pelvic ray count, however unimportant in itself, seems to provide the best practical indicator that the percoid level of organization has been attained.

A more important question zoologically, but one on which it is possible only to speculate, is why the percoid organization has been so successful. In no single way does it seem to differ from that of the now unimportant, perhaps relict, Beryciformes from which it was presumably derived. Possibly the percoids have developed some distinct, and as yet unknown, biological advantage over the Beryciformes, but for the moment one can only assume that the percoids represent a successful integration of a number of minor advances. Percoid advantage can be demonstrated only by comparing available beryciform and percoid fishes and assuming that the differences constitute percoid advances. One of the defects of this method is that if modern beryciform fishes represent only those forms which have survived competition with the percoids, then they may well provide an aberrant basis for comparison. Nevertheless, the method seems worth trying.

If, for whatever it is worth, one contrasts in nature basal percoids such as *Kuhlia* or carangids with members of the only inshore beryciform family, the holocentrids, one gets the impression that the percoids are much more actively swimming fishes. They dash about at greater speed. If one contrasts the morphology of *Kuhlia* with that of *Holocentrus,* one finds considerably less bone (and fewer bones) and a higher proportion of musculature in *Kuhlia.* Perhaps more important, the pelvics of *Kuhlia* are directly below the pectorals, where they can, and presumably do, assist in such maneuvers as stopping and turning more efficiently than do the more posteriorly placed pelvics of *Holocentrus* (Harris 1938; see also chap. 2). Both *Holocentrus* and *Kublia* are commonly found in obstructed reef areas, where any increase in swimming speed would be advantageous only if accompanied by equally increased maneuverability.

If, as provisionally hypothesized here, the main advance of the percoids has been increased swimming speed combined with maneuverability (or vice versa), this has been accomplished without significant loss of defensive structures. For though percoids are less generally spinous than *Holocentrus,* their pelvic spines are apparently more strategically placed and are equipped with a firmer abutment (see chap. 2).

Two other differences between percoids and berycoids are worth noting. In both groups the premaxillaries are protrusile. But in berycoids the final, variously adaptable percoid system of premaxillary protrusion appears to have been incompletely worked out, and these fish usually retain a bony roof, generally in the form of fixed nasal bones, over the ascending processes of the premaxillaries.

The second possible difference between the two groups is in life history. All modern beryciforms are marine fishes, and most of them have a specialized planktonic larval form that may grow to considerable size. Though the percoids are best represented in coral reef areas, it is at least notable that the groups generally considered to be most primitive in the Perciformes are largely fresh- and/or brackish-water forms (Gosline 1968). Furthermore, such fish develop directly from small eggs into miniature adults— *Lates* is an example (Hopson 1969). (Thus, though the freshwater percoids, like the freshwater salmonoids, have by-passed the larval form, they have done so in a different way [see, for example, Disler 1960]. The salmonids have, so to speak, absorbed the planktonic larval stage into the egg, whereas the freshwater percoids seem to have absorbed it into a precociously developed adult.)

If the perciform stage of structural organization is as nebulous as it appears to be, the question arises whether it may not have been attained independently a number of times. Indeed, Greenwood et al. (1966) postulated three independent arrivals at this state of organization, in addition to that leading from the Beryciformes to the Perciformes. Inasmuch as these three postulated arrivals involve separate questions of convergence vs.

inheritance, they can best be discussed individually under the particular groups involved. Despite the present author's disagreement with Greenwood et al. (1966) concerning the specific lineages these authors postulated, a whole series of aberrant orders (e.g., Mastacembeliformes, Synbranchiformes, Lophiiformes) are assumed, on the basis of rather scanty data, to have passed through a percoid stage of evolution. The possibility that this assumption is not true should at least be held in mind.

A rather different problem of polyphyletic origin for the Perciformes has been raised by Patterson (1964). He suggested that the basal perciform stock is made up of a number of parallel, related lines of independent origin, arising among different portions of the beryciform stock. (In this sense the Perciformes would seem to be "polyphyletic" in the same way that the mammals are thought to be; see, for example, Simpson 1959.) Though the particular lines of independent development postulated by Patterson (1964) do not seem to hold up (Gosline 1966*a*; Patterson 1968*b*), the possibility that this type of evolution has actually given rise to the Perciformes should not be discounted.

The classification of the higher teleostean groups themselves presents problems that are both zoological and philosophical. Historically, it developed as a method of sorting species. For this pigeonholing process the morphological gaps between groups provide the best approach. Unfortunately, the discrete groups of higher teleosts prove to be, on the one hand, a vast mass of percoid-like fishes and, on the other, a series of relatively small to very small clusters of aberrant forms (e.g., the Echeneidae, Dactylopteridae, Pegasidae). The unfortunate resemblance between the resulting classification and a planet with satellites has been alleviated to some extent by invocation of the dictum that the size of the morphological gap between groups should be inversely proportional to the size of the group.

Philosophically, it seems worthwhile to make two points about the morphological gaps between higher teleostean groups. First, a whole series of closely similar percoid families (see, for example, Danilchenko 1964) can be traced back as independent entities into the Paleocene, which is as far as the more aberrant groups can be traced. In other words, there is no reason to believe that, among higher teleosts, degree of morphological differentiation and age are positively correlated. Rather, it appears that many higher teleostean groups are about equally old and that morphological differentiation, at least in some instances, is related more closely to the extent to which a group has adopted a different mode of life than to age.

A hypothetical case in point is provided by the remoras (Echeneidae). Once the spinous dorsal fin of a percoid fish has somehow been rearranged into a sucking disk by means of which the fish obtains rides from other animals, a whole series of new selection pressures arises in connection with this transport system. In response to these pressures the animal will change drastically, providing it has the biological potentialities to do so.

The echeneids can be used also to illustrate a second point about the nature of morphological gaps between higher teleostean groups. A remora either adopts the new transportation system, successfully accommodating itself to the new selection pressures, or it does not. There would seem to be no ecological habitat available today for an inept remora, and intermediates between the remoras and their ancestral percoids do not exist. In short, both in mode of life and in morphology, the dividing lines between the remoras and percoids are sharp, and probably correlated.

By way of contrast, the differences between scorpaeniform and perciform fishes may be noted. To oversimplify, the scorpaeniform fishes seem to be percoids that sit on the bottom. This change in mode of life has led to a whole series of specializations in the more advanced forms. However, there also seems to be a place for a scorpaenoid that sometimes rests on the bottom and sometimes swims around. Some of the more generalized scorpaenoids continue to alternate between the two modes of life (and among flatfishes, the same apparently holds for the primitive *Psettodes*). Indeed, one scorpaeniform fish *(Anoplopoma)* seems, judging from appearance, to have reverted to a completely free-swimming existence. In both mode of life and morphology, the borders between the scorpaeniform and perciform fishes are not sharp.

Whether or not the higher teleostean groups are about equally related from the point of view of the relative times of divergence (Hennig 1966), it seems that morphological changes must have evolved sequentially. If this is so, it is possible to point to specialized types of structure and basal (or presumably ancestral) types. Because a series of transitional stages can often be demonstrated between the more aberrant forms and the percoid-type organization, it is postulated that the latter is the basal type among higher teleostean groups, and that the more aberrant forms have been derived from it.

Morphologically then, higher teleostean diversification may be considered as a half-wheel with spokes of varying length extending from a central percoid axle (Gosline 1968, fig. 1). In general, following this analogy, the axle comprises the superfamily Percoidae, the very short spokes together with the axle constitute the suborder Percoidei, and these together with the next longer series comprise the order Perciformes. The very long spokes (in terms of morphological differentiation) are separated out as separate higher teleostean orders. One practical problem that arises is how to determine where the axle ends and any particular spoke begins. The usual answer is to look for a convenient morphological gap in the series of transitional stages. A second problem is how to treat two closely associated spokes, such as the Acanthuridae and the Teuthididae (Siganidae). Gosline (1968) has advocated that, for purposes of classification, two or more be treated as one if they are closer to each other than to any other spokes.

To conclude, for the great assemblage of higher teleosts a classification has been developed that seems to meet two minimum standards: (1) the categories are more or less definable in morphological terms, and (2) totally unrelated forms are not included in a single taxon. Improvements in higher teleostean classification seem feasible along two lines. One is a greater emphasis on lineage differentiation within the higher teleosts. There are difficulties with this line of development: (1) The more deeply the lineages are differentiated toward their basal common ancestor, the more difficult the differentiation becomes; and (2) where differentiation becomes more difficult, the problem of whether it really exists at all or in the manner stated also becomes progressively greater. Thus the differentiation of lineages among the basal percoid families is not only difficult but such attempts as have been made along this line are of dubious validity.

The second possible improvement in higher teleostean classification lies in the direction of facilitating comprehension. If the present "planet-satellite" system could be broken into orders of more uniform size, a more assimilable classification would result. (Simply to combine the satellites with the planet, for example, the Echeneiformes and Icosteiformes with the Perciformes, is of no help in this regard.) The difficulties here are again of two sorts. First, any regroupings should not impair morphological definition and clarity. Second, from the point of view of human communication, the advantage to be gained from creating more assimilable groups should more than offset the confusion that would result from changing an existing classification.

To return from the mechanics of classification to zoology, there are two categories of higher teleostean groups for which the interrelationships remain to be worked out. One of these is the great mass of species within the superfamily Percoidae. The other contains a few aberrant orders, such as the Pegasiformes, for which the derivation remains unknown. These aberrant orders are relegated here to the end of the higher teleostean series.

17. Order PERCIFORMES

Suborder Mugiloidei
Superfamily Polynemoidae
Family Polynemidae
Superfamily Sphyraenoidae
Family Sphyraenidae
Superfamily Mugiloidae
Family Mugilidae
Superfamily Atherinoidae
Families Melanotaeniidae, Atherinidae, Isonidae, Neostethidae, and Phallostethidae
Suborder Anabantoidei
Superfamily Channoidae
Family Channidae
Superfamily Anabantoidae
Families Anabantidae, Belontidae, Helostomidae and Osphronemidae
Superfamily Luciocephaloidae
Family Luciocephalidae
Suborder Percoidei
Superfamily Percoidae
Families Badidae, Nandidae, Pristolepidae, Centropomidae, Bramidae, Pempheridae, Arripididae, Lutjanidae, Scorpididae, Nemipteridae, Pomadasyidae, Toxotidae, Monodactylidae, Lobotidae, Lethrinidae, Kyphosidae, Distichiidae, Girellidae, Sparidae, Centracanthidae, Emmelichthyidae, Leiognathidae, Sciaenidae, Mullidae, Chaetodipteridae, Drepanidae, Scatophagidae, Chaetodontidae, Enoplosidae, Histiopteridae, Oplegnathidae, Percichthyidae, Serranidae, Grammistidae, Plesiopidae, Acanthoclinidae, Opistogna-

thidae, Kuhliidae, Centrarchidae, Priacanthidae, Cepolidae, Rainfordiidae, Apogonidae, Percidae, Lactariidae, Labracoglossidae, Bathyclupeidae, Pomatomidae, Rachycentridae, Carangidae, Menidae, Coryphaenidae, Cichlidae, Sillaginidae, and Branchiostegidae

Superfamily Cirrhitoidae
Families Cirrhitidae, Aplodactylidae, Chironemidae, Cheilodactylidae, and Latridae

Superfamily Trichodontoidae
Family Trichodontidae

Superfamily Champsodontoidae
Family Champsodontidae

Superfamily Chiasmodontoidae
Family Chiasmodontidae

Superfamily Ammodytoidae
Families Ammodytidae and Hypoptychidae

Superfamily Embiotocoidae
Family Embiotocidae

Superfamily Pomacentroidae
Family Pomacentridae

Superfamily Labroidae
Families Labridae, Odacidae, and Scaridae

Suborder Ophidioidei
Superfamily Gadopsoidae
Family Gadopsidae

Superfamily Ophidioidae
Families Brotulidae, Aphyonidae, Ophidiidae, Pyramodontidae, and Carapidae

Suborder Kurtoidei
Family Kurtidae

Suborder Xiphioidei
Superfamily Xiphioidae
Families Xiphiidae and Istiophoridae

Superfamily Luvaroidae
Family Luvaridae

Suborder Scombroidei
Superfamily Trichiuroidae
Families Scombrolabracidae, Gempylidae, and Trichiuridae

Superfamily Scombroidae
Family Scombridae
Incertae sedis: Family Gasterochismatidae

Suborder Acanthuroidei

Superfamily Acanthuroidae
Families Acanthuridae and Zanclidae
Superfamily Teuthidoidae (Siganoidae)
Family Teuthididae (Siganidae)
Suborder Stromateoidei
Families Amarsipidae, Centrolophidae, Nomeidae, Ariommi-
dae, Tetragonuridae, and Stromateidae
Suborder Gobioidei
Families Gobiidae, Kraemeriidae, Microdesmidae, Rhyacic-
thyidae, Eleotridae, Taeniodidae, Benthophilidae, and
Psammichthyidae
Suborder Blennioidei
Superfamily Notothenioidae
Families Trichonotidae, Cheimarrichthyidae, Bovictidae,
Nototheniidae, Harpagiferidae, Bathydraconidae, and
Channichthyidae
Superfamily Trachinoidae
Families Trachinidae, Uranoscopidae, Leptoscopidae, and
Dactyloscopidae
Superfamily Congrogadoidae
Families Congrogadidae and Notograptidae
Incertae sedis: Family Peronedyidae
Superfamily Blennioidae
Families Tripterygiidae, Clinidae, Chaenopsidae, and Blenni-
idae
Superfamily Zoarceoidae
Families Bathymasteridae, Stichaeidae, Pholidae, Anarhichad-
idae, Ptylichthyidae, Zaproridae, Cryptacanthodidae and
Zoarcidae
Incertae sedis: Families Derepodichthyidae, Scytalinidae, and
Lycodapodidae
Suborder Schindlerioidei
Family Schindleriidae

No diagnostic traits are held in common by all of the thousands of
perciform species. Regan's (1913a, p. 111) definition is perhaps as
satisfactory as any: "Symmetrical acanthopterous physoclists with
normal dorsal fin, pelvic fin never more than 6-rayed, subabdominal, thoracic, jugular or mental in position, the pelvic bones
typically attached to the cleithra; principal caudal rays not more
than 17. No orbitosphenoid. Second suborbital not forming a stay
for the praeoperculum. Posttemporal more or less distinctly
forked."

Although perciform fishes have been recorded from the Cretaceous a number of times, most of these records have proved to belong to lower orders, or (e.g., Blochiidae) remain incertae sedis. Indeed, the first solidly established perciform record is from the Tertiary (Andrews et al. 1967).

The problems of classifying higher teleostean fishes have been dealt with above. So far as the Perciformes are concerned, the practical problem is to determine how much of the basic higher teleostean diversification should be included in the group (see also Gosline 1968). Within rather broad limits, the decision to include or exclude individual peripheral groups is primarily based on human convenience. Suffice it to note that certain groups here included in the Perciformes have sometimes been excluded, among them the Mugiloidei (Gosline 1962), Ophidioidei (Mead, Bertelsen, and Cohen 1964), and Gobioidei (Regan 1936). Conversely, certain groups here treated as separate orders have sometimes been included in the Perciformes, for example, the Scorpaeniformes (Berg 1940) and the Icosteiformes and Mastacembeliformes (Greenwood et al. 1966). Here the greatest novelty in the treatment of perciform borders is (following Gosline, in Press) the transferal of the callionymoid fishes from the Perciformes to the Gobiesociformes.

The basic percoid organization has been extremely successful and has also permitted an adaptive radiation into almost every habitat ever occupied by fishes. The success of the percoid construction is adequately demonstrated by the fact that today the percoids dominate what has probably always been the single major habitat for fishes—the inshore marine areas.

The percoids have adaptively radiated in many directions, of which only two will be mentioned. In swimming ability the percoids, at one extreme, have given rise to the xiphioids and scombroids, which are among the fastest moving of all fishes. At the other extreme are those innumerable percoid derivatives that have become semisedentary bottom forms. This adaptation to an existence in direct contact with the bottom is a curious one for several reasons. It is undoubtedly a secondary development among teleosts. However, the lower and intermediate teleostean groups, aside from the eels, certain myctophiform fishes, and perhaps the catfishes, seem never to have had much success with this adaptation. By contrast, group after group of the higher teleosts have successfully adopted this mode of life—cirrhitoids, blennioids, gobioids, scorpaenoids, flatfishes, and many others. One can only wonder why the higher teleosts have been so diversely successful at a mode of life rarely adopted by lower teleostean forms.

Certain thoughts bearing on this matter will be noted for what they are worth. First, it might be that there once were numerous lower and intermediate teleostean groups that lived in direct contact with the bottom, but that competition from the percoid derivatives exterminated many of them. This possibility does not seem to be borne out by the fossil record. The alternative possibility is that certain aspects of percoid construction preadapt them to a semisedentary existence. Two percoid structural systems might belong in this category. One is the mechanism for pumping water over the gills. So long as the oral, opercular, and branchiostegal pumps are integrally associated, as they are in lower teleosts, respiration involves rather gross changes in head configuration, including alternate lowering and raising of the floor of the oral cavity (chap. 3). However, among at least some percoid derivatives, for example, the trachinids and uranoscopids (Baglioni 1907), a separate branchiostegal pump is developed to the point where respiration can be carried on without any distortion of the head configuration at all. The second possible preadaptation for a semisedentary existence among percoids is their paired-fin structure. With the pectorals shifted to a vertical axis, an expansion of the partly extended pectorals will serve two functions. The lower rays can be used as lateral struts to hold the body in fixed position on the bottom, that is, they tend to prevent the fish from rolling over onto its side. But also, in the event of danger, these pectorals can be clapped back sharply against the sides, providing an efficient standing start for forward locomotion.

A very different type of percoid adaptive radiation is that associated with freshwater and saltwater habitats. As mentioned in the introduction to this chapter, the basal percoid families today are mostly represented by euryhaline or freshwater forms. On the basis of what may be envisioned as a euryhaline basal type, it may be at least speculated that the perciform fishes have evolved in two ecological directions. One is toward the now abundant and diverse coral-reef perciform fauna. The other is to forms completely restricted to fresh water, notably the percids and centrarchids in the northern temperate regions and the anabantoids and cichlids in the tropics. Of the tropical groups the cichlids appear to be a relatively recent development. By contrast, bits of evidence are accumulating that the anabantoids may be a part of a relatively early freshwater diversification that includes such other groups as the nandids, pristolepids (Gosline 1968), badids (Barlow, Liem, and Wickler 1968), and quite possibly the mastacembelids (Nelson 1969*a*). In addition, one may at least wonder whether the synbranchids do not also belong here.

Suborder MUGILOIDEI

This suborder is understood here as including the Polynemidae and phallostethoid families as well as the percesocine families *sensu stricto* (Gosline 1962). The principal characteristic held in common by all members of the group is that, unlike most perciform fishes, the pelvic girdle is not attached to the cleithra.

Most authors (except Rosen 1964) are agreed that the major morphological separation within the suborder lies between the polynemids and the remaining forms (Regan 1912*b*). The polynemids are bottom-living fishes that have developed the lower pectoral rays as probes for locating food. Probably in association with this, the mouth tends to be subterminal. The head and back are relatively high; the head has well-developed cranial crests, and there is a separate anterior spinous dorsal fin in its usual percoid position (Gosline 1962). All the other mugiloid fishes spend much of their time near the surface of the water, and they are flat headed and flat backed. Crests on the dorsal surface of the skull are rudimentary or lacking, and at least in the larger forms they have been functionally replaced (see chap. 2) by bony, brushlike extensions from the posterior face of the cranium (Starks 1899). The anterior spinous dorsal, when retained, has become a small, collapsible, brushlike affair.

In character after character (except pelvic structure), it is possible to trace, within the Mugiloidei, a series of stages from its basal percoid condition, usually in polynemids and sphyraenids, through to its most specialized development, usually in atherinids or phallostethoids (see Hubbs 1944, for the fin structure; Gosline 1963*a*, for the caudal skeleton; and Gosline 1962, for vertebral number, etc.). The feeding habits of the different mugiloid groups are quite distinctive; the differences in the jaws and associated structures are probably at least partly related to the fact that the mouth opens forward and downward in polynemids and mugilids, directly forward in sphyraenids, and forward and somewhat upward in atherinids and phallostethoids.

Suborder ANABANTOIDEI

For various reasons the anabantoids appear to be an early freshwater offshoot of the perciform stock. Thus the Channidae (Ophiocephalidae) have a pelvic fin (when present) made up of six soft rays, and the pelvic girdle is remote from the cleithra. As long as the groups included in the Anabantoidei are limited to the Channidae, the anabantoid families (Liem 1963), and *Luciocephalus,* their peculiarities set them off distinctively from the Percoidei. But it is becoming increasingly clear (Barlow, Liem, and Wickler 1968; Gosline 1968) that these groups are somehow related to the less specialized Badidae, Nandidae, and Pristolepidae. If these last three families are removed from the Percoidei and placed in the Anabantoidei, as they perhaps should be, then the question arises of how to define the Anabantoidei. In the absence of specimens for the three families in question, only certain possible morphological indicators of affinity between them and the anabantoids can be suggested—enlarged nasal bones, an expanded auditory bulla, and the presence of a single epural in the caudal skeleton. *Pristolepis* (Gosline 1968, fig. 2*b*) and *Polycentropsis* (Monod 1968, fig. 655) have developed, like anabantoids, a round-tailed type of caudal skeleton in which the parahypural lacks a hypurapophysis (Nursall 1963) and a basal articulation with a centrum element, but in *Badis* (Barlow, Liem, and Wickler 1968, fig. 11) the parahypural has become fused basally with the caudal skeleton. In short, the basal members of what would seem to be the anabantoid lineage are morphologically percoids.

Suborder PERCOIDEI

About the only attempt ever made to classify the Percoidei on more than external features is that of Regan (1913*a*). He divided the group into divisions (= superfamilies), of which the Percoidae comprise the central mass of families and the other divisions are peripheral offshoots characterized by peculiarities of one sort or another. Such attempts to separate out lineages among the Percoidei as have been made—for example, by Jordan (1923) and Matsubara (1955, 1963)—are not backed by morphological differences and seem to be based primarily on intuition. In osteology as well as in superficial characters the more than 50 families of Percoidae are so similar that they can be separated only by trivia. Some of these, for example the peculiar arrangement of opercular spines in the serranid-grammistid group (Gosline 1966*b*), are obviously useful only for pigeonholing purposes. Others may or may not have more general phylogenetic significance: the presence or absence of axillary scales at the base of the pelvic fins (Regan 1913*a*); scale structure (McCully 1961); the caudal skeleton (Gosline 1961); the pattern of configuration of the recurrent facial nerve (Freihofer 1963); the jaw structure (Gosline 1966a); and the nature of the supraoccipital crest (Gosline 1966a; but see Patterson 1968b). It may be that the use of some as yet untried characteristic, such as plasma proteins or chromosome number, will prove of equal or greater value in sorting percoid lineages. When a number of these lines of investigation together are brought to bear on the classification of the Percoidei, it may well prove advisable to alter it drastically. Meanwhile, the classification followed here is that of Regan (1913a), as modified by Gosline (1968).

Suborder OPHIDIOIDEI

The primary specialization of the members of this suborder seems to have been the development of filamentous pelvic rays, which are presumably used for probing the bottom for food. Other, secondary specializations, for example, the carapid habit of living in the cavities of echinoderms, have been superimposed. Gosline (1968) traced the development of the major ophidioid peculiarities back to a fish, *Gadopsis,* that is intermediate between the percoids and the more specialized ophidioids. The reasons for believing that the ophidioids, gadoids, and zoarcids represent lines of convergent evolution, rather than related groups as has been postulated by Greenwood et al. (1966) and by Rosen and Patterson (1969), are also summarized by Gosline (1968).

Suborder Kurtoidei

This suborder is made up of two species of the single genus *Kurtus,* about which relatively little has been published (de Beaufort 1914).

Suborder XIPHIOIDEI

Gosline (1968) and others have shown that the similarities between the spearfishes and scombroids are undoubtedly due to convergent development in large, fast-swimming forms, and that the two groups are most probably unrelated. *Luvarus* is provisionally placed with the xiphioids, but whether it really belongs there is open to question.

Suborder SCOMBROIDEI

Gosline (1968) recently traced the typical scombroids and the trichiuroids back to a form, *Scombrolabrax,* that has some of the attributes of both groups, and of the percoids as well. Whether

Gasterochisma, placed at the base of the scombroid series by Fraser-Brunner (1950), is even related to the suborder seems questionable.

Suborder ACANTHUROIDEI

This suborder and the Teuthidoidei (Siganoidei) have usually been considered distinct, but Gosline (1968) combined them since it is generally agreed that they are more closely related to each other than to any other group.

Suborder STROMATEOIDEI

The stromateoids, with one exception (Haedrich 1969), are unique in possessing teeth on the lining of the oesophagus. All members of the group are marine and many are high-seas forms. Haedrich (1967) has recently reviewed the group.

Suborder GOBIOIDEI

So far as known, all gobies are quite distinctive in the configuration of both the suspensorium (Regan 1911*d*) and the caudal skeleton (Gosline 1955). There seems to be just as much justification for giving separate ordinal status to the gobioids, as suggested by Regan (1936), as to the Scorpaeniformes. Traditionally, however, they have been considered a suborder of perciform fishes, as they are here.

Within this very large and widespread suborder of fishes, however, the classification is chaotic. Though there are numerous regional treatments, the one attempt to review the genera of one section of the suborder on a world-wide basis (Koumans 1931) has proved gravely inadequate.

Suborder BLENNIOIDEI

The blennioids constitute another large group of seemingly related fishes that are not necessarily, however, of strictly monophyletic origin. The classification of Gosline (1968) is followed here. The placement by Greenwood et al. (1966) and Rosen and Patterson (1969) of the family Zoarcidae in a different superorder from the closely related Bathymasteridae seems unjustifiable.

Suborder SCHINDLERIOIDEI

This suborder is made up of the small oceanic, paedomorphic fishes of the genus *Schindleria.* About all that can be said about them is that they seem to be percoid derivatives (Gosline 1959), possibly related to the ammodytoids (Gosline 1963*b*).

18. Order PLEURONECTIFORMES

Suborder Psettodoidei
  Family Psettodidae
Suborder Pleuronectoidei
  Families Citharidae, Scophthalmidae, Bothidae and Pleuro-
    nectidae
Suborder Soleoidei
  Families Soleidae and Cynoglossidae

Adults of all members of the order have both eyes on the same side of the head—a feature that distinguishes them immediately from all other fishes. In the larva the eyes have the usual symmetry, but at the time of transformation and before the bones of the head ossify, the eye of the future blind side migrates across the top of the head. Except for this adult peculiarity, flatfishes range from forms *(Psettodes)* closely resembling the percoid fishes to the tapering, practically eyeless tongue soles (Cynoglossidae). Partly because of general interest and partly because a number of temperate-zone flatfishes have great commercial importance, there is a very extensive literature on the group. Fortunately, most of this literature is adequately summarized for systematic and evolutionary purposes by Norman (1934), Hubbs (1945), and Ochiai (1959 [in Japanese] and 1963).

Except for the asymmetrical eyes, *Psettodes* resembles such percoids as the serranid *Epinephelus* (Norman 1934). The thoracic pelvics have a spine and five soft rays, and the pelvic girdle articulates with the cleithra in the usual manner. Unlike all other flatfishes, the dorsal fin does not extend forward onto the head, and its anterior portion has about 10 spines. The anal is said to have from one to three spines. There are 15 branched rays in the caudal fin. In the pectoral girdle there are two postcleithra and well-developed actinosts. The maxillary has a supramaxillary. The vomer and palatine are toothed. The nasal organs of the two sides of the head are nearly symmetrical. Unlike other flatfishes, some specimens of *Psettodes* have the eyes on one side of the head and some on the other; furthermore sometimes the right optic nerve passes above the left and sometimes vice versa in the optic chiasma, regardless of which side the eyes are on (i.e., the chiasma is dimorphic: Hubbs 1945, p. 16). There are 24 vertebrae, 10 abdominal and 14 caudal. Though nothing is known of the behavior of *Psettodes* in life, Regan (1910*c*, p. 491) has suggested, on the basis of structure, that "this is evidently a predaceous fish, which probably lies on the bottom concealed from its prey, and then darts out, swimming rapidly for a short distance by lateral movements of the tail," and, "Probably it has retained so many Percoid features because it has not adopted progression by undulating movements of the body and marginal fins to the same extent as other fishes of this order."

From the quite percoid-like structural organization of *Psettodes,* there has evolved a whole series of flatfishes that move across the bottom by a series of undulations, as do the skates and rays. There seems to be a purely physical reason why a flatfish moving over the bottom, as a flounder or a skate does, should develop an undulating type of movement and become secondarily bilaterally symmetrical. Consider a tail-swinging fish that turns on its side and swims close to the bottom. The upstroke of the tail is not limited but the downstroke is limited by the proximity of the bottom; furthermore, the water displaced by the upstroke can move outward in various directions, but the direction of displacement from the downstroke is again limited by the presence of the bottom. On the other hand, a thin cushion of relatively nondisplaceable water between a flat body and the bottom could quite possibly prove advantageous for undulating locomotion, provided the body is bilaterally symmetrical. In any event, most of the flatfish peculiarities seem to be associated with their habit of undulating close to the bottom. The fins become spineless (a single pelvic "spine" is retained in the Citharidae) and tend to enclose the body: the dorsal fin moves forward onto the head, and the anal is continued forward at least functionally by the pelvic fin of the eyed side, which may become median and many rayed (e.g., 13 rayed in *Ammotretis elongatus:* Norman 1934, p. 424).

Though these modifications and many others have taken place repeatedly in flatfishes, two main lines of development are usually traced back to separate origins in a *Psettodes*-like stock. One includes the mostly diurnal flounders and their relatives (Citharidae, Bothidae, and Pleuronectidae), and the other the nocturnal soles (Soleidae and Cynoglossidae). In the flounders and soles, unlike *Psettodes,* all of the members of a genus and in most cases of a family, have the eyes either on the right side (Pleuronectidae, Soleidae) or on the left side (Bothidae, Cynoglossidae) of the head. In the flounders the crossing of the optic nerves in the optic chiasma is so arranged that when the eye crosses over to the eyed side the chiasma untwists (i.e., it is monomorphic). All flounders investigated have the eye and the optic nerve relatively large, and the olfactory lobes of the brain relatively small. The nasal organ of the blind side is displaced to or toward the eyed side. The jaws are symmetrical or nearly so and the lower is prominent. Within the same species of sole, by contrast, in the optic chiasma sometimes one nerve is on top and sometimes the other (the dimorphic condition, as in *Psettodes*). The eyes and the optic nerves are small, but the olfactory lobes are relatively large. The nasal organ of the blind side is not displaced. The jaws are asymmetrical and the lower is never prominent. Many of the soles have become much more specialized than the flounders: some are naked, some are covered with dermal projections, and some taper to a point posteriorly.

The recorded members of the Pleuronectiformes extend back to the Eocene (Chabanaud 1937). Today, members of the order are to be found from the Arctic nearly to the Antarctic. They are abundant over banks, rare over bare rocks. Some live in rather deep water. Groups represented in the more insular areas (e.g., the Bothidae) seem to have forms with relatively long-lived planktonic larval stages. At another geographical extreme the achirine soles are limited to America, where they ascend rivers—sometimes, as in the Amazon, to considerable distances.

19. Order **SCORPAENIFORMES**

Group 1. Families Scorpaenidae, Synanceidae, Triglidae, Peristedi-
idae, Caracanthidae, Aploactidae, Pataecidae, Platy-
cephalidae, Hoplichthyidae, and Congiopodidae
Group 2. Anoplopomatidae
Group 3. Hexagrammidae, Zaniolepidae, Cottidae, Cottunculidae,
Psychrolutidae, Comephoridae, and Agonidae
Group 4. Cyclopteridae and Liparidae
Group 5. Dactylopteridae

So far as can be determined from the literature the only character that more or less consistently distinguishes the scorpaeniform fishes from the percoids is the presence in the Scorpaeniformes of a strut extending posteriorly from the second suborbital bone (not counting the lacrimal) to (or toward) an abutment on the outer surface of the preopercle. The lacrimal and the first and second suborbitals together usually form a firm and frequently spinous stay extending longitudinally across the cheek (Matsubara 1943). Certain other trends of development in the scorpaeniform fishes may be noted. The head and body tend to be spiny or bony plated; the pectoral fin is usually rounded, with the membranes between the lower rays more or less deeply incised; and the caudal fin is rarely forked.

The classification of the group appears to be in an advanced state of confusion. Though a great deal has been recorded concerning individual members, only two attempts have been made to classify the group as a whole. Of these, Matsubara's (1955, 1963) seems to bear little resemblance to that of Regan (1913*b*). Regan (p. 170) stated that "the group is a natural one" but then proceeded to include the Gasterosteiformes. Conversely, Quast (1965, p. 564) working from a narrow base of northern forms concluded, "The mail-cheeked fishes may be an assemblage containing at least three different evolutionary lines, scorpaenid, anoplopomatid, and hexagrammid-cottid."

Here, as a provisional measure, the views of the three authors cited have been combined to the extent that each major subdivision of the order advocated by any of them has been assigned its own group. Group 5, the Dactylopteridae, has sometimes been allocated to a separate order (e.g., by Berg, 1940). Its relationship to the other scorpaeniform fishes seems to be problematic.

20. Order GOBIESOCIFORMES

Suborder Callionymoidei
   Superfamily Callionymoidae
      Family Callionymidae
   Superfamily Draconettoidae
      Family Draconettidae
Suborder Gobiesocoidei
   Family Gobiesocidae

Head and body without normally developed scales. Articular processes of the premaxillaries either fused with the ascending processes or absent. Opercular bones extending back into a spine, except in some gobiesocids. Metapterygoid absent. Circumorbital bones represented only by a lacrimal. Ribs from the second vertebra. Spinous dorsal, if present, separate from the soft dorsal. Soft dorsal and anal rays equal in number to the vertebrae between them. Caudal rounded or brushlike, with fewer than 15 branched rays. Pelvics with 4 or 5 branched rays, united into a sucking disk in gobiesocids, inserted ahead of the rounded pectorals.

Gosline (in Press) has pointed out the derivation of the families Callionymidae, Draconettidae, and Gobiesocidae from the notothenioid section of the perciform suborder Blennioidei (see also Gosline 1968). As might be expected from such a derivation, all three families are strictly bottom-living forms, but beyond that the three groups have become specialized in quite different ways. The draconettids are high-headed forms with the orbits so greatly enlarged as to have affected (and presumably weakened) the preorbital portion of the skull. Callionymids have developed peculiar lateral–line extensions. Gobiesocids have transformed the pelvic fins into the lateral borders of a complex sucking disk (Briggs 1955).

21. Order **TETRAODONTIFORMES**

Suborder Balistoidei
  Superfamily Triacanthoidae
    Families Triacanthodidae, Triacanthidae
  Superfamily Balistoidae
    Families Monacanthidae, Balistidae, and Aluteridae
  Superfamily Ostraciontoidae
    Families Ostraciontidae, Aracanidae
Suborder Tetraodontoidei
  Superfamily Triodontoidae
    Family Triodontidae
  Superfamily Tetraodontoidae
    Families Canthigasteridae, Tetraodontidae
  Superfamily Diodontoidae
    Family Diodontidae
  Superfamily Moloidae
    Family Molidae

The order Tetraodontiformes is an easily definable group. The following diagnosis is drawn mostly from Tyler (1968).

No parietal, intercalar, supramaxillary, nasal, suborbital, or tabular bones. Suspensorium more or less firmly attached to the cranium anteriorly and posteriorly. Posttemporal bone, if present, fused to the cranium. Gill openings restricted, never extending far below the pectoral base. No lateral line on the body. Vertebrae 23 or fewer. Pelvic fins, if present, with no more than 2 soft rays. No anal spines. Caudal fin rounded, truncate, or absent (except *Triodon*), with 10 or fewer branched rays.

Though certain tetraodontiform fishes, particularly the Triacanthoidae, are somewhat intermediate between the Perciformes and the Tetraodontiformes, the more specialized members are among the most advanced of all fishes.

The general direction of evolution, except in the Molidae, has been toward the development of powerfully leveraged, if small, shearing jaws. With these a monacanthid can and will attack a crab almost as large as itself, and, after nipping off the eyestalks, will pull it apart piece by piece. No tetraodontiform fish can swim rapidly, but the monacanthids at least are capable of very accurate maneuvering, which they accomplish partly by appropriate pectoral movement and partly by passing undulations backward or forward along the dorsal and anal fins. In this group, as in other fishes that use dorsal and/or anal undulation, each ray is simple and inserted over a basal ball-and-socket articulation; there are several rays per vertebra. The tetraodontiform fishes, again apparently excepting the Molidae, but like other slow-moving fishes, have ample protective devices—spines, bony armor, poisonous flesh (Tetraodontidae), or poisons that they exude into the water on becoming excited (Ostraciontidae).

The subordinal and superfamily classification adopted here is from Tyler (1968); the families are those of Fraser-Brunner (1951 and earlier papers).

22. Order ECHENEIFORMES

Family Echeneidae

The Echeneiformes comprises a handful of species of perciform derivation in which the spinous dorsal fin has been transformed into a sucking disc, by means of which they ride along on fishes, turtles, and whales. Just what value this transport service is to the echeneids is not always clear. In any event, the whole echeneid structure and much of the life history and even the physiology of these fishes are associated with this unique mode of life. The lower jaw, for example, extends forward of the upper. Associated with elongation of the lower jaw is an increase in branchiostegal rays, unique among acanthopteran fishes, to as many as 11 (McAllister 1968).

The echeneids are immediately separable from all other fishes, but whether their peculiarities merit ordinal status is perhaps open to question. The lineage has been distinct since Eocene times, but so have a great many lineages within the Perciformes.

Despite their specializations, there seems to be no reason to believe that the echeneids have not been derived from some percoid fish such as *Rachycentron* (see, for example, Nelson 1969*a*).

23. Order MASTACEMBELIFORMES

Suborder Mastacembeloidei
    Family Mastacembelidae
Suborder Chaudhurioidei
    Family Chaudhuriidae

Nasal bones greatly enlarged, meeting on the midline. Premaxillaries excluding the maxillaries from the gape. Pectoral girdle not attached to the skull. Dorsal and anal usually with spines. Vertebrae numerous. No pelvic fins. (For accounts of the osteology of the Mastacembeliformes, see Regan 1912*d*; Sufi 1956; Maheshwari 1967).

The mastacembeliform fishes are peculiar, mostly spiny,eel-like fishes of the fresh waters of tropical Asia and Africa. They have no known accessory air-breathing apparatus, but apparently are able to aestivate.

Chaudhuria appears in many respects to be a dwarf, spineless mastacembelid, (Annandale and Hora 1923) but it also lacks the peculiar "trunk" of the Mastacembelidae.

The relationships of the Mastacembeliformes are obscure. Their eellike shape, large nasal organs, and posteriorly displaced pectoral girdles recall the Anguilliformes, but such similarities are surely the result of convergence. Indeed, it is generally agreed that the mastacembeliform fishes are perciform derivatives. On the basis of certain peculiarities of gill-arch structure (paired tooth plates fused with the third hypobranchials), Nelson (1969*a*) has suggested a possible relationship between the Mastacembeliformes and the anabantoid fishes—a suggestion perhaps supported by the enlarged nasal bones, the fact that the dorsal and anal soft rays are somewhat more numerous than the vertebrae, and the old-world tropical freshwater distribution.

24. Order SYNBRANCHIFORMES

Families Synbranchidae, Amphipnoidae
Incertae sedis: Family Alabetidae

Gape bordered by the premaxillaries above. Gill openings confluent, restricted above, and typically appearing as a transverse slit. No ribs. Dorsal and anal without rays; pectorals absent; pelvics minute and jugular *(Alabes)* or absent.

The Synbranchiformes, as here defined, comprise two eel-shaped groups without any trace of dorsal or anal rays. The two groups are certainly not eels and most probably are not related to one another.

The Synbranchidae and Amphipnoidae are primarily freshwater fishes occurring world wide across the tropics. All seem to have accessory air-breathing structures of one type or another, and their vascular system is highly specialized (Liem 1961). Thus in *Fluta,* as in the eel *Moringua* (Trewavas 1932), the heart is well posterior to the cleithral symphysis. The eyes may be greatly reduced.

Alabes is a small Australian coastal fish of unknown affinities. In certain respects, for example, the jugular pelvics and the long premaxillary ascending processes, *Alabes* resembles the blennioids. However, those working on blennioids (e.g., Gosline 1968) are convinced it does not belong with that group. In certain respects, for example, the single, ventral gill opening and the rayless dorsal and anal fins, *Alabes* resembles the synbranchids. However, those working on symbranchids (e.g., Liem 1968) are convinced it does not belong with that group.

25. Order ICOSTEIFORMES

Family Icosteidae

This order and family is made up of one species, *Icosteus aenigmaticus,* from the North Pacific. This strange creature, said to reach 7 feet in length, has a limp, flabby body and poorly ossified skeleton. The pelvics are lost with growth.

Regan (1923) has stated that there is no reason why *Icosteus* should not be considered a perciform derivative, but beyond this no suggestions as to relationships have been offered.

26. Order PEGASIFORMES

Family Pegasidae

This order, made up of some half-dozen tropical species of little armor-plated fishes, does not seem to fit anywhere. Judging from

Berg's (1940) summary of earlier papers, the anterior part of the suspensorium is attached to the vomer rather than to the posterior part of the suspensorium; the infraorbitals are attached to the preopercle; the pelvics are subadominal, with 1 to 3 soft rays, and the pelvis is ligamentously attached to the cleithra; the vertebrae number 19 to 24.

In life *Pegasus papilio* looks like a butterfly creeping over the bottom, but its relationships remain problematic.

27. Order **LOPHIIFORMES**

Suborder Batrachoidei
    Family Batrachidae
Suborder Lophioidei
    Superfamily Lophioidae
        Family Lophiidae
    Superfamily Antennarioidae
        Families Brachionichthyidae, Antennariidae, Chaunacidae, and Ogcocephalidae
    Superfamily Ceratioidae
        Families Melanocetidae, Diceratiidae, Himantolophidae, Oneirodidae, Gigantactidae, Centrophrynidae, Ceratiidae, and Linophrynidae

Premaxillaries with separate ascending and articular processes. Posttemporal firmly united to or fused into the skull. Gills 2 or 3; none on the 4th arch. First vertebra rigidly attached to the skull, its neural arch suturally united to the exoccipitals. Pleural ribs absent. Upper pectoral ray articulating basally with an actinost. Pelvics inserted ahead of the pectorals. At least the parahypural and the lower hypurals fused basally with a centrum element.

The batrachoid and lophioid fishes are here combined in a single order, following Regan (1912*a*), because they seem to be more closely related to one another than to any other fish group. Though in many respects the batrachoids are less peculiar than the lophioids, both groups are so specialized that their origin is obscure. A number of derivations have been suggested, but all seem unsatisfactory. The basic difficulty is that the various lophiiform peculiarities suggest quite different relationships. Regan (1912*a*) noted the similarity in the caudal skeleton between the batrachoids and the Percopsiformes. Unlike most teleosts but like many percopsiform and lampridiform fishes, the lower hypurals are fused to a centrum element basally, but the upper hypurals articulate with the back of this same element by means of what appears to be an intervertebral articulation (see Monod 1968, fig. 805; Rosen and Patterson 1969, fig. 4 A–D). If the expansion at the base of the upper hypurals is really a centrum element, then it must be the centrum from the second ural vertebra, which is usually absent in the Perciformes. However, the batrachoid pelvics seem to be percoid: they are inserted ahead of the pectorals, they may have a spine and up to 5 soft rays, and the pelvic girdle articulates directly with the cleithra. The loss of articulation between the uppermost pectoral ray and the scapula recalls the blenniids and the goby *Periophthalmus*. Starks (1923) called attention to similarities between the flattened skulls of batrachoids and uranoscopoids.

The Lophiiformes have certainly developed as sedentary, bottom-living fishes, as is indicated by their pectoral actinost structure, reduction in gill surfaces (Gray 1954), and a host of other characters. However, once the lophioids developed a lure technique for capturing prey, many of them secondarily became midwater forms.

The present author has no familiarity with the deep-water members of this order. The family classification followed is that of Greenwood et al. (1966). So far as the ceratioids are concerned, this represents some reduction in the number of families recognized by Bertelsen (1951).

Literature Cited

Abe, T., R. Marumo, and K. Kawaguchi. 1965. Description of a new cetomimid fish from Suruga Bay. Japanese Journal of Ichthyology, vol. 12, pp. 57–63, 2 figs.

Aleev, Y. G. 1963. [Functional Basis of the Exterior Structure in Fish.] Moscow: Akademiia Nauk SSSR. 247 pp., 162 figs. [In Russian.]

Alexander, R. McN. 1965. Structure and function in the catfish. Journal of Zoology, vol. 148, pp. 88–152, 18 figs.

—— 1966. The functions and mechanisms of the protrusible upper jaws of two species of cyprinid fish. Journal of Zoology, vol. 149, pp. 288–296.

—— 1967a. Functional Design in Fishes. London: Hutchinson University Library. 160 pp., 16 figs.

—— 1967b. The functions and mechanisms of the protrusible upper jaws of some acanthopterygian fish. Journal of Zoology, vol. 151, pp. 43–64, 9 figs.

—— 1967c. Mechanisms of the jaws of some atheriniform fish. Journal of Zoology, vol. 151, pp. 233–255, 10 figs.

—— 1968. Animal Mechanics. London: Sidgwick and Jackson. xi + 346 pp., 135 figs.

—— 1969. The orientation of muscle fibers in the myomeres of fishes. Journal of the Marine Biological Association of the United Kingdom, vol. 49, pp. 263–290, 12 figs.

Al-Hussaini, A. H. 1949. On the functional morphology of the alimentary tract of some fish in relation to differences in their feeding habits. Quarterly Journal of the Microscopical Society of London, vol. 90, pp. 109–139, 323–354, 7 pls., 6 text figs.

Allis, E. P., Jr. 1897. The cranial muscles and cranial and first spinal nerves in Amia calva. Journal of Morphology, vol. 12, pp. 487–808, pls. 20–38.

—— 1903. The lateral sensory system in the Muraenidae. Internationale Monatsschrift für Anatomie und Physiologie, vol. 20, pp. 125–170, pls. 6–8.

—— 1905. The latero-sensory canals and related bones in fishes. Internationale Monatsschrift für Anatomie und Physiologie, vol. 21, pp. 401–500, pls. 8–20.

—— 1909. The cranial anatomy of the mail-cheeked fishes. Zoologica, vol. 22, pp. 1–219, 5 pls.

175

Andrews, S. M., B. G. Gardiner, R. S. Miles, and C. Patterson. 1967. Pisces. *In* A. B. Harland et al., eds., The Fossil Record, a Symposium with Documentation. Chapter 26, pp. 637–683, 6 figs.

Annandale, N., and S. L. Hora. 1923. On the systematic position of the Burmese fish *Chaudhuria*. Annals and Magazine of Natural History, ser. 9, vol. 11, pp. 327–333, 4 figs.

Arambourg, C., and L. Bertin. 1958. Super-ordres des holostéens et des halécostomes (Holostei et Halecostomi). *In* P.-P. Grassé, ed., Traité de zoologie. Vol. 13, pt. 3, pp. 2173–2203, figs. 1536–1660.

Baglioni, S. 1907. Der Atmungsmechanismus der Fische. Zeitschrift für allgemeine Physiologie, vol. 7, pp. 177–282, pls. 5–9, 6 text figs.

Bainbridge, R. 1963. Caudal fin and body movement in the propulsion of some fish. Journal of Experimental Biology, vol. 40, pp. 23–56, pl. 1, 21 text figs.

Ballintijn, C. M. 1969. Functional anatomy and movement coordination of the respiratory pump of the carp *(Cyprinus carpio* L.*)*. Journal of Experimental Biology, vol. 50, pp. 547–567, 6 figs.

Ballintijn, C. M., and G. M. Hughes. 1965. The muscular basis of the respiratory pumps in the trout. Journal of Experimental Biology, vol. 43, pp. 349–362, 7 figs.

Bannister, K. E. 1970. The anatomy and taxonomy of *Indostomus paradoxus* Prashad and Mukerji. Bulletin of the British Museum (Natural History), Zoology, vol. 19, pp. 181–209, 15 figs.

Bardach, J. E., and J. Case. 1965. Sensory capabilities of the modified fins of squirrel hake *(Urophycis chuss)* and searobins *(Prionotus carolinus* and *P. evolans)*. Copeia, 1965, pp. 194–206, 10 figs.

Bardach, J. E., H. E. Winn, and D. G. Menzel. 1959. The role of the senses in the feeding of the nocturnal reef predators *Gymnothorax moringa* and *G. vicinus*. Copeia, 1959, pp. 133–139, 3 figs.

Barlow, G. W., K. F. Liem, and W. Wickler. 1968. Badidae, a new fish family—behavioural, osteological, and developmental evidence. Journal of Zoology, vol. 156, pp. 415–447, 2 pls., 13 figs.

Bath, H. 1962. Vergleichende biologisch-anatomische Untersuchungen über die Leistungsfähigkeit der Sinnesorgane für den Nahrungserwerb, ihre gegenseitige Abhangigkeit und ihre Beziehungen zum Bau des Gehirns bei verschiedenen Knochenfischarten. Zeitschrift für wissenschaftliche Zoologie, vol. 167, pp. 238–290, 37 figs.

Berg, L. S. 1936. On the suborder Esocoidei. Bulletin de l'Institut de recherches biologiques . . . de Perm, vol. 10, pp. 389–391.

—— 1940. Classification of fishes, both recent and fossil. Travaux de l'Institut zoologique de l'Academie des sciences de l'URSS, vol. 5, pt. 2, pp. 87–517, figs. 1–190.

Berghe, L. van den. 1928. Recherches sur la déglutition chez les poissons téléostéens. Bulletin de la Classe des sciences de l'Académie Royale de Belgique, ser. 5, vol. 14, pp. 322–332, 2 figs.

Berry, F. H. 1964. Aspects of the development of the upper jaw bones in teleosts. Copeia, 1964, pp. 375–384, 10 figs.

Berry, F. H., and C. R. Robins. 1967. *Macristiella perlucens,* a new clupeiform fish from the Gulf of Mexico. Copeia, 1967, pp. 46–50, 4 figs.

Bertelsen, E. 1951. The Ceratioid Fishes: Ontogeny, Taxonomy, Distribution and Biology. Dana-Report No. 39, 276 pp., 141 figs.

Bertelsen, E., and N. B. Marshall. 1956. The Miripinnati, a new order of fishes. Dana-Report No. 42, 34 pp., 1 pl., 14 text figs.

—— 1958. Notes on Miripinnati. Dana-Report No. 45, pp. 9–10, 1 fig.

Bertin, L., and C. Arambourg. 1958. Super-ordre des téléostéens. *In* P.-P. Grassé, ed., Traité de zoologie. Vol. 13, pt. 3, pp. 2204–2500, figs. 1561–1788.

Bertmar, G. 1959. On the ontogeny of the chondral skull in Characidae, with a discussion on the chondrocranial base and the visceral chondrocranium in fishes. Acta Zoologica, vol. 40, pp. 203–364, 85 figs.

Bierbaum, G. 1914. Untersuchungen über den Bau der Gehörorgane von Tiefseefischen. Zeitschrift für wissenschaftliche Zoologie, vol. 111, pp. 281–380, 2 pls., 17 text figs.

Böhlke, J. E. 1966. Order Lyomeri. *In* Fishes of the Western North Atlantic. Yale University. Sears Foundation for Marine Research, Memoir No. 1, pt. 5, pp. 603–628, figs. 219, 220.

Bolin, R. L. 1936. The systematic position of *Indostomus paradoxus* Prashad and Mukerji, a fresh water fish from Burma. Journal of the Washington Academy of Sciences, vol. 26, pp. 420–423.

Borcea, I. 1907. Observations sur la musculature branchiostégale des téléostéens. Annales scientifiques de l'Université de Jassy, vol. 4, pp. 203–225, 17 figs.

Boulenger, G. A. 1904. Fishes (systematic account of the Teleostei). *In* A. E. Shipley and S. F. Harmer, eds., The Cambridge Natural History. Vol. 7, pp. 541–727, figs. 325–440.

Brauer, A. 1908. Die Tiefseefische. II. Anatomischer Teil. *In* C. Chun, ed., Wissenschaftliche Ergebnisse der Deutschen Tiefsee-Expedition "Valdivia." Vol. 15, pp. 1–266, 24 pls.

Braus, H. 1900. Die Muskeln und Nerven der Ceratodusflosse. *In* R. Semon, Zoologischen Forschungsreisen in Australien und den Malayischen Archipel . . . . Vol. 1, pp. 137–300, 9 pls., 25 text figs.

Breder, C. M., Jr. 1926. The locomotion of fishes. Zoologica, vol. 4, pp. 159–297, figs. 39–83.

—— 1947. An analysis of the geometry of symmetry with especial reference to the squamation of fishes. Bulletin of the American Museum of Natural History, vol. 88, pp. 325–412, 43 figs.

Breder, C. M., Jr., and P. Rasquin. 1950. A preliminary report on the role of the pineal organ in the control of pigment cells and light reactions in recent teleost fishes. Science, vol. 111, pp. 10–12, 1 fig.

Bridge, T. W. 1896. The mesial fins of ganoids and teleosts. Journal of the Linnean Society, Zoology, vol. 25, pp. 530–602, 3 pls.

Briggs, J. C. 1955. A monograph of the clingfishes. Stanford Ichthyological Bulletin, vol. 6, pp. 1–224, 114 figs.

Brundin, L. 1966. Transantarctic relationships and their significance, as evidenced by chironomid midges. Kungliga Svenska Vetenskapsakademiens Handlingar, ser. 4, vol. 11, no. 1, 472 pp., 30 pls.

Burne, R. H. 1909. The anatomy of the olfactory organ of teleostean fishes. Proceedings of the Zoological Society of London, May–Dec. 1909, pp. 610–663, figs. 188–213.

Castro, G. de Oliveira. 1961. Morphological data on the brain of *Electrophorus electricus* (L.). *In* Carlos Chagas and Antonio Paes de Carvalho, eds., Symposium on Comparative Bioelectrogenesis, Rio de Janeiro, 1959, Proceedings. Bioelectrogenesis, a Comparative Survey of Its Mechanisms with Particular Emphasis on Electric Fishes. Pp. 173–184, 15 figs.

Cavender, T. 1966. Systematic position of the North American Eocene fish, *"Leuciscus" rosei* Hussakof. Copeia, 1966, pp. 311–320, 6 figs.

——— 1969. An Oligocene mudminnow (family Umbridae) from Oregon with remarks on relationships within the Esocoidei. Occasional Papers of the Museum of Zoology, University of Michigan, No. 660, 33 pp., 2 pls., 6 text figs.

Chabanaud, P. 1937. Les téléostéens dyssymétriques du Mokattam Inférieur de Tourah. Mémoires de l'Institut égyptien (d'Égypte), vol. 32, pp. 1–121, 4 pls.

Chapman, G. 1958. The hydrostatic skeleton in invertebrates. Biological Reviews, vol. 33, pp. 338–364.

Chapman, W. M. 1934. The osteology of the haplimous fish *Novumbra hubbsi* Schultz with comparative notes on related species. Journal of Morphology, vol. 56, pp. 371–405.

——— 1942. The osteology and relationship of the bathypelagic fish *Macropinna microstoma*, with notes on its visceral anatomy. Annals and Magazine of Natural History, ser. 11, vol. 9, pp. 272–304, 9 figs.

Clark, R. B. 1964. Dynamics in Metazoan Evolution: the Origin of the Coelom and Segments. Oxford: Clarendon Press. x + 313 pp., 123 figs.

Cohen, D. M. 1964. Suborder Argentinoidea. *In* Fishes of the Western North Atlantic. Yale University. Sears Foundation for Marine Research. Memoir No. 1, pt. 4, pp. 1–70, 20 figs.

Collette, B. B. 1966. *Belonion*, a new genus of fresh-water needlefishes from South America. American Museum Novitates No. 2274, 22 pp., 7 figs.

d'Aubenton, F. 1961. Morphologie du crâne de *Cromeria nilotica occidentalis* Daget 1954. Bulletin de l'Institut français d'Afrique Noire, ser. A, vol. 23, pp. 131–164, 14 figs.

Daget, J. 1964. Le crâne des téléostéens. Mémoires du Muséum national d'histoire naturelle, ser. A, vol. 31, pp. 163–341.

Danilchenko, P. G. 1964. Teleostei. *In* Y. A. Orlov, ed., Fundamentals of Paleontology. Vol. 11, pp. 396–472, figs. 101–197. [In Russian; English translation by Israel Program for Scientific Translations, 1967]

Davis, B. G., and R. J. Miller. 1967. Brain patterns in minnows of the genus *Hybopsis* in relation to feeding habits and habitat. Copeia, 1967, pp. 1–39, 34 figs.

de Beaufort, L. F. 1914. Die Anatomie und systematische Stellung des Genus *Kurtus* Bloch. Gegenbaurs morphologisches Jahrbuch, vol. 48, pp. 391–410, pl. 12, 3 text figs.

de Beer, G. R. 1937. The Development of the Vertebrate Skull. Oxford: Oxford University Press. xxiv + 552 pp., 143 pls.

Dehadrai, P. V. 1962. Respiratory function of the swimbladder of *Notopterus* (Lacépède). Proceedings of the Zoological Society of London, vol. 139, pp. 341–357.

Delsman, H. C. 1926. Fish eggs and larvae from the Java Sea. 10. On a few larvae of empang fishes. Treubia, vol. 8, pp. 401–412, 17 figs.

Denton, E. J., and N. B. Marshall. 1958. The buoyancy of bathypelagic fishes without a gas-filled swimbladder. Journal of the Marine Biological Association of the United Kingdom, vol. 37, pp. 753–767, 2 pls., 3 text figs.

Derschied, J.-M. 1924. Contributions à la morphologie céphalique des vertébrés. A.—Structure de l'organe olfactif chez les poissons. Annales de la Société Royale zoologique de Belgique, vol. 54, pp. 79–162, 26 figs.

Devillers, C. 1958. Le crâne des poissons. *In* P.-P. Grassé, ed., Traité de zoologie. Vol. 13, pt. 1, pp. 551–687, figs. 345–443.

Dietz, P. A. 1914. Beiträge zur Kenntnis der Kiefer- und Kiemenbogenmuskulatur der Teleostier. I. Die Kiefer- und Kiemenbogenmuskeln der Acanthopterygier. Mitteilungen aus der Zoologischen Station zu Neapel, vol. 22, pp. 99–162, 45 figs.

Dijkgraaf, S. 1963. The functioning and significance of the lateral line organs. Biological Reviews, vol. 38, pp. 51–105.

Disler, N. N. 1960. Organy chuvstv sistemy bokovoi linii i ikh znachenie rpovedenii ryb. [The Sense Organs of the Lateral Line System and Their Significance in the Behavior of Fishes]. Moscow: Institute of Animal Morphology, Academy of Sciences. 310 pp. [In Russian]

Dunkle, D. H. 1940. The cranial osteology of Notelops brama (Agassiz), an elopid fish from the Cretaceous of Brazil. Lloydia, vol. 3, pp. 157–190, 9 figs.

Eaton, T. H., Jr. 1935. Evolution of the upper jaw mechanism in teleost fishes. Journal of Morphology, vol. 58, pp. 157–172, 2 pls.

Eigenmann, C. H. 1909. Cave Vertebrates of America. Carnegie Institution of Washington, Publication No. 104, ix + 241 pp., 29 pls.

Evans, H. M. 1940. Brain and Body of Fish. London: Blakiston. 164 pp.

Fishelson, L. 1968. Structure of the vertebral column in *Lepadichthys lineatus*, a clingfish associated with crinoids. Copeia, 1968, pp. 859–861, 5 figs.

Flock, A. 1967. Ultrastructure and function in the lateral line organs. *In* P. H. Cahn, ed., Lateral Line Detectors. Pp. 163–197, 19 figs.

Foster, R. 1967. Trends in the evolution of reproductive behavior in killifishes. Studies in Tropical Oceanography No. 5, pp. 549–566, 2 figs.

François, Y. 1956. Quelques particularités de la nageoire dorsale des larves de clupéidés. Bulletin de la Société zoologique de France, vol. 81, pp. 175–182, 6 figs.

Franz, V. 1911. Das Mormyridenhirn. Zoologische Jahrbücher: Abteilung für Anatomie und Ontogenie der Tiere, vol. 32, pp. 465–540, 63 figs.

Fraser-Brunner, A. 1950. The fishes of the family Scombridae. Annals and Magazine of Natural History, ser. 12, vol. 3, pp. 131–189, 35 figs.

—— 1951. The ocean sunfishes (family Molidae). Bulletin of the British Museum (Natural History), Zoology, vol. 1, pp. 89–121, 18 figs.

Freihofer, W. C. 1963. Patterns of the ramus lateralis accessorius and their systematic significance in teleostean fishes. Stanford Ichthyological Bulletin, vol. 8, pp. 80–189, 29 figs.

Fridberg, G., and H. A. Bern. 1968. The urophysis and the caudal neurosecretory system of fishes. Biological Reviews, vol. 43, pp. 175–199, 4 figs.

Frost, G. A. 1930. A comparative study of the otoliths of the neopterygian fishes. Annals and Magazine of Natural History, ser. 5, vol. 9, pp. 621–627.

Fry, F. E. J. 1957. The aquatic respiration of fish. In M. Brown, ed., The Physiology of Fishes. Vol. 1, pp. 1–63, 27 figs.

Gabriel, M. L. 1940. The inflation mechanism of Spheroides maculatus. Biological Bulletin, vol. 79, p. 372.

Gadd, G. E. 1952. Some hydrodynamical aspects of the swimming of snakes and eels. Philosophical Magazine, ser. 7, vol. 43, pp. 663–670, 5 figs.

Gardiner, B. G. 1960. A revision of certain actinopterygian and coelacanth fishes, chiefly from the Lower Lias. Bulletin of the British Museum (Natural History), Geology, vol. 4, pp. 241–384, 8 pls., 81 text figs.

Gegenbaur, C. 1878. Ueber das Kopfskelet von Alepocephalus rostratus, Risso. Gegenbaurs Morphologisches Jahrbuch, vol. 4, suppl., pp. 1–42, 2 pls., 1 text fig.

Goodrich, E. S. 1904. On the dermal fin-rays of fishes, living and extinct. Quarterly Journal of Microscopical Science, vol. 47, pp. 465–522.

—— 1906. Notes on the development, structure and origin of the median and paired fins of fish. Quarterly Journal of Microscopical Science, vol. 50, pp. 333–376.

—— 1909. Cyclostomes and fishes. In R. Lankester, ed., A Treatise on Zoology. Part IX, fasc. 1, xvi + 518 pp., 515 figs.

—— 1930. Studies on the Structure and Development of Vertebrates. London: Macmillan. xxx + 837 pp., 754 figs.

Goody, P. C. 1968. The skull of Enchodus faujasi from the Maastricht of southern Holland. Koninklijke Nederlandse Akademie van Wetenschappen, Amsterdam, Proceedings, ser. B, vol. 71, pp. 209–231, 9 figs.

—— 1969. The relationships of certain Upper Cretaceous teleosts with special reference to the myctophoids. Bulletin of the British Museum (Natural History), Geology, suppl. 7, 255 pp., 102 figs.

Gosline, W. A. 1955. The osteology and relationships of certain gobioid fishes, with particular reference to the genera *Kraemeria* and *Microdesmus*. Pacific Science, vol. 9, pp. 158–170, 7 figs.

—— 1959. Four new species, a new genus, and a new suborder of Hawaiian fishes. Pacific Science, vol. 13, pp. 67–77, 6 figs.

—— 1960*a*. Contributions toward a classification of modern isospondylous fishes. Bulletin of the British Museum (Natural History), Zoology, vol. 6, pp. 327–365, 15 figs.

—— 1960*b*. Mode of life, functional morphology, and the classification of modern teleostean fishes. Systematic Zoology, vol. 8, pp. 160–164.

—— 1960*c*. A new Hawaiian percoid fish, *Suttonia lineata*, with a discussion of its relationships and a definition of the family Grammistidae. Pacific Science, vol. 14, pp. 28–38, 8 figs.

—— 1961. Some osteological features of modern lower teleostean fishes. Smithsonian Miscellaneous Collections, vol. 142, no. 3, pp. 1–42, 8 figs.

—— 1962. Systematic position and relationships of the percesocine fishes. Pacific Science, vol. 16, pp. 207–217, 3 figs.

—— 1963*a*. Considerations regarding the relationships of the percopsiform, cyprinodontiform, and gadiform fishes. Occasional Papers of the Museum of Zoology, University of Michigan, No. 629, 38 pp., 11 figs.

—— 1963*b*. Notes on the osteology and systematic position of *Hypoptychus dybowskii* Steindachner and other elongate perciform fishes. Pacific Science, vol. 17, pp. 90–101, 8 figs.

—— 1965. Teleostean phylogeny. Copeia, 1965, pp. 186–194, 1 fig.

—— 1966*a*. Comments on the classification of the percoid fishes. Pacific Science, vol. 20, pp. 409–418, 2 figs.

—— 1966*b*. The limits of the fish family Serranidae, with notes on other lower percoids. Proceedings of the California Academy of Sciences, vol. 33, pp. 91–112, 10 figs.

—— 1967. Reduction in branchiostegal ray number. Copeia, 1967, pp. 237–239, 1 fig.

—— 1968. The suborders of perciform fishes. Proceedings of the United States National Museum, vol. 124, pp. 1–77, 12 figs.

—— 1969. The morphology and systematic position of the alepocephaloid fishes. Bulletin of the British Museum (Natural History), Zoology, vol. 18, no. 6, pp. 183–218, 14 figs.

—— In press. The Gobiesociformes: a Reinterpretation.

Gosline, W. A., N. B. Marshall, and G. W. Mead. 1966. Order Iniomi: characters and synopsis of families. *In* Fishes of the Western North Atlantic. Yale University. Sears Foundation for Marine Research, Memoir No. 1, pt. 5, pp. 1–18, 6 figs.

Gray, I. E. 1954. Comparative study of the gill area of marine fishes. Biological Bulletin, vol. 107, pp. 219–225.

Gray, J. 1933. Studies in animal locomotion. I. The movement of fish with special reference to the eel. Journal of Experimental Biology, vol. 10, pp. 88–101.

Greenwood, P. H. 1963. The swimbladder in African Notopteridae (Pisces) and its bearing on the taxonomy of the family. Bulletin of the British Museum (Natural History), Zoology, vol. 11, pp. 377–412, 4 pls., 5 figs.

—— 1966. The caudal fin skeleton in osteoglossoid fishes. Annals and Magazine of Natural History, ser. 13, vol. 9, pp. 581–597.

—— 1968. The osteology and relationships of the Denticipitidae, a family of clupeomorph fishes. Bulletin of the British Museum (Natural History), Zoology, vol. 16, pp. 215–273, 34 figs.

Greenwood, P. H., and C. Patterson. 1967. A fossil osteoglossoid fish from Tanzania (E. Africa). Journal of the Linnean Society, Zoology, vol. 47, pp. 211–223, 3 pls., 3 text figs.

Greenwood, P. H., D. E. Rosen, S. H. Weitzman, and G. S. Myers. 1966. Phyletic studies of teleostean fishes, with a provisional classification of living forms. Bulletin of the American Museum of Natural History, vol. 131, pp. 345–455, pls. 21–23, 9 text figs.

Greenwood, P. H., and K. S. Thomson. 1960. The pectoral anatomy of *Pantodon buchholzi* Peters (a freshwater flying fish) and the related Osteoglossidae. Proceedings of the Zoological Society of London, vol. 135, pp. 283–301, 9 figs.

Gregory, W. K. 1933. Fish skulls: a study of the evolution of natural mechanisms. Transactions of the American Philosophical Society, new ser., vol. 23, pp. 75–481, 302 figs.

Grenholm, Å. 1923. Studien über die Flossenmuskulatur der Teleostier. Uppsala Universitets Årsskrift, vol. 2, pp. i–ix, 1–296, 168 figs.

Griffith, J., and C. Patterson. 1963. The structure and relationships of the Jurassic fish *Ichthyokentema purbeckensis*. Bulletin of the British Museum (Natural History), Geology, vol. 8, pp. 1–43, 4 pls., 14 text figs.

Gudger, E. W. 1946. Oral breathing valves in fishes. Journal of Morphology, vol. 79, pp. 263–285, 11 figs.

Günther, K., and K. Deckert. 1953. Morphologisch-anatomische und vergleichend ökologische Untersuchungen über die Leistungen des Viszeralapparates bei Tiefseefischen der Gattung *Cyclothone* (Teleostei, Isospondyli). Zeitschrift für Morphologie und Ökologie der Tiere, vol. 42, pp. 1–66, 25 figs.

—— 1959. Morphologie und Funktion des Kiefer- und Kiemenapparates von Tiefseefischen der Gattungen Malacosteus und Photostomias (Teleostei, Isospondyli, Stomiatoidea, Malacosteidae). Dana-Report No. 49, 54 pp., 33 figs.

Gutman, W. F. 1966. Coelomgliederung, Myomerie und die Frage der Vertebraten-Antezedenten. Zeitschrift für zoologische Systematik und Evolutionsforschung, vol. 4, pp. 13–57, 8 figs.

—— 1967. Das Dermalskelett der fossilen "Panzerfische" funktionell und phylogenetisch interpretiert. Senckenbergiana Lethaea, vol. 48, pp. 277–283, 2 figs.

Haedrich, R. L. 1967. The stromateoid fishes: systematics and classification. Bulletin of the Museum of Comparative Zoology, Harvard, vol. 135, pp. 31–139, 56 figs.

—— 1969. A new family of aberrant stromateoid fishes from the equatorial Indo-Pacific. Dana-Report No. 76, 14 pp., 10 figs.

Harrington, R. W. 1961. Oviparous hermaphroditic fish with internal self-fertilization. Science, vol. 134, pp. 1749–1750.

Harris, G. G., and W. A. van Bergeijk. 1962. Evidence that the lateral line organ responds to near-field displacements of sound sources in the water. Journal of the Acoustical Society of America, vol. 34, pp. 1831–1841.

Harris, J. E. 1938. The role of the fins in the equilibrium of the swimming fish. II. The role of the pelvic fins. Journal of Experimental Biology, vol. 15, pp. 32–47, 7 figs.

—— 1953. Fin patterns and mode of life in fishes. *In* S. M. Marshall and A. P. Orr, eds., Essays in Marine Biology. Pp. 17–28, 4 figs.

Harrison, R. G. 1895. Die Entwicklung der unpaaren und paarigen Flossen der Teleostier. Archiv für mikroskopische Anatomie, vol. 46, pp. 500–576.

Harry, R. R. 1952. Deep-sea fishes of the Bermuda Oceanographic Expeditions. Families Cetomimidae and Rondeletiidae. Zoologica, vol. 37, pp. 55–71, 1 pl., 4 figs.

Hasler, A. D. 1957. The sense organs: olfactory and gustatory senses of fishes. *In* M. E. Brown, ed., The Physiology of Fishes. Vol. 2, pp. 187–209, 9 figs.

Hennig, W. 1966. Phylogenetic Systematics. Urbana: University of Illinois Press. 263 pp.

Henschel, J. 1939. Der Atmungsmechanismus der Teleosteer. Journal du Conseil . . . pour l'exploration de la mer, vol. 14, pp. 249–260.

—— 1941. Neue Untersuchungen über den Atemmechanismus mariner Teleosteer. Helgoländer wissenschaftliche Meeresuntersuchungen, vol. 2, pp. 244–278, 12 figs.

Herrick, C. J. 1908. On the phylogenetic differentiation of the organs of smell and taste. Journal of Comparative Neurology and Psychology, vol. 18, pp. 155–166.

Hertel, H. 1966. Structure, Form, Movement. New York: Reinhold. 251 pp., 297 figs.

Hobson, E. S. 1968. Predatory behavior of some shore fishes in the Gulf of California. United States Fish and Wildlife Service, Bureau of Sport Fisheries and Wildlife, Research Report 73, vi + 92 pp., 26 figs.

Hoedeman, J. J. 1960. Studies on callichthyid fishes. 5. Development of the skull of *Callichthys* and *Hoplosternum* (Pisces - Siluriformes). Bulletin of Aquatic Biology, vol. 2, no. 13 pp. 21–36, figs. 20–31.

Holl, A. 1965. Vergleichende morphologische und histologische Untersuchungen am Geruchsorgan der Knochenfische. Zeitschrift für Morphologie und Ökologie der Tiere, vol. 54, pp. 707–782, 50 figs.

Hollister, G. 1936. Caudal skeleton of Bermuda shallow water fishes. I. Order Isospondyli: Elopidae, Megalopidae, Albulidae, Clupeidae, Dussumieriidae, Engraulidae. Zoologica, vol. 22, pp. 385–399, 18 figs.

Holmgren, N., and E. Stensiö. 1936. Kranium und Visceralskelett der Akranier, Cyclostomen und Fische. *In* L. Bolk, et al., eds., Handbuch der vergleichenden Anatomie der Wirbeltiere. Vol. 4, pp. 233–500, figs. 203–373.

Holstvoogd, C. 1965. The pharyngeal bones and muscles in Teleostei, a taxonomic study. Koninklijke Nederlandse Akademie Van Wetenschappen, Proceedings, ser. C, vol. 68, pp. 209–218, 5 pls., 11 text figs.

Hopson, A. J. A. 1969. A description of the pelagic embryos and larval stages of *Lates niloticus* (L.) (Pisces: Centropomidae) from Lake Chad, with a review of early development in lower percoid fishes. Zoological Journal of the Linnean Society, vol. 48, no. 1, pp. 117–134, 8 figs.

Hubbs, C. L. 1920. A comparative study of the bones forming the opercular series of fishes. Journal of Morphology, vol. 33, pp. 61–71.

—— 1924. Studies of the fishes of the order Cyprinodontes. Miscellaneous Publications of the Museum of Zoology, University of Michigan, no. 13, pp. 1–31, pls. 1–4.

—— 1944. Fin structure and the relationships of the phallostethid fishes. Copeia, 1944, pp. 69–79.

—— 1945. Phylogenetic position of the Citharidae, a family of flatfishes. Miscellaneous Publications of the Museum of Zoology, University of Michigan, no. 63, pp. 1–38.

Hughes, G. M. 1960. A comparative study of gill ventilation in marine teleosts. Journal of Experimental Biology, vol. 37, pp. 28–45, 10 figs.

—— 1963. Comparative Physiology of Vertebrate Respiration. Cambridge: Harvard University Press. xii + 146 pp., 39 figs.

Iwai, T. 1967. Structure and development of lateral line cupulae in teleost larvae. *In* P. H. Cahn, ed., Lateral Line Detectors. Pp. 27–43, 9 figs.

Jacobshagen, E. 1911–1913. Untersuchungen über das Darmsystem der Fische und Dipnoer. Jenaische Zeitschrift für Naturwissenschaft, vol. 47, pp. 529–568, 3 figs.; and vol. 49, pp. 373–810, pl. 18, 164 text figs.

Jakubowski, M. 1958. The structure and vascularization of the skin of the pond-loach (*Misgurnus fossilis* L.). Acta Biologica Cracoviensia: sér. Zoologique, vol. 1, pp. 113–126, 4 figs.

—— 1963. Cutaneous sense organs of fishes. 1. The lateral line organs in the stone perch (*Acerina cernua* L.). Acta Biologica Cracoviensia, sér. Zoologique, vol. 6, pp. 59–78, pls. 8–11, 5 text figs.

Jarvik, E. 1944. On the exoskeletal shoulder-girdle of teleostomian fishes. Kungliga Svenska Vetenskapsakademiens Handlingar, ser. 3, vol. 21, no. 7, pp. 1–32.

—— 1954. On the visceral skeleton in *Eusthenopteron* with a discussion of the parasphenoid and palatoquadrate in fishes. Kungliga Svenska Vetenskapsakademiens Handlingar, ser. 4, vol. 5, no. 1, 104 pp., 47 figs.

—— 1959. Dermal fin-rays and Holmgren's principle of delamination. Kungliga Svenska Vetenskapsakademiens Handlingar, ser. 4, vol. 6, no. 1, pp. 3–50, 5 pls., 22 text figs.

John, K. R. 1957. Observations on the behavior of blind and blinded fishes. Copeia, 1957, pp. 123–132.

Jones, F. R. H., and N. B. Marshall. 1953. The structure and functions of the teleostean swim bladder. Biological Reviews, vol. 28, pp. 16–83, 7 figs.

Jordan, D. S. 1923. Classification of fishes including families and genera as far as known. Stanford University Publications, University Series, Biological Sciences, vol. 3, pp. 77–243.

Jungersen, H. F. E. 1908. Ichthyotomical contributions. I. The structure of the genera *Amphisile* and *Centriscus*. Mémoires de l'Académie des sciences et des lettres de Danemark, ser. 7, Sciences, vol. 6, pp. 41–109, 2 pls., 33 text figs.

—— 1910. Ichthyotomical contributions. II. The structure of the *Aulostomidae, Syngnathidae* and *Solenostomidae*. Mémoires de l'Académie des sciences et des lettres de Danemark, ser. 7, Sciences, vol. 8, pp. 269–363, 7 pls.

Kirkhoff, H. 1958. Funktionell-anatomische Untersuchung des Visceralapparates von *Clupea harengus* L. Zoologische Jahrbücher: Abteilung für Anatomie und Ontogenie der Tiere, vol. 76, pp. 461–540, 63 figs.

Kishinouye, K. 1923. Contributions to the comparative study of the so-called scombroid fishes. Journal of the College of Agriculture, University of Tokyo, vol. 8, pp. 293–475, pls. 13–34, 26 text figs.

Kleerekoper, H. 1967. Some aspects of olfaction in fishes, with special reference to orientation. American Zoologist, vol. 7, pp. 385–395, 13 figs.

—— 1969. Olfaction in Fishes. Bloomington: Indiana University Press. viii + 222 pp., 24 pls., 86 text figs.

Koumans, F. P. 1931. A Preliminary Revision of the Genera of the Gobioid Fishes with United Ventral Fins. Lisse: Drukkerij "Imperator." 174 pp.

Kuiper, J. W. 1967. Frequency characteristics and functional significance of the lateral line organ. *In* P. J. Cahn, ed., Lateral Line Detectors. Pp. 105–117, 6 figs.

Leiner, M. 1937. Die Physiologie der Fischatmung. Bronn's Klassen und Ordnungen des Tierreichs, vol. 6, pt. 1, book 2, sect. 1, pp. 827–910, figs. 707–756.

Leong, R. J. H., and C. P. O'Connell. 1969. A laboratory study of particulate and filter feeding of the northern anchovy (*Engraulis mordax*). Journal of the Fisheries Research Board of Canada, vol. 26, pp. 557–582, 6 figs.

Liem, K. F. 1961. Tetrapod parallelisms and other features in the functional morphology of the blood vascular system of *Fluta alba* Zuiew (Pisces: Teleostei). Journal of Morphology, vol. 108, pp. 131–143, 6 figs.

—— 1963. The comparative osteology and phylogeny of the Anabantoidei (Teleostei, Pisces). Illinois Biological Monographs, No. 30, viii + 149 pp., 104 figs.

—— 1968. Geographical and taxonomic variation in the pattern of natural sex reversal in the teleost fish order Synbranchiformes. Journal of Zoology, vol. 156, pp. 225–238, 3 figs.

Liermann, K. 1933. Über den Bau des Geruchsorgans der Teleostier. Zeitschrift für Anatomie und Entwicklungsgeschichte, vol. 100, pp. 1–39, 17 figs.

Lissman, H. W. 1961. Ecological studies on gymnotids. *In* Carlos Chagas and

Antonio Paes de Carvalho, eds., Symposium on Comparative Bioelectrogenesis, Rio de Janeiro, 1959, Proceedings. Bioelectrogenesis, a Comparative Survey of Its Mechanisms with Particular Emphasis on Electric Fishes. Pp. 215–223.

—— 1963. Electric location by fishes. Scientific American, March, 1963, pp. 50–59, figs.

Lissman, H. W., and K. E. Machin. 1958. The mechanism of object location in *Gymnarchus niloticus* and similar fish. Journal of Experimental Biology, vol. 35, pp. 451–486, 21 figs.

Maheshwari, S. C. 1967. The head skeleton of *Mastacembelus armatus* (Lacep.). Journal of the Zoological Society of India, vol. 8, pp. 107–118, 7 figs.

Makushok, V. M. 1961. [Some peculiarities in the structure of the seismosensory system in northern blennioid fishes (Stichaeoidae, Blennioidei, Pisces)]. Trudy Instituta Okeanologii, vol. 43, pp. 225–269, 9 figs. [In Russian]

Mansueti, A. J., and J. D. Hardy, Jr. 1967. Development of Fishes of the Chesapeake Bay Region. An Atlas of Egg, Larval, and Juvenile Stages. Part 1. Natural Resources Institute, University of Maryland. 202 pp., 90 figs.

Manton, S. M. 1959. Functional morphology and the evolution of diagnostic characters of arthropodian groups. Proceedings of the XVth International Congress of Zoology, London, pp. 390–393.

Marshall, N. B. 1953. Egg size in Arctic, Antarctic and deep-sea fishes. Evolution, vol. 7, pp. 328–341.

—— 1954. Aspects of Deep-Sea Biology. New York: Philosophical Library. 380 pp., illus.

—— 1955. Alepisauroid fishes. Discovery Reports, vol. 27, pp. 303–336, pl. 19, text figs.

—— 1960. Swimbladder structure of deep-sea fishes in relation to their systematics and biology. Discovery Reports, vol. 31, pp. 1–121, 47 figs.

—— 1961. A young *Macristium* and the ctenothrissid fishes. Bulletin of the British Museum (Natural History), Zoology, vol. 7, pp. 353–370, 4 figs.

—— 1962a. The biology of sound-producing fishes. Symposia of the Zoological Society of London No. 7, pp. 45–60.

—— 1962b. Observations on the Heteromi, an order of teleost fishes. Bulletin of the British Museum (Natural History), Zoology, vol. 9, pp. 251–270, 5 figs.

—— 1965a. The Life of Fishes. London: Weidenfeld and Nicolson. 402 pp., 86 figs.

—— 1965b. Systematic and biological studies of the macrourid fishes (Anacanthini-Teleostei). Deep-Sea Research, vol. 12, pp. 229–322, 9 figs.

—— 1967. The olfactory organs of bathypelagic fishes. Symposia of the Zoological Society of London No. 19, pp. 57–70.

Matsubara, K. 1943. Studies on the scorpaenoid fishes of Japan. Transactions of the Sigenkagaku Kenyusyo, nos. 1 and 2, 486 pp., 3 pls., 156 figs.

—— 1955. [Fish Morphology and Hierarchy.] Tokyo: Ishizaki Shoten. 1605 pp., 135 pls., 536 text figs. [In Japanese]

—— 1963. Fishes. *In* [Animal Systematic Taxonomy]. Vol. 9, pt. 2, Vertebrata (Ib). Pp. 197–531, figs. 197–657. [In Japanese]

Matthes, H. 1963. A comparative study of the feeding mechanisms of some African Cyprinidae (Pisces, Cypriniformes). Bijdragen tot de dierkunde, vol. 33, pp. 1–35, 12 pls.

Maul, G. E. 1954. Monografia dos peixes do Museu Municipal do Funchal. Ordem Berycomorphi. Boletim do Museu municipal do Funchal, no. 7, art. 17, pp. 5–41, 15 figs.

McAllister, D. E. 1968. Evolution of branchiostegals and classification of teleostome fishes. National Museum of Canada Bulletin 221, pp. i–xiv, 1–239, 21 pls., 3 text figs.

McCully, H. H. 1961. The comparative anatomy of the scales of the serranid fishes. Dissertation Abstracts, vol. 22, no. 5, 3 pp.

McDowall, R. M. 1969. Relationships of galaxioid fishes with a further discussion of salmoniform classification. Copeia, 1969, pp. 796–824, 10 figs.

Mead, G. W. 1965. The larval form of the Heteromi. Breviora, vol. 226, pp. 1–5, 1 fig.

Mead, G. W., E. Bertelsen, and D. M. Cohen. 1964. Reproduction among deep-sea fishes. Deep-Sea Research, vol. 11, pp. 569–596.

Mead, G. W., and G. E. Maul. 1958. *Taractes asper* and the systematic relationships of the Steinegeriidae and Trachyberycidae. Bulletin of the Museum of Comparative Zoology, Harvard, vol. 119, pp. 393–417, 1 pl., 7 text figs.

Miller, R. R. 1945. *Hyporhamphus patris,* a new species of hemiramphid fish from Sinaloa, Mexico, with an analysis of the generic characters of *Hyporhamphus* and *Hemiramphus.* Proceedings of the United States National Museum, vol. 96, pp. 185–193, pl. 11, text fig. 9.

Monod, T. 1960. A propos du *pseudobrachium* des *Antennarius* (Pisces, Lophiiformes). Bulletin de l'Institut Français d'Afrique Noire, ser. A, vol. 22, pp. 620–698, 83 figs.

—— 1967. Le complexe urophore des Téléostéens: typologie et évolution (note préliminaire). Colloques internationaux du Centre national de la recherche scientifique, no. 163, pp. 111–131, 16 figs.

—— 1968. Le complexe urophore des poissons téléostéens. Mémoires de l'Institut Fondamental d'Afrique Noire, No. 81, vi + 705 pp., 989 figs.

Moore, G. A. 1950. The cutaneous sense organs of barbeled minnows adapted to life in the muddy waters of the Great Plains region. Transactions of the American Microscopical Society, vol. 69, pp. 69–95, 20 figs.

Morrow, J. E. 1964. Suborder Stomiatoidea. General discussion and key to families. *In* Fishes of the Western North Atlantic. Yale University. Sears Foundation for Marine Research. Memoir No. 1, pt. 4, pp. 71–76.

Moy-Thomas, J. A. 1940. The Devonian fish *Palaeospondylus gunni* Traquair. Philosophical Transactions of the Royal Society of London, ser. B, vol. 230, pp. 391–413, pls. 22–25, 7 text figs.

Munk, O. 1966. Ocular anatomy of some deep-sea teleosts. Dana-Report No. 70, 71 pp., 16 pls., 27 text figs.

Myers, G. S., and W. C. Freihofer. 1966. Megalomycteridae, a previously unrecognized family of deep-sea cetomimiform fishes based on two new genera from the North Atlantic. Stanford Ichthyological Bulletin, vol. 8, pp. 193–201, 5 figs.

Nelson, E. M. 1955. The morphology of the swim bladder and auditory bulla in the Holocentridae. Fieldiana, Zoology, vol. 37, pp. 121–137, 3 pls.

Nelson, G. J. 1966. Gill arches of teleostean fishes of the order Anguilliformes. Pacific Science, vol. 20, pp. 391–408, 58 figs.

—— 1967a. Branchial muscles in representatives of five eel families. Pacific Science, vol. 21, pp. 348–363, 12 figs.

—— 1967b. Branchial muscles of some generalized teleostean fishes. Acta Zoologica, vol. 48, pp. 277–288, 2 figs.

—— 1967c. Epibranchial organs in lower teleostean fishes. Journal of Zoology, vol. 153, pp. 71–89, 1 pl., 3 figs.

—— 1968. Gill arches of teleostean fishes of the division Osteoglossomorpha. Journal of the Linnean Society, Zoology, vol. 47, pp. 261–277, 11 figs.

—— 1969a. Gill arches and the phylogeny of fishes, with notes on the classification of vertebrates. Bulletin of the American Museum of Natural History, vol. 141, pp. 479–552, pls. 79–92, 26 text figs.

—— 1969b. Infraorbital bones and their bearing on the phylogeny and geography of osteoglossomorph fishes. American Museum Novitates No. 2394, 37 pp., 22 figs.

Nichols, J. T., and C. M. Breder. 1928. An annotated list of the Synentognathi with remarks on their development and relationships. Zoologica, vol. 8, pp. 423–448.

Nielsen, E. 1942. Studies on Triassic fishes. I. Meddelelser om Grønland, vol. 138, pp. 1–394, 30 pls., 78 figs.

Nielsen, J. G., and V. Larsen. 1968. Synopsis of the Bathylaconidae (Pisces, Isospondyli), with a new eastern Pacific species. Galathea Report, vol. 9, pp. 221–238, pls. 13–15, 10 text figs.

Norden, C. R. 1961. Comparative osteology of representative salmonid fishes, with particular reference to the grayling (*Thymallus arcticus*) and its phylogeny. Journal of the Fishery Research Board of Canada, vol. 18, pp. 679–791, 16 pls., 2 text figs.

Norman, J. R. 1934. A Systematic Monograph of the Flatfishes (Heterosomata). Vol. 1. London: British Museum (Natural History). viii + 459 pp., 317 figs.

Nursall, J. R. 1962a. The caudal musculature of *Hoplopagrus guntheri* Gill (Perciformes: Lutjanidae). Canadian Journal of Zoology, vol. 41, pp. 865–880, 6 figs.

—— 1962b. Swimming and the origin of paired appendages. American Zoologist, vol. 2, pp. 127–141, 8 figs.

—— 1963. The hypurapophysis, an important element of the caudal skeleton. Copeia, 1963, pp. 458–459, 1 fig.

Nybelin, O. 1956. Les canaux sensoriels du museau chez *Elops saurus*. Arkiv för zoologi, ser. 2, vol. 10, pp. 453–458, 3 figs.

—— 1961. Über die Frage der Abstammung der rezenten primitiver Teleostier. Paläontologische Zeitschrift, vol. 35, pp. 114–117.

—— 1968. The dentition in the mouth cavity of *Elops. In* T. Ørvig, ed., Current Problems of Lower Vertebrate Phylogeny. Pp. 439–443, 3 figs.

Nysten, M. 1962. Étude anatomique des rapports de la vessie aérienne avec l'axe vertébral chez *Pantodon buchholzi* Peters. Annales du Musée Royale de l'Afrique Central, ser. 8, Sciences Zoologiques, pp. 187–220.

Ochiai, A. 1959. Morphology, Taxonomy and Ecology of the Soles of Japan. Mimeographed. 236 pp., 2 pls. [In Japanese]

—— 1963. Fauna Japonica, Soleina (Pisces). Tokyo: Biogeographical Society of Japan. 114 pp., 24 pls.

Orton, G. L. 1963. Notes on larval anatomy of fishes of the order Lyomeri. Copeia, 1963, pp. 6–15, 4 figs.

Ørvig, T. 1958. *Pycnaspis splendens*, new genus, new species, a new ostracoderm from the Upper Ordovician of North America. Proceedings of the United States National Museum, vol. 108, no. 3391, pp. 1–23, 3 pls., 5 text figs.

—— 1967. Phylogeny of tooth tissues: evolution of some calcified tissues in early vertebrates. *In* A. E. W. Miles, ed., Structural and Chemical Organization of Teeth. Vol. 1, pp. 45–110, 53 figs.

Parin, N. V. 1961. [Principles of classification of flying fishes.] Trudy Instituta Okeanologii, Akademiya Nauk SSSR, vol. 43, pp. 92–183, 45 figs. [In Russian]

Parr, A. E. 1929. A contribution to the osteology and classification of the orders Iniomi and Xenoberyces. Occasional Papers of the Bingham Oceanographic Collection, no. 2, 45 pp.

—— 1930*a*. Jugostegalia, an accessory skeleton in the gill cover of the eels of the genus *Myrophis*. Copeia, 1930, pp. 71–73, fig. 2.

—— 1930*b*. A note on the classification of the stomiatoid fishes. Copeia, 1930, p. 136.

—— 1933. Deep sea Berycomorphi and Percomorphi from the waters around the Bahama and Bermuda islands. Bulletin of the Bingham Oceanographic Collection, vol. 3, pt. 6, pp. 1–51, 22 figs.

—— 1934. Report on experimental use of a triangular trawl for bathypelagic collecting. Bulletin of the Bingham Oceanographic Collection, vol. 4, pt. 6, pp. 1–59.

Patterson, C. 1964. A review of Mesozoic acanthopterygian fishes, with special reference to those of the English Chalk. Philosophical Transactions of the Royal Society of London, ser. B, vol. 247, pp. 213–482, 114 figs.

—— 1967*a*. Are the teleosts a polyphyletic group? Colloques internationaux du Centre national de la recherche scientifique, no. 163, pp. 93–109, 11 figs.

—— 1967*b*. New Cretaceous berycoid fishes from Lebanon. Bulletin of the

British Museum (Natural History), Geology, vol. 14, pp. 69–109, 4 pls., 11 text figs.

—— 1967c. A second specimen of the Cretaceous teleost *Protobrama* and the relationships of the sub-order Tselfatioidei. Arkiv för zoologi, ser. 2, vol. 19, pp. 215–234, 8 figs.

—— 1968a. The caudal skeleton in Lower Liassic pholidophoroid fishes. Bulletin of the British Museum (Natural History), Geology, vol. 16, pp. 203–239, 5 pls., 12 text figs.

—— 1968b. The caudal skeleton in Mesozoic acanthopterygian fishes. Bulletin of the British Museum (Natural History), Geology, vol. 17, pp. 49–102, 28 figs.

Peyer, B. 1968. Comparative Odontology. Chicago: University of Chicago Press. xiv + 347 pp., 8 colored pls., 88 black and white pls., 220 text figs.

Pfeiffer, W. 1963. Alarm substances. Experientia, vol. 19, pp. 113–123, 10 figs.

—— 1967. Schreckreaktion und Schreckstoffzellen bei Ostariophysi und Gonorhynchiformes. Zeitschrift für vergleichende Physiologie, vol. 56, pp. 380–396, 6 figs.

Pfüller, A. 1914. Beiträge zur Kenntniss der Seitensinnesorgane und Kopfana-tomie der Macruriden. Jenaische Zeitschrift für Naturwissenschaft, vol. 52 (45 of new series), pp. 1–132, 2 pls., 38 text figs.

Pipping, M. 1927. Der Geruchssin der Fische mit besonderer Berücksichtigung seiner Bedeutung für das Aufsuchung des Futters. Commentationes biologicae (Societas scientiarum Fennica), vol. 2, no. 4, 28 pp., 2 figs.

Poulsen, T. C. 1963. Cave adaptations in amblyopsoid fishes. American Midland Naturalist, vol. 70, pp. 257–290, 4 figs.

Quast, J. C. 1965. Osteological characteristics and affinities of the hexa-grammid fishes. Proceedings of the California Academy of Sciences, ser. 4, vol. 31, pp. 563–600, 3 figs.

Rass, T. S. 1941. Analogous or parallel variations in structure and development of fishes in northern and Arctic seas. Jubilee Publications of the Moscow Society of Naturalists 1805–1940, pp. 1–60. (Not seen; cited from Marshall, 1953.)

Rayner, D. M. 1948. The structure of certain Jurassic holostean fishes with special reference to their neurocrania. Philosophical Transactions of the Royal Society of London, ser. B, vol. 233, pp. 287–345, pls. 1–4.

Regan, C. T. 1903. On the systematic position and classification of the gadoid or anacanthine fishes. Annals and Magazine of Natural History, ser. 7, vol. 11, pp. 459–466, 2 figs.

—— 1907. On the anatomy, classification and systematic position of the teleostean fishes of the suborder Allotriognathi. Proceedings of the Zoological Society of London, 1907, pt. 2, pp. 634–643, figs. 166–171.

—— 1910a. The anatomy and classification of the teleostean fishes of the order Zeomorphi. Annals and Magazine of Natural History, ser. 8, vol. 6, pp. 481–484.

—— 1910b. On the caudal fin of the Clupeidae, and on the teleostean urostyle. Annals and Magazine of Natural History, ser. 8, vol. 5, pp. 531–533, 2 figs.

—— 1910c. The origin and evolution of the teleostean fishes of the order Heterosomata. Annals and Magazine of Natural History, ser. 8, vol. 6, pp. 484–496, 3 figs.

—— 1911a. The anatomy and classification of the teleostean fishes of the order Iniomi. Annals and Magazine of Natural History, ser. 8, vol. 7, pp. 120–131.

—— 1911b. The anatomy and classification of the teleostean fishes of the orders Berycomorphi and Xenoberyces. Annals and Magazine of Natural History, ser. 8, vol. 7, pp. 1–9, 1 pl., 2 text figs.

—— 1911c. The classification of the teleostean fishes of the order Synentognathi. Annals and Magazine of Natural History, ser. 8, vol. 7, pp. 327–334, pl. 9, 1 text fig.

—— 1911d. The osteology and classification of the gobioid fishes. Annals and Magazine of Natural History, ser. 8, vol. 8, pp. 729–733, 2 figs.

—— 1911e. The osteology and classification of the teleostean fishes of the order Microcyprini. Annals and Magazine of Natural History, ser. 8, vol. 7, pp. 320–327, pl. 8.

—— 1911f. On the systematic position of *Macristium chavesi*. Annals and Magazine of Natural History, ser. 8, vol. 7, pp. 204–205.

—— 1912a. The classification of the teleostean fishes of the order Pediculati. Annals and Magazine of Natural History, ser. 8, vol. 9, pp. 277–289, 6 figs.

—— 1912b. Notes on the classification of the teleostean fishes. Proceedings of the 7th International Zoological Congress, Boston, 1907, pp. 838–853.

—— 1912c. The osteology and classification of the teleostean fishes of the order Apodes. Annals and Magazine of Natural History, ser. 8, vol. 10, pp. 377–387, 2 figs.

—— 1912d. The osteology of the teleostean fishes of the order Opisthomi. Annals and Magazine of Natural History, ser. 8, vol. 9, pp. 217–219.

—— 1913a. The classification of the percoid fishes. Annals and Magazine of Natural History, ser. 8, vol. 12, pp. 111–145.

—— 1913b. The osteology and classification of the teleostean fishes of the order Scleroparei. Annals and Magazine of Natural History, ser. 8, vol. 11, pp. 169–184, 5 figs.

—— 1922. The distribution of the fishes of the order Ostariophysi. Bijdragen tot de Dierkunde, vol. 22, pp. 203–207.

—— 1923. The fishes of the family Icosteidae. Annals and Magazine of Natural History, ser. 9, vol. 11, pp. 610–612.

—— 1924. The morphology of a rare oceanic fish, *Stylophorus chordatus*, Shaw. Proceedings of the Royal Society, London, ser. B, vol. 96, pp. 193–207.

—— 1929. Fishes. *In* Encyclopaedia Britannica. 14th ed., vol. 9, pp. 305–328.

—— 1936. Natural History. London: Ward Lock & Co. 896 pp., illus.

Reno, H. W. 1969. Cephalic lateral-line systems of the cyprinid genus *Hybopsis*. Copeia, 1969, pp. 736–773, 32 figs.

Retzius, M. G. 1881. Das Gehörorgan der Wirbelthiere. Vol. 1. Das Gehörorgan der Fische und Amphibien. Stockholm. 150 pp., 24 pls.

Ride, W. D. L. 1954. A possible selective mechanism in the evolution of the vertebrate heart. Proceedings of the Zoological Society of London, vol. 123, pp. 753–755.

Ridewood, W. G. 1904a. On the cranial osteology of the fishes of the families Elopidae and Albulidae, with remarks on the morphology of the skull in the lower teleostean fishes generally. Proceedings of the Zoological Society of London, 1904, pt. 2, pp. 35–81, figs. 8–18.

—— 1904b. On the cranial osteology of the fishes of the families Mormyridae, Notopteridae, and Hyodontidae. Journal of the Linnean Society, Zoology, vol. 29, pp. 188–217, pls. 22–25.

—— 1905a. On the cranial osteology of the clupeoid fishes. Proceedings of the Zoological Society of London, 1904, pt. 2, pp. 448–493, figs. 118–143.

—— 1905b. On the cranial osteology of the families *Osteoglossidae, Pantodontidae,* and *Phractolaemidae.* Journal of the Linnean Society, Zoology, vol. 29, pp. 252–282, pls. 30–32.

—— 1905c. On the skull of *Gonorhynchus greyi.* Annals and Magazine of Natural History, ser. 7, vol. 15, pp. 361–372, pl. 16, 1 text fig.

Rivas, L. R. 1953. The pineal apparatus of tunas and relative scombrid fishes as a possible light receptor controlling phototactic movements. Bulletin of Marine Science of the Gulf and Caribbean, vol. 3, pp. 168–180, 5 figs.

Robertson, J. D. 1957. The habitat of the early vertebrates. Biological Reviews, vol. 32, pp. 156–187.

Robins, C. R. 1966. Additional comments on the structure and relationships of the mirapinniform fish family Kasidoridae. Bulletin of Marine Science, vol. 16, pp. 696–701, 3 figs.

Robins, C. R., and D. P. de Sylva. 1965. The Kasidoridae, a new family of mirapinniform fishes from the western Atlantic Ocean. Bulletin of Marine Science, vol. 15, pp. 189–201, 2 figs.

Rosen, D. E. 1962. Comments on the relationships of the North American cave fishes of the family Amblyopsidae. American Museum Novitates No. 2109, 35 pp., 24 figs.

—— 1964. The relationships and taxonomic position of the halfbeaks, killifishes, silversides, and their relatives. Bulletin of the American Museum of Natural History, vol. 127, pp. 217–268, pls. 14, 15, text figs. 1–23.

Rosen, D. E., and C. Patterson. 1969. The structure and relationships of the paracanthopterygian fishes. Bulletin of the American Museum of Natural History, vol. 141, pp. 357–474, pls. 52–78, text figs. 1–74.

Sagemehl, M. 1885. Beiträge zur vergleichenden Anatomie der Fische. III. Das Cranium der Characiniden nebst allgemeinen Bemerkungen über die mit einem Weber'schen Apparat versehenen Physostomenfamilien. Gegenbaurs morphologisches Jahrbuch, vol. 10, pp. 1–119, pls. 1, 2.

—— 1891. Beiträge zur vergleichenden Anatomie der Fische. IV. Das Cranium der Cyprinoiden. Gegenbaurs morphologisches Jahrbuch, vol. 17, pp. 489–595, 3 pls.

Saunders, R. L. 1961. The irrigation of the gills of fishes. I. Studies of the mechanism of branchial irrigation. Canadian Journal of Zoology, vol. 39, pp. 637–653, 9 figs.

Schaeffer, B. 1961. Differential ossification in the fishes. Transactions of the New York Academy of Sciences, ser. 2, vol. 23, pp. 501–505.

Schaeffer, B., and D. E. Rosen. 1961. Major adaptive levels in the evolution of the actinopterygian feeding mechanism. American Zoologist, vol. 1, pp. 187–204, 7 figs.

Schemmel, C. 1967. Vergleichende Untersuchungen an den Hautsinnes-organen ober- und unterirdisch lebender *Astyanax* Formen. Zeitschrift für Morphologie und Ökologie der Tiere, vol. 61, pp. 255–316, 25 figs.

Schultz, L. P. 1948. A revision of six subfamilies of atherine fishes, with descriptions of new genera and species. Proceedings of the United States National Museum, vol. 98, pp. 1–48, pls. 1, 2.

—— 1958. Review of the parrotfishes family Scaridae. United States National Museum Bulletin 214, 143 pp., 27 pls., 30 text figs.

Schultz, L. P., et al. 1953. Fishes of the Marshall and Marianas islands. United States National Museum Bulletin 202, vol. 1, xxxii + 685 pp., 74 pls., 90 figs.

Schultz, L. P., and E. M. Stern. 1948. The Ways of Fishes. New York: Van Nostrand. xii + 264 pp., 80 figs.

Schwartz, E. 1965. Bau und Funktion der Seitenlinie des Streifhechtlings *Aplocheilus lineatus.* Zeitschrift für vergleichende Physiologie, vol. 50, pp. 55–87.

Sethi, R. P. 1960. Osteology and Phylogeny of Oviparous Cyprinodont Fishes (order Cyprinodontiformes). Ph.D. thesis, University of Florida. Repro-duced by University Microfilms, Ann Arbor, Michigan. Mic 60–1909, xiii + 275 pp., 59 figs.

Sewertzoff, A. N. 1926. Die Morphologie der Brustflosse der Fische. Jenaische Zeitschrift für Naturwissenschaft, vol. 62 (55 of new series), pp. 343–392, 26 figs.

—— 1934. Evolution der Bauchflossen der Fische. Zoologische Jahrbücher, Abteilung für Anatomie und Ontogenie, vol. 58, pp. 415–500, 59 figs.

Simpson, G. G. 1959. Mesozoic mammals and the polyphyletic origin of mammals. Evolution, vol. 13, pp. 405–414.

Souché, G. 1932. Morphologie comparative des muscles élévateurs de la mandibule chez les poissons. Mémoires de la Société des sciences physiques et naturelles de Bordeaux, vol. 3, no. 2, pp. 1–292, 3 pls., 191 text figs.

Starks, E. C. 1899. The osteological characters of the suborder Percesoces. Proceedings of the United States National Museum, vol. 22, pp. 1–10, pls. 1–3.

—— 1904a. The osteology of *Dallia pectoralis.* Zoologische Jahrbücher, Abteilung für Systematik, vol. 21, pp. 249–262, 2 figs.

―――― 1904b. A synopsis of characters of some fishes belonging to the order Haplomi. Biological Bulletin, vol. 7, pp. 254–262.

―――― 1923. The osteology and relationships of the uranoscopoid fishes. Stanford University Publications, University Series, Biological Sciences, vol. 3, pp. 259–290, 5 pls.

―――― 1930. The primary shoulder girdle of the bony fishes. Stanford University Publications, University Series, Biological Sciences, vol. 6, pp. 149–239, 38 figs.

Stensiö, E. A. 1947. The sensory lines and dermal bones of the cheek in fishes and amphibians. Kungliga Svenska Vetenskapsakademiens Handlingar, ser. 3, vol. 24, no. 3, 195 pp., 38 figs.

―――― 1958. Les cyclostomes fossiles ou ostracoderms. In P.-P. Grassé, ed., Traité de zoologie. Vol. 13, pt. 1, pp. 172–425, figs. 107–219.

―――― 1963. Anatomical studies on the arthrodiran head. Pt. I. Kungliga Svenska Vetenskapsakademiens Handlingar, ser. 4, vol. 9, no. 2, pp. 1–419, 62 pls., 124 text figs.

Stokell, G. 1941. A revision of the genus Retropinna. Records of the Canterbury Museum, vol. 7, pp. 361–372, pls. 55–57.

Studnicka, F. K. 1916. Über den Knochen von Orthagoriscus. Anatomischer Anzeiger, vol. 49, pp. 151–169, 177–194.

Sufi, S. M. K. 1956. A revision of the Oriental fishes of the family Mastacembelidae. Bulletin of the Raffles Museum, no. 27, pp. 92–146, pls. 13–26.

Suyehiro, Y. 1942. A study of the digestive system and feeding habits of fish. Japanese Journal of Zoology, vol. 10, pp. 1–303, 15 pls., 190 text figs.

Svetovidov, A. N. 1946. [Morphological principles of the classification of the Gadidae.] Akademiya Nauk SSSR, Izvestiya, Seriya Biologicheskaya [Bulletin of the Academy of Sciences, USSR, Biology], 1946, pts. 2–3, pp. 183–198, 4 figs. [In Russian with English summary]

―――― 1948. Gadiformes. Fauna of the USSR, Fishes, vol. 9, no. 4, 222 pp., 72 pls., 39 text figs. [In Russian; English translation by Israel Program for Scientific Translations, 1962]

―――― 1952. Clupeidae. Fauna of the USSR, Fishes, vol. 2, no. 1, 323 pp., 52 pls., 52 text figs. [In Russian; English translation by Israel Program for Scientific Translations, 1963]

―――― 1953. [Materials on the structure of the fish brain. 1. Structure of the brain of codfishes.] Trudy Zoologicheskogo Instituta, Akademiya Nauk SSSR, vol. 13, pp. 390–412, 25 figs. [In Russian]

―――― 1968. Peculiarities in the microscopic structure of the cerebellum in Eleginus navaga (Pallas) and Gadus morhua marisailbi Derjugin in respect to their mode of life. Zoologicheskii Zhurnal, vol. 47, no. 12, pp. 1823–1828. [In Russian, with English summary]

Szabo, T. 1965. Sense organs of the lateral line system in some electric fish of the Gymnotidae, Mormyridae and Gymnarchidae. Journal of Morphology, vol. 117, pp. 229–249, 12 figs.

Takahasi, N. 1925. On the homology of the cranial muscles of the cypriniform fishes. Journal of Morphology and Physiology, vol. 40, pp. 1–103, 3 pls., 20 text figs.

Taverne, L. 1967. Le squelette caudal des Mormyriformes et des Ostéoglossomorphes. Bulletin de la Classe des sciences de l'Académie Royale de Belgique, ser. 5, vol. 53, pp. 663–678, 10 figs.

Tavolga, W. N., and J. Wodinsky. 1963. Auditory capacities in fishes. Bulletin of the American Museum of Natural History, vol. 126, pp. 177–239, 24 figs.

Taylor, G. 1952. Analysis of the swimming of long and narrow animals. Proceedings of the Royal Society of London, ser. A, vol. 214, pp. 158–183, 12 figs.

Tchernavin, V. V. 1938. The absorption of bones in the skull of the salmon during their migration to rivers. Fishery Board for Scotland, Salmon Fisheries, 1938, no. 6, 4 pp.

—— 1947. Six specimens of Lyomeri in the British Museum (with notes on the skeleton of Lyomeri). Journal of the Linnean Society, Zoology, vol. 41, pp. 287–350, 3 pls., 15 text figs.

—— 1948. On the mechanical working of the head of bony fishes. Proceedings of the Zoological Society of London, vol. 118, pp. 129–143, 11 figs.

—— 1949. On the lateral line system of some cyprinodonts. Annals and Magazine of Natural History, ser. 11, vol. 13, pp. 429–432.

—— 1953. The Feeding Mechanisms of the Deep Sea Fish *Chauliodus sloani* Schneider. London: British Museum (Natural History). viii + 101 pp., 10 pls., 53 text figs.

Teichman, H. 1962. Die Chemorezeption der Fische. Ergebnisse der Biologie, vol. 25, pp. 177–205, 2 figs.

Te Winkel, L. E. 1935. A study of Mistichthys luzonensis with special reference to conditions correlated with reduced size. Journal of Morphology, vol. 58, pp. 463–509, 13 pls.

Thorp, C. H. 1969. A new species of myrapinniform fish (family Kasidoridae) from the western Indian Ocean. Journal of Natural History, vol. 3, pp. 61–70, 4 figs.

Thorson, G. 1950. Reproduction and larval ecology of marine bottom invertebrates. Biological Reviews, vol. 25, pp. 1–25.

Thys van den Audenaerde, D. F. E. 1961. L'anatomie de *Phractolaemus ansorgei* Blgr. et la position systématique des Phractolaemidae. Annales du Musée Royale de l'Afrique Central, ser. 8vo, Sciences zoologiques, no. 103, pp. 101–167, 9 pls., 27 text figs.

Tretiakov, D. K. 1944.[Outlines of the Phylogeny of Fishes.] Akademiya Nauk SSSR. 176 pp. [In Russian]

Trewavas, E. 1932. A contribution to the classification of the fishes of the order Apodes, based on the osteology of some rare eels. Proceedings of the Zoological Society of London, 1932, pp. 639–659, 4 pls., 6 text figs.

Tucker, D. W. 1954. Fishes. Part I. *In* The "Rosaura" Expedition, Bulletin of the British Museum (Natural History), Zoology, vol. 2, no. 6, pp. 163–214, 19 text figs, pls. 7, 8.

Tuge, H., K. Uchihashi, and H. Shimamure. 1968. An Atlas of the Brains of the Fishes of Japan. Tokyo: Tsukiji Shokan Publishing Co. 240 pp., illus.

Tyler, J. C. 1968. A monograph on plectognath fishes of the superfamily Triacanthoidea. Academy of Natural Sciences of Philadelphia Monograph 16, 364 pp., 209 figs.

van Bergeijk, W. A. 1967. The evolution of vertebrate hearing. *In* W. Neff, ed., Contributions to Sensory Physiology. Vol. 2.

Van Dobben, W. H. 1935. Über den Kiefermechanismus der Knochenfische. Archives néerlandaises de zoologie, vol. 2, pp. 1–72, 50 figs.

Vetter, B. 1878. Untersuchungen zur vergleichenden Anatomie der Kiemen- und Kiefermusculatur der Fische. II. Theil. Jenaische Zeitschrift für Naturwissenschaft, vol. 12, pp. 431–550, pls. 12–14.

Walls, G. L. 1942. The Vertebrate Eye and Its Adaptive Radiation. Cranbrook Institute of Science. Bulletin No. 19, xiv + 785 pp., 196 figs.

Walters, V. 1961. A contribution to the biology of the Giganturidae, with description of a new genus and species. Bulletin of the Museum of Comparative Zoology, Harvard, vol. 125, pp. 297–319, 7 figs.

——— 1964. Order Giganturoidei. Yale University. Sears Foundation for Marine Research, Memoir No. 1, pt. 4, pp. 566–577, figs. 152–155.

Wassnetzov, W. W. 1935. Zur Morphologie der Fettflosse. Travaux du Laboratoire de morphologie évolutive, Institut de Morphologie Évolutive et de Palaeozoologie, Academie des Sciences de l'URSS, Moscou, vol. 2, pt. 3, pp. 53–75, 20 figs. [In Russian, with German summary]

Weisel, G. F. 1968. The salmonoid adipose fin. Copeia, 1968, pp. 626–627, 3 figs.

Weitzman, S. H. 1962. The osteology of *Brycon meeki*, a generalized characid fish, with an osteological definition of the family. Stanford Ichthyological Bulletin, vol. 8, no. 1, pp. 1–77, 21 figs.

——— 1964. Osteology and relationships of South American characid fishes of subfamilies Lebiasininae and Erythrininae with special reference to subtribe Nannostomatina. Proceedings of the United States National Museum, vol. 116, pp. 127–169, 10 figs.

——— 1967*a*. The origin of the stomiatoid fishes with comments on the classification of the salmoniform fishes. Copeia, 1967, pp. 507–540, 18 figs.

——— 1967*b*. The osteology and relationships of the Astronesthidae, a family of oceanic fishes. Dana-Report No. 71, 54 pp., 31 figs.

White, E. G. 1937. Interrelationships of the elasmobranchs with a key to the order Galea. Bulletin of the American Museum of Natural History, vol. 74, pp. 25–138, 51 pls., 65 text figs.

White, E. I. 1946. *Jamoytius kerwoodi*, a new chordate from the Silurian of Lanarkshire. Geological Magazine, vol. 83, pp. 89–97, 2 figs.

Wiedersheim, R. 1887. Über rudimentare Fischnasen. Anatomischer Anzeiger, vol. 2, pp. 652–657, 4 figs.

Willem, V. 1931. Les manoeuvres respiratoires chez les poissons et les amphibiens. Académie Royale de Belgique, Classe des sciences, Mémoires, collection in 4°, ser. 2, vol. 10, no. 7, 194 pp., 75 figs.

—— 1947. Contributions è l'étude des organes respiratoires chez les téléostéens plectognathes. 5e Partie: Tetraodontes et Diodon. Bulletin du Musée Royal d'histoire naturelle de Belgique, vol. 23, no. 17, 17 pp., 10 figs.

Wohlfahrt, T. A. 1936. Das Ohrlabyrinth der Sardine *(Clupea pilchardus* Walb.) und seine Beziehungen zur Schwimmblase und Seitenlinie. Zietschrift für Morphologie und Ökologie der Tiere, vol. 31, pp. 371–410, 28 figs.

—— 1937. Anatomische Untersuchungen über die Seitenkanäle der Sardine *(Clupea pilchardus* Walb.). Zeitschrift für Morphologie und Ökologie der Tiere, vol. 33, pp. 381–411, 15 figs.

Woodward, A. S. 1895. Catalogue of the Fossil Fishes in the British Museum (Natural History). Vol. 3. London: British Museum (Natural History). xlii + 544 pp., 18 pls.

Woskoboinikoff, M. M. 1932. Der Apparat der Kiemenatmung bei den Fischen. Zoologische Jahrbücher, Abteilung für Anatomie und Ontogenie, vol. 55, pp. 315–488, 15 figs.

Index

199